THE MIRACLE OF INTERVALE AVENUE

T · H · E
MIRACLE OF
INTERVALE
A·V·E·N·U·E

THE STORY OF A
JEWISH CONGREGATION
IN THE SOUTH BRONX

Jack Kugelmass

With photographs by the author

SCHOCKEN BOOKS · NEW YORK

Portions of this book were originally published in
Natural History, Moment, and *Prooftexts.*

Library of Congress Cataloging-in-Publication Data
Kugelmass, Jack.
The miracle of Intervale Avenue.
1. Intervale Jewish Center (Bronx, New York, N. Y.)
2. Jews—New York (N. Y.)—Social conditions. 3. Bronx
(N. Y.)—Religious and ecclesiastical institutions.
4. New York (N. Y.)—Religious and ecclesiastical
institutions. I. Title.
BM225.N51575   1986   296.8'3'09747275   85–26094

Design by Richard Oriolo
ISBN 0–8052–4010–1 (hardcover)
ISBN 0–8052-0845–3 (paperback)

CONTENTS

CONTENTS

ACKNOWLEDGMENTS

I am deeply indebted to the members of the Intervale Jewish Center who allowed me to enter their lives. Believing that their story is a gift, I have decided not to change their names, as a way that I might give them in return a kind of coauthorship of this book. The names of other individuals more peripheral to the story have been changed.

There were many people who helped me in the course of this project and encouraged me to pursue it until its completion. I would like to thank my agent, Edy Selman, for excellent advice, and my editor, Bonny Fetterman, for generous commitment of her time both to me and my work. Nancy Erlich devoted considerable effort to reading and editing early drafts of the manuscript. Marilyn Stern gave generously of her photographic expertise and equipment. Janet Belcove Shalin, Jonathan Boyarin, Adrienne Cooper, Jenna Weissman Joselit, Marc Kaminsky, Barbara Kirshenblatt-Gimblett, David Roskies, Moishe Sacks, Roger Sanjek, Billy Seroken, and Emanuel Tobier either listened to or read and commented on individual chapters. Sharon Kugelmass, among her many other contributions to this project, listened while I tried to piece this story together. My parents, Fay and David Kugelmass, lent a good deal of support and interest, committed as ever to their son's pursuit of Jewish studies.

Finally, I would like to acknowledge two contributions which made this book that much more feasible: the pioneering work of Barbara Myerhoff, without which I might never have attempted this study; and the Wenner Gren Foundation for Anthropological Research, Inc., which awarded me three very generous postdoctoral grants-in-aid.

THE MIRACLE OF INTERVALE AVENUE

· 1 ·

FORT APACHE: THE BRONX

Two men, one sipping sweet kosher wine, the other taking his regular Sabbath shot of Scotch, both nibbling on an assortment of honey, sponge, and marble cakes, were engaged in the usual conversation that accompanies the *kiddush,* the benediction over wine that follows the Saturday morning services.

MR. ABRAHAM: I'm telling you, Moishe, if they put a cop in the building, it's more trouble than it's worth. We had a cop in our old *shul* before it closed. He used to make long-distance phone calls, put the heat up until it was ninety degrees, put the air conditioning on, and sleep on the benches using *taleysim* [prayer shawls] for a cover.

MR. SACKS: Mr. Abraham, we got nothing to worry about. They aren't going to put a cop in here. And if they do, he can't put the heat up to ninety degrees because we don't have a boiler. If he wants air conditioning he'll have to open the windows. And if he wants to sleep on these hard benches, I wouldn't deny him the taleysim for a pillow.

The question of increased police protection for the building was the main topic of conversation on this particular Sabbath because, two days earlier, several youths had been arrested on charges of breaking and entering. They did not take much since there was little to take. Mr.

Sacks's prayer shawl and prayer book were the only things missing, and these were now in police custody being held as evidence. Most of the damage resulted from petty vandalism. Some old and tattered Hebrew books had been swept off the shelves and scattered on the floor, kosher wine had been sprinkled on the carpet, and the cloth hangings separating the men's section from the women's section had been torn down.

The shul—the Intervale Jewish Center—stands in the heart of the South Bronx, a part of New York City inhabited predominantly by Puerto Ricans, interspersed with pockets of black residents and here and there a few remaining elderly Jews. Crime, arson, and hostility toward the police were once so widespread in this area that the 41st Precinct, in which the shul is located, was nicknamed "Fort Apache." Like all institutions, the shul is subjected to repeated attempts at pilferage and vandalism, although it is so denuded of artifacts that there is scarcely anything left to steal. The silver ornaments that decorated the Torah scrolls were placed in someone's hands for safekeeping years ago and, with little prospect of the area being revitalized as a Jewish neighborhood, the artifacts have since been sold.

The Intervale Jewish Center lies wedged between two vacant lots, each of which is strewn with bricks and pieces of white, blue, and pink mosaic floors, the only traces of the six-story apartment buildings that once stood there. The main entrance of the synagogue is barricaded with metal sheets. Many of the wooden letters on an ancient sign ensconced above the doors that spell out "Intervale Jewish Center" are missing; others hang limply, attached by a single rotting nail.

Inside, the building is as raw as its exterior. The only decorations are scribbled red-and-blue Hebrew signs, the work of Intervale's caretaker and resident "graffiti artist," David Lentin. Dave, or "Davíd Lentín, the Jewish Puerto Rican," as he likes to call himself, is also responsible for the Ten Commandments and the words "Thank you, come again" painted on adjoining doors dividing the hallway from the sanctuary. Other decorations are meant to mask the decay: on one side of the main hall the windows are boarded over with plywood. Two velvet Torah covers, white and purple, hang beside a large red cloth tacked onto one of the sheets of plywood. The Torah scrolls they once contained were donated to a synagogue in Israel.

The evidence of decay is so overwhelming that it mocks the feeble efforts to hide it. Inside the main room, long oak pews—some facing forward, some backward—are covered with dust and splotches of white paint, their wide plank seats cracked straight down the middle from years of constant use. Piles of debris cover the benches in various corners of the synagogue, evidence of periodic efforts to patch and repaint holes in the ceiling. Under the benches lie scraps of crumbling yellow Hebrew texts, tattered fragments from ancient holy books. The wood plank floors are giving way in parts, rotted from frequent leaks. And the Ark, unprotected from the rain, its dignity further assaulted by doors that need a good deal of coaxing to open or close, doubles as a closet for Dave's hand-me-down clothes, utility knives, and packages of food. To protect them from the moisture, the Torahs are covered with either plastic garbage bags or shiny white shopping bags worn upside down like party hats. Their "I love New York" slogan printed in bold red type is an ironic message considering their current use. First-time visitors to Intervale look inside and say, "This must have been beautiful at one time." It probably never was.

In 1917, the year the synagogue was incorporated as the Minsker Congregation, worshipers used the president's home as their sanctuary. In 1922, Herman Wouk, then a boy of five, laid the present building's cornerstone (his father was a founder of the shul and his grandfather was for many years its rabbi). Originally, the building committee intended to erect a basement study hall (*besmedresh*) and, when funds became available, the main sanctuary. At the time, the South and Central Bronx contained between a quarter-million and a half-million Jews.[1] Nearby, on Westchester Avenue, rows of stores catered to the culinary needs of observant Jews. But the Great Depression, the Second World War, and the subsequent decline of the Bronx transformed an ambitious dream into an ironic reality, a one-story building with a two-story facade. The synagogue's front steps, leading to a completely barricaded main entrance behind which lies the roof of the sanctuary, are a constant reminder that the building leapfrogged from adolescence to old age. With only the basement built, and exposed on either side, the shul looks as if it's huddling beneath the surface, too frightened to stand out. Passersby assume the building is just another abandoned synagogue in the South Bronx. It very nearly became just that.

Twenty years ago, the congregation was dwindling and the prospects for new members few. Alarmed by the growing incidence of crime and convinced that the community had no future, the rabbi moved out of the neighborhood. Although services were still held, he was anxious to close the building and receive a proper sum as severance pay. The money could come only from selling the building. As the current secretary of the synagogue recalls, the rabbi conspired with members of the Board of Directors to call a secret meeting at which they would vote to dissolve the congregation's assets. Unfortunately for the conspirators, one woman got wind of what was about to happen when she saw one of the board members heading toward the synagogue. Suspecting that something was in the works, she saw to it that several diehards were there to keep careful tabs on the proceedings. Included in the counterconspiracy was Herman Wouk's mother, who, though no longer a resident of the neighborhood, could be counted among the congregation's supporters.

The proposal to sell the building was rejected. The woman who was instrumental in thwarting the board's intentions became Intervale's secretary. Moishe Sacks gradually assumed a greater role in the shul's activities. Like almost all the others, Sacks joined the Intervale Jewish Center only after his own shul, a few blocks from his home, had closed. His was a Conservative shul, while the Intervale Jewish Center is Orthodox. Gradually he began modifying his religious observance to accommodate the Orthodox congregants. When he first arrived, Sacks's offer to provide cake for the kiddush was rejected since congregants preferred to patronize a nearby *shomer shabes* bakery (one that is closed on the Sabbath). When the *baal koyre* (Torah reader) left, Sacks was asked to assume the role, with the stipulation that he would have to forgo all work on the Sabbath. Sacks complied, and assumed the dual role of reader and caterer, and in the course of time other roles, too, as those who had previously filled them moved away or died.

Once home to five hundred worshipers, with weeknight study groups for adults and an afternoon religious school for children, the building now remains empty during the week. Only on weekends does it show any signs of life. Saturdays, when services are held, twelve to fifteen men and women appear. Most are regulars, but once in a while one or another of the remaining few dozen Jews in the area drops by. The regulars sit scattered throughout the room, either alone or in small groups. One or two roam about the hall, checking for needed repairs, while others busy themselves at the rear of the shul, preparing the food that accompanies the kiddush. For the most part, they are elderly Jews who still live in the area. Very often a Jewish storeowner from Southern Boulevard, the nearby commercial strip, joins the congregation. And from time to time a policeman from the 41st Precinct or a newspaper reporter drops by too. As members of the only synagogue still in regular use in the South Bronx, over the years the congregants have been the subject of numerous newspaper, magazine, and television stories.

Sundays the congregation expands, incorporating people from other neighborhoods, many of whom are former residents of the area. Others are residents of Hunts Point, who spend weekdays in the senior citizen centers and come to Intervale for the brunch of rolls, cream cheese, and cake, followed by the review of the *parshe* (Torah reading).

In the face of the decay, Mr. Sacks's defiantly humorous remarks about having a policeman in the building reveal a seemingly incongruous optimism in the shul's future. The optimism, however, is justified: the shul suffers from financial problems and the constant threat of vandalism, but neither poses an insurmountable risk. Over the years, the most serious question the shul has faced is whether or not it can assemble the *minyan*—the ten adult Jewish males who constitute a quorum for ritual purposes. Despite the age and frailty of the congregants and the neighborhood's reputation, the minyan has, with few exceptions, continued week after week, year after year. As Mr. Sacks explained to me during our first conversation, "When one person leaves or dies, someone else always seems to come along to take his place. This is the miracle of Intervale Avenue." I had come to the shul to study it as an anthropologist. But since I visited the shul on a regular basis, and I am an adult Jewish male, I was regarded as a regular member of the minyan. I quickly learned that I, too, was part of the miracle. In Sacks's view, God had sent me after the death of another congregant. When my study ended, someone else would appear in my stead.

The first time I saw the Intervale Jewish Center was on a Sunday morning in February 1980. I remember the day because it was bitterly cold outside and the synagogue was not much warmer inside. The steam from the boiler couldn't reach the radiators because the brass pipes had been ripped from the walls by vandals only a few days before. I had gone there to write a magazine article about elderly Jews living in "Fort Apache." Chilled to the bone by damp air, my fingers too numb to take notes, I had hoped this would be one of very few visits to the synagogue. Nor was the frigid temperature the only thing that bothered me. I had already begun work on another book; incorrectly anticipating that fieldwork might be less to my liking than library research, I did not look forward to making regular journeys to a place where my abilities to forgo creature comforts would be sorely tested. Moreover, the project had a distinctly ominous side to it, namely its location in one of the world's most famous slums. I had lived in New York City for almost ten years, having moved there to attend graduate school in anthropology. Growing up in Montreal, I was accustomed to a pleasant, safe environment where crime was not of much concern. In New York City of the early 1970s it was constantly on people's minds. There were rules about how to dress, how to walk, where to keep your money, and most of all, where not to go. After watching the nightly newscasts, to me the very words "South Bronx" spelled disaster, conjuring up images of arson, murder, and heinous attacks by gangs of youths upon elderly Jews. Even today most New Yorkers visit the area only if they accidentally take a wrong turn off of an expressway. Even former Bronxites, the ones who now live in suburban communities in Westchester and Long Island, seldom return to see the

The Intervale Jewish Center,
the last synagogue in use
in the South Bronx, is a
one-story building with a
two-story facade.

Members of the congre-
gation take in the sun outside
the *shul* before the
Sunday brunch.

In a burst of zeal, David Lentin takes on the task of sweeping up the South Bronx.

(*Overleaf*) Dave escorts Lucy home along Intervale Avenue.

Dave sits by his artwork in the Intervale Jewish Center.

old neighborhood. And for good reason: in most cases there is no old neighborhood—only acres of empty lots or blocks of abandoned buildings left standing as stark shells like monuments to an apocalypse.

Despite my apprehension about the area, the project had its attractions. In a way, the location was ideal: third world by way of underemployment and population, understudied, and only a half-hour subway ride from Manhattan. Possible danger notwithstanding, the project sounded like an easy one. All I had to do, I thought, was document the lives of elderly Jews living in a world-famous slum: a few photographs, some interviews, a little commentary, and my study would be complete. I was wrong, of course. A project that I assumed required no more than a year of work managed to hold my interest for over five years. My initial assessment of the amount of time required for this project stemmed less from naiveté about field research in general than from a rather skewed notion that I, like so many other New Yorkers, held about the area and its inhabitants.

At the time, the Paul Newman film *Fort Apache: the Bronx* had just been released, and the omission of old Jews from the film suggested to me how remarkable the phenomenon of elderly Jewish holdouts would seem to be. It was a portrait of the area during the early 1970s, when the 41st Precinct led the city in every major crime, and the filmmakers very likely assumed that old Jews would be much too frail to endure the crime-ridden environment. Indeed, the popular image of elderly Jews in the South Bronx is that the few who remain are hidden and invisible, locked behind heavy metal gates and multilatched doors, desperate for someone to rescue them. Yet upon my first encounter with the congregants of the Intervale Jewish Center, it immediately became apparent that there was much more to this story than I had thought. Most of these elderly Jews remain not because they have no alternative but because they enjoy the neighborhood. To them, the Bronx is stimulating. It enhances their sense of dignity and self-worth. And it allows them to feel brave and resourceful, particularly when others see the area as too dangerous to visit, let alone inhabit.

There is a time lag in our views of the world. The violent South Bronx I had pictured in February 1980 was actually the South Bronx of the late 1960s and early 1970s. The images I had of the area were cast from the same mold as the Paul Newman film. The South Bronx the elderly Jews know is of a still earlier time when the East Bronx (the former term for areas such as Hunts Point and Longwood) was a desirable place to live—a long step up the ladder for immigrant or first-generation Jews from Lower Manhattan tenements. Despite the years of change, they continue to see the area as the location of homes they have shared with spouses and children, homes they now maintain almost like shrines to loved ones no longer living or worlds that now exist only in memory.

The South Bronx they still cherish was once a thriving Jewish area, holding half of the borough's Jewish population.[2] In the decades preceding the Second World War, according to the historian Deborah Dash Moore, "it was the most economically heterogeneous of the immigrant neighborhoods." Besides being an immigrant area, it also housed many middle-class Jews attracted to the many "fine brick apartment houses, some with elevators, with embossed tin and carved granite, wrought-iron rails, polished-brass mailboxes and marble lobbies."[3]

It wasn't only the large, airy, and relatively inexpensive housing that attracted Jews to the East Bronx. It was also the fact that Jewish life, particularly in its secular form, thrived there.[4] Today, of course, these attractions are gone. One of the few traces of the hundreds of thousands of Jews who once inhabited the South Bronx is a huge fading wall mural that reads, "Moe Levy, Outfitter to Man and Boy," visible from the elevated train only a stop or two from the Intervale station. Aside from the peeling paint, the sign has remained intact, unaltered by a changing neighborhood. The other remnant of Jewish life, the dozens of former synagogues, have had to adapt to change. Almost all are now churches. They retain, however, Marrano-like traces of Jewish identity. Some still display the congregation's name in Hebrew lettering carved in red or beige granite, their stony timelessness an ironic reminder that while the building would withstand the forces of nature, the congregation would give way under a torrent of social and ethnic change. Other former synagogues still display the stone tablets with the Ten Commandments in Hebrew above the entrance and here and there a large stained-glass Star of David. Everywhere, surrounding these relics, are the empty lots upon which not very long ago stood substantial apartment buildings, now reduced to piles of used brick and clusters of ornate mosaic hallway tiles.

Why did it all disappear? That a once-thriving Jewish neighborhood would become a non-Jewish one is not an unusual occurrence. Jews are mobile, and they are long accustomed to abandoning former homes in search of safer, nicer, or more prosperous places in which to live. As Marshall Berman reflects in his study of modernism, "the Bronx of my youth was possessed, inspired by the great modern dream of mobility. To live well meant to move up socially, and this in turn meant to move out physically; to live one's life close to home was not to be alive at all."[5]

So the mentality of its upwardly mobile Jewish residents made the Bronx particularly susceptible to change. But that a vast area should physically collapse, that a section of an American metropolis should become a suitable locale for a German film crew to shoot look-alike shots of

THE MIRACLE OF INTERVALE AVENUE

Dresden after the bombing, or that a New York City councilman should tour the area with a group of Russian diplomats and ask for Soviet foreign aid[6] gives ample cause for disturbing speculation. I have not set out in this book to explain why or how it happened. The task I have chosen is to relate the contemporary story of one tiny community within the South Bronx. So I must rely here on the work done by others to decipher these events.[7]

The settlement of the Bronx in the nineteenth century for the most part followed the construction of the railroad stations. The area was populated by Irish and German immigrant villages, with country homes and estates for wealthy New Yorkers. In 1888 the Third Avenue El was extended from Manhattan to 133rd Street in the Bronx, attracting added population particularly to the Mott Haven section of the Bronx. In 1898 the Bronx became a borough of New York City. In the next few decades, when the subway was extended from Manhattan, developers bought up large tracts of land lining the Westchester Avenue route of the elevated line and erected apartment buildings, which attracted ever-increasing numbers of people to the area. The same period coincided with the mass migration of East European Jews to America. Seeking less congested neighborhoods, the immigrants eventually ventured away from their original Lower East Side settlement and moved to the newer neighborhoods of East New York in Brooklyn and Mott Haven in the Bronx.[8] From 1920 to 1930 the Bronx gained half a million residents, many of them Jews. By 1930 there were 600,000 Jews living in the Bronx, or about half the borough's residents.[9]

For roughly two decades prior to the Second World War, the South Bronx remained a stable area populated by Jews, Italians, Irish, and Germans.[10] The Second World War brought the first seeds of change, since the scarcity of labor, as elsewhere in the industrial regions of the East and Midwest, brought Puerto Ricans to the city, including several neighborhoods in the Bronx. Blacks had already settled in Morrisania by the 1930s, and their numbers increased significantly during the war. The war years also brought rent control, first instituted by the federal government and later taken over by the state. Rent control's tight lid on escalating housing prices encouraged a change in housing choices since older residents were reluctant to leave desirable units. Moreover, young families armed with automobiles were attracted to newer suburban neighborhoods by federally subsidized mortgages at low interest rates and by a rapidly expanding freeway system that provided easy access to the city. Shortly after the war, the middle class began its exodus from the urban core. The same freeway system that promoted the outmigration by encouraging the growth of the suburbs also hurt the city directly. Subsidized through the interstate highway system in 1959, the Cross Bronx Expressway carved a huge chunk out of many stable working-class South Bronx neighborhoods. It undermined once tightly knit communities and planted the seeds of blight that eventually spread throughout the southern portion of the borough.[11]

In and of themselves, neither the Cross Bronx Expressway nor the ethnic transformation of the South Bronx caused the area's destruction. The history of New York neighborhoods is one of constant shifts as one ethnic group succeeds another.[12] The end of the European mass migration to New York in 1924 meant that there would not be a succeeding group of Jews to occupy the apartments that the previous generation was leaving. Indeed, other immigrants came in their stead. But unlike the European migration to America, which corresponded to America's industrialization and New York City's emergence as a world metropolis, the black and Puerto Rican migration northward was an internal migration. Though stimulated by the possibility of jobs (which many immigrants did find), they also entered industries that were losing their economic vigor. Consequently, upward mobility was not as certain as in the case of the European migration. During the 1960s when the Bronx was becoming a predominantly Puerto Rican borough, it was continually losing jobs. The trend continued throughout the 1970s when New York City lost over 600,000 manufacturing jobs, largely due to the flow of capital southward, where tax and labor policies were more favorable to management. By 1974 the South Bronx had lost 650 of the manufacturers who had been in the area in 1959. As the job market collapsed, welfare rolls expanded. In 1962 Hunts Point had 11,000 welfare recipients; ten years later the figure was 53,000.[13]

Critical, too, for understanding what happened to the South Bronx, is the social climate of the 1960s. The United States at the time was transformed by a new ethic as drugs became a mainstay of a counterculture and an increasingly unpopular war undermined the moral authority of political and social institutions. Both the war and drugs played large roles in shaping the American counterculture; they had much grimmer consequences for the less privileged groups within American society, contributing much to the values and worldview of the underclass that came to form the population of the urban core. Crime became a way of life for some, with profound consequences for once-stable working-class neighborhoods. As Robert Jensen writes:

Heroin addiction rose dramatically in New York City in the 1960s, particularly in poor neighborhoods. In 1972, the city's police commis-

THE MIRACLE OF INTERVALE AVENUE

sioner estimated that seventy percent of the crime in New York was drug related, usually addicts trying anything to get money for a fix. The number of reported assaults in the Bronx rose from 998 in 1960 to 4,256 in 1969; burglaries rose from 1,765 to 29,276. The principal increase in these boroughwide statistics came from the South Bronx.[14]

Ultimately the destruction of something as vast as the South Bronx could not have happened unless some people profited from it. In the 1960s landlords no longer found rents sufficient return on their investments. Suffering from the spiraling costs of maintenance, some landlords had their buildings torched to collect insurance on them, while others sold theirs to unscrupulous investors who purchased the buildings with only one thing in mind: to milk them for revenue. Apartments were rented to anyone who would pay the price without regard to his or her suitability as a tenant. At the same time, short-sighted public agencies[15] used the Bronx as a dumping ground for welfare clients. Since the landlords were offered finder's fees and paid directly by city agencies, these new tenants were just what the landlords wished for: passive tenants who demanded and got very little and yet, through the welfare system, had their rents paid on time. By closing down basic services, landlords could keep costs to a minimum and profits to a maximum.

While most tenants suffered terrible hardships, a few tenants profited from the destruction: welfare recipients anxious to move to the top of the list for public housing torched their buildings and immediately became eligible for $1,000 to $3,000 in assistance to cover clothing, furniture, and moving expenses. Others destroyed buildings, too: fixture strippers to cover their tracks and street gangs who did it just for fun. Between 1970 and 1975 there were 68,456 fires in the Bronx—more than 33 each night, most of these in the South Bronx.[16] In the 1977 television documentary "The Fire Next Door," Bill Moyers refers to the flames of the South Bronx as "a signal of a national disaster" in which 50,000 buildings have been gutted since the 1960s.[17]

The late 1960s and early 1970s were a devastating period during which literally tens of thousands of buildings were destroyed. The media began to discover the Bronx, and over the course of a decade the area rose to national and even international notoriety. But the Bronx the media discovered was a strange place, quite different from the one its residents knew. Indeed, the media's Bronx was hardly a place fit for human habitation. In 1972 Stewart Alsop, writing in *Newsweek,* pronounced the South Bronx dying "as though to some loathsome, lethal disease" and pinned much of the blame on the addicts. In the article Alsop predicted:

FORT APACHE: THE BRONX

The Bronx, in fact, seems destined to become a rubble-filled semidesert. Drive down almost any street, and you see apartment houses that have just been abandoned—you can always tell by the broken windows. Others are sagging wrecks, and some have been bulldozed to the ground. In fact, the South Bronx looks a lot like London after the blitz.[18]

In 1975, David Black reported in the *New York Times* that in one three-hour period forty fires were reported in the Bronx. With 30,000 drug addicts reputed to be residing in the area, the pockets of white ethnics who remained saw "the surrounding neighborhood as a jungle filled with beasts."[19] Herbert E. Meyer, in the November 1975 issue of *Fortune,* suggested that the South Bronx "may be the closest men have yet come to creating hell on earth."[20]

Despite the attention the South Bronx received, not all would agree about the implications of the area's problems. Writing for the *New York Times,* Roger Wilkins reported that so extensive was the devastation in the South Bronx that some urban experts believe that its "Dresden-like quality" was "in no way typical of America's urban problems in general. To take the moonscape of the South Bronx as a metaphor for the nation's urban needs is to inflate an already horrendous problem to a scale that would defy even the most ambitious political imagination." The South Bronx serves merely as a warning. Wilkins went on to quote John Patterson, Jr., then president of the South Bronx Overall Economic Development Corporation, who argued, "People ought to visit the South Bronx and see it as symbolic. Whatever stage your own local brand of urban decay has reached, the South Bronx will show you just where it's going to go if you don't do the things you have to do to reverse it."[21]

Whether typical or not of America's urban problems, the South Bronx has become a national shrine, a new Gettysburg. In his 1976 campaign Jimmy Carter toured the area and promised to rebuild it. Four years later both contenders for the presidency visited Charlotte Street—one to mock the incumbent's idle promises, the other to defend the record. Despite such visits, few concrete programs emerged to match the grandiose promises of presidential candidates. Here and there some buildings have been renovated and new buildings have gone up. For the most part, the area, now tranquil, waits much like the fallow land it once was. Residents know that one day the Bronx will be rebuilt. Visitors do not. To them the area is a thing to be gawked at, but from a distance, safe behind a car windshield. Very, very few outsiders really know the South Bronx. "The way people talk, you would think we live in a jungle," one member of the Intervale Jewish Center remarks. "Like we don't got no roads or things and you have to hack your way through to get here."

THE MIRACLE OF INTERVALE AVENUE

Given the grim appraisals of the area, perhaps the most astonishing thing about my first visit to the South Bronx on that bitter cold day in 1980 was my sense of disappointment. I had expected to see burning buildings, violent youth gangs, and perhaps even a shootout. I saw nothing of the kind. I had come a few years too late. The fires had stopped. The gangs had disappeared. The drugs addicts had died. Gone, too, were the angry inhabitants who, having laid siege to the 41st Precinct, helped change the area's nickname from "Korea" to "Fort Apache." In the words of one police officer, "They used to call this place Fort Apache. That was before they tore it all down. Now we call it the Little House on the Prairie." Despite the miles of devastated buildings and empty lots, some streets surprisingly are relatively intact. Major thoroughfares such as Southern Boulevard and parts of Westchester Avenue are crowded with stores and shoppers. And the old Jews I met at the Intervale Jewish Center did not appear frightened. Nor did they recall being in any danger during the period in the early 1970s when all the fires occurred. When I asked them about it, they generally appeared more shocked by what they considered the silliness of the question than by their recollections of the events.

"Of course I remember the fires," Mordechai Parkes responded to my question. "Sometimes the fumes were so bad you couldn't breathe at night. We used to feel like we were choking."

"Did you feel threatened?" I asked.

"No. To us it seemed like it was normal. You looked out your window, and every day you could see two five-story buildings that were burning. Maybe in your neighborhood that would be unusual and people would be concerned. But to us that was normal."

I asked Mr. Abraham whether the reports in the newspapers about how dangerous the area was were true.

"B.S.," he responded.

"They weren't true?" I asked once more.

"No. It was all bull!" A strange comment from a man whose wife was recently abducted at gunpoint while waiting for him inside the car just a few blocks from the shul! Individual incidents are one thing, a sense of persecution is something else entirely. The mass media never made such distinctions. And yet, had the South Bronx been what the media made it out to be, these elderly people could never have survived there.

If there is any one theme in this book, it is this: there is life where we least expect it: in the heart of the South Bronx and, too, in old age. But there is an underlying theme here that speaks to a lust for the "good fight"—that for some people life consists not of a series of misfortunes or lucky breaks but of a constant challenge to overcome adversity by actively imagining reality and imposing their will upon it. Indeed, for the handful of Jews that are left in the Intervale vicinity, surviving in an area where few dare to venture represents a personal triumph over the physiological tyranny of advanced age, an affirmation of life in the face of death.

The Miracle of Intervale Avenue emerged from five years of participant observation. The study began as an examination of how people survive in what appears to be a forbidding environment; it evolved, however, into an account of how people impute sense and meaning into the fact of their survival. "I'll tell you a story," Mrs. Miroff tells me after drawing me away from the other congregants. "From it you can write a book. It's the story of a life."

The Miracle of Intervale Avenue is largely the story of one man, Moishe Sacks, the Intervale Jewish Center's charismatic leader, acting rabbi, master baker, and storyteller. Yet, although the book tells the story of Sacks's determination to duel with blind happenstance and to creatively impose his will upon it, the story is much broader than a biography of one individual; it tells the story of a tiny group of mostly elderly Jews who frequent the Intervale Jewish Center, each of whom has assumed a key role in making the miracle possible. And it tells a universal story of the human quest for meaning in the face of death: that such meaning could be found in the heart of the South Bronx among an aged remnant of a once-thriving community is sufficient proof that there indeed exists a miracle of Intervale Avenue.

· 2 ·

"I'M A BAKER,
I KNOW VINEGAR"

A short, rather squat man with a round, ruddy face hurries to leave the synagogue. I help him with his coat as one arm reaches blindly for a sleeve. The man accepts the offer without protest. "Tell me your name once more," he asks. "You've told it to me before, but I have a very bad memory for names. I have a son who is a psychologist. He tells me that the reason I don't remember names is because I'm too much of an egotist. I don't pay attention to other people."

"My name is Jack."

"Jack. And in Hebrew that's Yakov."

"It should be. But my Hebrew name is Yoysef."

"Yoysef? Good. That's my grandson's name, so when I need to remember your name all I got to do is think of my grandson and I'll remember that your name is Yoysef. My name is Moishe. In English it's Maurice or Morris. Maurice Sacks is my official name. But most people call me Moish. Anyway I'm pleased to meet you even though you've been here before and we've been introduced before. Tell me again why you're here. You're a journalist or something to that effect?"

"I'm an anthropologist."

"An anthropologist. Good. This is a good place for an anthropologist.

They call this area Fort Apache. The only thing is you won't find any Apache Indians here. The area is too dangerous. They left."

"I'm not looking for Indians."

"You would like to study us?" The tone of Sacks's voice suggests that he's not terribly surprised by the idea. More than personal vanity is at work here. An avid reader of popular science magazines, Sacks has a pretty good idea about what it is that anthropologists do.

"Yes."

"Well, I got nothing against it. You're welcome to come here as you've already been doing. You can attend our services on Saturday. You're more than welcome because we can always use another man for the minyan and you can join us for the Sunday morning brunch and *dvar Torah* [explications of the weekly Torah reading]. The only thing is right now I've got to go. You know what they say, *malokhe varubo vehayom*— the work is long and the day is short. I have plenty of work yet to do in the bakery." Sacks struggles to insert the buttons of his coat into the proper holes. He gives up after closing only one or two. "Those buttons don't want to go into the holes they're supposed to go into. Anyway it's not too cold outside. I better get going. I want to try something out. I have a new order to make rugelakh three hundred for an old-age home. And they're supposed to be not as big as a danish, but bigger than rugelakh. They should not be so big that my boss will say, 'This is a sixty-cent not a thirty-cent item!' And it has to be big enough for people to take one portion and be satisfied. *Dayenu*. So this is a tricky size to accomplish. You know something? I'm a firm believer in *amuno* [faith]. I actually believe I will get the right size that will satisfy everyone."

"I'm sure you will."

"Your faith [in me] is overwhelming."

"Well. Should it not be?"

"Definitely! Let me tell you the story of opera fudge."

"Wait a minute. Let me get out my tape recorder so I can tape it."

"Listen, Jack. I don't got time for no tape recorders. I told you I'm going back to the bakery. I got work to do."

"Can I walk with you?"

"You can walk with me until the bakery. But once we get there I won't have time for you because I have to get to work. O.K.?"

"Do I have a choice?"

"Sure, you do. You can always not go. Now tell me why you want to record all this."

"I told you that I'm an anthropologist. I would like to write a book about the Intervale Jewish Center."

THE MIRACLE OF INTERVALE AVENUE

"So why record me?"

"I can't record the shul."

"That's not what I meant. Today is Sunday. So we have our usual brunch in shul and then we go over the Torah reading for the week. Why don't you write about that? Isn't that important?"

"I intend to. And I agree it's important. But sometimes you can learn as much about a community by listening to how individuals talk about their lives as you can from observing the whole group."

"So what should I talk about?"

"Why don't you just continue with the story you were telling me."

"About opera fudge?"

"Yes. Tell me about opera fudge."

"Well this is a true story. It happened years ago. Maybe forty or forty-five years ago. I was still a youngster. At least I think I was still a youngster forty-five years ago. It was before the time when you had your ingredients ready-made. I was making a chocolate icing for cupcakes and something was wrong with the consistency because it wouldn't stay on the cake. One of the other bakers who used to work with me says, 'Wait till the boss finds out!' So I tell him, 'Let him find out! What can I do, spend all day here?' So I send the cupcakes out the way they are. And the boss is giving them out with the icing sliding off. So all of a sudden he comes running back and wants to know what's going on with the cupcakes. So I tell him, 'Mr. So-and-So, those aren't cupcakes. They're opera fudge.' 'What's opera fudge?' he asks. 'Something special,' I tell him. 'It's a little more expensive than a cupcake and you have to serve it on a plate.' So the boss turns around and starts yelling at his wife, 'What's the matter with you? Those aren't cupcakes. They're opera fudge. You're charging too little!' The next day, sure enough, people are coming in and asking for opera fudge. Did you get that on tape?"

"Yes. I think so."

"Good. Now tell me, of what value to you is such a story?"

"That's not a fair question."

"Why isn't it fair?"

"How can I know right now what value that story will have for my book? Sometimes details which seem at first to be of no significance become very important only after you reflect on them for a while. At any rate, even if the story isn't useful for the book, it's already taught me something about you."

"What?"

"That you're resilient and imaginative."

"I could have told you that myself."

"Maybe. But there's something else the story tells me. You're a hood-winker. You know how to make people behave in ways that suit you rather than them."

"Who do I hoodwink?"

"Well, you just told me about hoodwinking a boss. I suppose you do the same thing at Intervale. But if I'm wrong, I'll know that in time. And maybe, too, I'll discover other meanings in the story. So for now let's just say that one should never underestimate the role that chance plays in research."

"I wouldn't dream of it. I already know the role that chance plays in baking. Look at the story about opera fudge. That was chance. You know, in baking, all the things we take for granted came about by accident. It's like marble cake. How do you think marble cake came about? Someone was making a pound cake and a can of chocolate accidentally fell into the batter. Anyway, if you're walking me to the bakery, let's walk. As I told you, I have a lot of work to do yet."

Once outside the shul, Sacks sets a brisk pace. He is anxious to get to the bakery, but he manages to point out various landmarks in the area as we walk: a former shul ("I used to *daven* [pray] there when I first came to Hunts Point"); an abandoned building ("My uncle used to live there"); the 41st Precinct ("Sometimes they send down a man to look in on the shul. If he's Jewish we count him in the minyan"); a spot where he was mugged ("They didn't get nothing because they only looked in my pockets. I keep my valuables in this shopping bag, not in my pockets"); Southern Boule-vard ("Every bit as crowded now as when this was a Jewish area—even more so"); a small park where he often goes to relax ("They all know me here so no one gives me a hard time"). The walk gives me a chance to see the South Bronx through the eyes of a native. It looks strangely unthreat-ening. Individual streets look abandoned; the neighborhood does not.

"Don't you have an assistant?" I ask, responding to Sacks's concern over the amount of work before him.

"I have. More than one. But the assistants I have I would be better off not having. I tell one of them to do something and he just laughs at me. If I don't tell him exactly what he should do, he sits and waits till I give him another order. I got so upset the other day that I started to yell, not at him but at Elye Markraykh."

"Who is Elye Markraykh?"

"That's what they wanted to know, too. They thought I must be losing my marbles or something like that. Anyway, I'll tell you about Elye Markraykh, and you'll have another story to think about. Elye Markraykh is the baker that broke me in over here when I came from Europe. I had to serve as his helper. This Elye took all the advantages of being foreman.

THE MIRACLE OF INTERVALE AVENUE

Not only in his position of manager, but in the *yikhes* [status] that came from it. He was actually a graduate from the old tradition. He was a master baker. He used to come in, he'd put on a red shirt to show that he was tops. He walked around in the bakery with a *royte gartl,* a red handkerchief hanging down from the side. If he had to do anything which required manual work, even putting the bread on the wooden peal to go into the oven, he had a porter that had to take the bread off from the box and put it on the peal. Then he put the peal gracefully into the oven. In other words, in whatever he did, the service that was coming to him as a master baker from an apprentice, he demanded. If there was a can of eggs on the table and he needed a quart of eggs, he used to say, 'Moishele, give me a quart of eggs.' So I said, 'Elye Markraykh, the eggs are right there. I'm busy cleaning the stove.' Or I was doing something else. He said, 'Moishele, I'm asking for the quart of eggs. You give me that quart of eggs!' And he says, 'Besides, you'll get to my age, to my status, there'll be another Moishele and he'll do the same thing for you.' Now, where I work, I don't have to ask for the quart of eggs. If I want the can of eggs, all I have to do is go and move a three-hundred-pound bag of flour myself just to get to the can of eggs. And every time I do that I say, 'Elye Markraykh, turn around in your grave! Elye,' I say, 'I need a bag of flour. Elye, where is the boy to give it to me?' The helpers just stand there and they laugh. They say, 'You can't get yourself a bag of flour?' "

"So they give you a hard time."

"It's not just them that give me a hard time in there. I got plenty of other aggravation from the bakery. There's another bit of aggravation I got that comes from the bakery that has also to do with the Social Security system, the way they keep bugging me about my age. You know, in Europe not only did they not keep records of the year you were born, they didn't even remember the exact day. When I came to Ellis Island and they asked for my birth date, I told them what my mother would say: '*Dray teg nokh Rosheshone* [Three days after Rosh Hashanah].' So the officer looks up when Rosh Hashanah was in 1923, the year I arrived here, and that became my official birth date. Now I got a new problem. But this has nothing to do with documents about my age. Apparently the boss's wife has done something wrong with the deductions for Social Security. She may have deducted a certain amount from my check but never turned it in to the Social Security system. Now they say at SSI, I owe them money. So I had to go in there for a hearing. They called me for an early-morning meeting with them. I arrived a little early for the appointment. But since I had been up all night working, I used the time to catch up on my sleep. When the officer came to get me, he had to wake me up because I was fast asleep. The guy sees me, he says, 'If you're able to sleep then I can tell already that you have nothing to worry about because you got nothing on your conscience.'

"You see, I never worry. Even about the minyan. Even about whether we'll have the ten men for the service. This will change and that will change. One man leaves, another comes along. It's like an equation. You move something on one side to the other, it looks a little different, but the equation is still the same."

"How do you explain your optimism?"

"How do I explain it? It's very simple. It comes from experience. It's from the calamities in life. I've lost my wife. I've lost children. One died in my arms. He was two years old. I've lost good friends that died. You learn, too, that if you can make someone else feel better, some of it will rub off and make you feel better.

"You know, there's always a bright side to things. It's like the problem we have with the leaking roof in the shul. So now we have part of the shul blocked off by two-by-fours so nobody should stand near where the plaster is falling in from the ceiling. That leak is nothing new. It's been fixed before. But it's still leaking. That's all in God's reckoning. It's just like cosmetics. Supposing they came up with a kind of makeup and mascara that you put it on once and it makes you beautiful forever. The cosmetic companies would go out of business. Well, God figures the same way. If we repaired it once and everything was O.K., no one would be able to make a living. This way the repairman makes a living every time there's a new leak. And if the roof falls in and hits someone, the doctor makes a living, and if the person decides to sue, a lawyer can make a good living, too."

We cross underneath the cavernous concrete skyway, the Bruckner Expressway. We walk another block and Sacks points to his store up ahead. I see the green-painted facade. Above the silver-painted metal gates sits a huge sign that reads "Moshman's Garrison Bakery." Aside from one or two signs advertising a nearby kosher meat-packing plant, the Moshman sign is the only remaining trace of the once-thriving Jewish commercial enterprises on Hunts Point Boulevard: it stands out like a thing frozen in time. I feign a willingness to leave, but Sacks motions me over to see something. His cat, Spotty, is waiting impatiently. He stares at us through the store window. "Come inside. You'll meet Spotty. And I'll give you both something to eat." Sacks puts his plastic shopping bag down beside the metal gate covering the door. He pulls an enormous set of keys from his pocket, turns the cylinder on a heavy metal lock, and lifts the upward-sliding metal gate at first by hand then by a metal prod until it is comfortably perched inside its mount several feet above the doorway.

We enter and Sacks locks the door behind us. "Spotty looks pretty hungry, so let me find him some food. Then I'll get us something to eat. After that I'll get to work. Why don't you meantime set the table here with some silverware and cups?" The front part of the bakery is a store and restaurant. It is actually quite large, with rows of white Formica-covered tables and red vinyl-covered chairs. On one wall, over the serving counter, hangs a huge hand-painted sign listing the various sandwiches sold in the bakery. The sign is old, its edges frayed, the blue and red writing slowly fading. The prices on beige masking tape are recent additions. They pay hommage to the reach of inflation even here in the South Bronx, and indeed to the economic vitality of an institution intricately linked to the Hunts Point Market. The other walls are covered with oil paintings and wood engravings. The bakery's owner has a hobby of copying paintings. The themes he chooses are eclectic: Hasidim at the Western Wall in Jerusalem, a bouquet of flowers, a Spanish-looking woman lying naked on a bed, a gorilla framed with metal bars covering its head and sporting a button that reads "I eat at Moshman's."

After Sacks finishes with Spotty, he sits down with a plate of rolls, a bin of tuna salad, and some cans of diet soft drinks. He tells me to serve myself while he replaces his street hat with a baker's work hat. Then he begins to struggle with the tab of the can of soda. Unable to open the top with his pudgy fingers, he inserts the plastic knife between the tab and the metal rim, using it as a lever to pry it open.

"You see, it's not only me that feels my age but even inanimate objects."

"What do you mean?"

"Take this can, for example. For some reason, either because my fingers are too stiff or because I don't have enough strength, the cover is giving me a hard time. It's like it's getting pleasure from the advance of my age. Does that sound strange to you? A little bit? Well, it's true! It's like the trouble I had in shul buttoning my coat up. It's hard to button a button. And those buttons know, goddamn them, they know that the older you get, the harder it is, and they just stay out of the hole, like they don't want to go in. The same way even with the keys. I have my keys tied up with garbage ties that you can't tear. The only time it breaks is when I open the door to the store twelve-thirty in the morning, with the policemen who drove me standing right there. And all the keys spill in the dark onto the floor."

"Were you able to find them?"

"I had no trouble at all. The police put on all their flashlights. And I crawl around feeling the sidewalk with my hands, and I manage to find them myself. I pick up all the keys."

"If you come in at twelve-thirty A.M. and stay until four P.M., I can't see what you're complaining about. Your age doesn't seem to be interfering with your stamina for work."

"Well, it's true I can still do the work I used to, but the difference is that now I feel it. I'm much more tired now than I used to be. The other day I was hunting through the cupboard for a can of something and I had to move a bag in front of it that weighed maybe two hundred pounds. And it was giving me a hard time like it was making fun of me. Even my body rebels. I tell it to bend over and lift up the bag, my body tells me it doesn't want to do it. It's tired. So I have to force it, and all the while it complains and gives me a hard time. You'll know what I'm talking about when you get old."

"I already have some idea. The older I get, the more my body rebels when I go outside in winter. I don't look forward to winter one bit."

"I'm not the same. Winters in New York are much colder than in Russia. Not the temperature but the way it feels because of the dampness. But even so, I actually look forward to winter. Once it gets to autumn and then winter, you can use the hours of the day differently. In summer, although you may be tired and you would like to settle down in bed with a book at five or six o'clock, you somehow feel that you would be denying yourself some pleasure, like you would be missing something by not staying up. As it gets colder and the days get shorter, it is cold in the apartment. So I get into bed with three blankets and the heating pad underneath, and just my nose sticks out far enough so I can see the book I'm holding and I read.

"The other night I was reading the Bible, in Hebrew just the way I learned it in *kheyder* [Jewish elementary school] in Russia. You're a writer. Have you ever read the Bible?"

"When I was young. But not in recent years," I admit.

"Well, you should. Let me tell you something. The way they should teach people to write in school is just by sitting down and reading *Breshis*, Genesis. It is so beautiful and concise. In a few short sentences it tells the story of a thousand years."

"I heard you say the same thing this morning in shul when you were going over the parshe. The Bible must have been a very important part of your childhood."

"The Bible, of course! Look, I was four years old when I went to kheyder."

"Your father was very Orthodox?"

"My father had nothing to do with it. My father at that time was already in America. So he had no part in it. My mother with her four children stayed in Russia. And she made sure I had a proper Jewish education. On *shabes* [the Sabbath] I would be examined for what I learned in kheyder not by my father, since he was in America, but by my mother, to the best of her capacity, or by my uncle, her brother, who also worked in the bakery. I also had private tutors since I was born into a comparatively wealthy family. The Kovner *maggid* [preacher] was my private tutor."

"Your mother came here much after your father?"

"Much after? My mother never came here. My father and mother never saw each other after he went to America. He got a job as a baker, but he never made quite enough to bring her over with the four children. She died in Russia."

"So you learned baking from your father?"

"I learned not from my father, because like I told you, he was already in America when I was growing up. Besides, I had my mother's bakery to learn from. That's where my father learned, too. In fact he wasn't a baker until he married my mother.

"My grandfather, Moishe Gershon, owned a bakery. He was my mother's father. And his father owned a bakery. And the generation before him owned a bakery. They were all bakers. My mother happened to be the daughter of a wealthy baker who was looking for a suitable husband for her. She was a girl of, I don't know how old but she was much younger than he was. He was a yeshiva *bokher* [student] who came from Poland and studied in Kovno. He remained a bokher till he was forty, when he married my mother. My father was a student in a gymnasium [secular school of higher education]. He was in his secular studies advanced enough to be an accountant in Russia. He was also a musician and could even write music. So the yeshiva education was only one of the things he did. How he made a living before he married my mother I don't know. In those days you didn't ask questions from *lamdonim* [scholars] on how they made livings. Their work was to study. Other people made sure they had what to eat. And from all the prospective suitors, they preferred my father because he was a scholar. He was a yeshiva bokher, a *lamdn*. And don't forget the family was wealthy. So he would have nothing to do except be the father of the children of Khaye-Sore *bas* Moshe-Gershon ha-Kohen. That was his job. He had nothing else to do."

"So what made him decide to come to America?"

"He didn't decide. It was decided for him. In 1914 when he would have been drafted into the army because Russia was at war. That's when my father came to America along with other male members of the family. Over here, all of them were bakers. He couldn't be an accountant because he didn't know the language. And as a musician he would have starved. Since the relatives knew he was from a baker's family, they made him a baker and he worked the rest of his life as a baker. You see, being an intelligent man and having been around a bakery, he would have known the process of baking. But the bakery here in New York and in Europe were completely different. Completely different. In Europe we made candies, we made challahs, we made big black breads, and we made *pirishkes*. Pirishki is like rugelakh with prune and jelly filling. That's it. That was the baking in Europe.

"In America, there was a melting pot of the bakers from all over. The ones who came from Germany, from Austria, from Galicia knew German Jewish baking. So they introduced the Vienna roll, the kaiser roll. The ones from Galicia also introduced things. So a hodgepodge of different baking developed here. I remember, in my time yet, when a Jewish baker could make a jelly roll or a metropolitan cupcake, he was considered an artist. Even the Vienna roll could take a baker years to learn. The problem is shaping it with your hands. I didn't know how to make it till I came here. The first night I worked in my father's bakery, he says, 'Now you make Vienna rolls.' I says, 'Vienna rolls I never made.' 'Oh', he says, 'it's terrible. It's so hard to make.' I says, 'Why is it so terrible? Show me and I'll make it.' I didn't know that I was talking presumptuously or something to that effect. He gave me a piece of dough and he showed me. The way my father showed me the first night, that's the way I'm making it now. And if he's down in his grave there in the *gan eyden* [Paradise], he's turning over and he still wouldn't believe it. He used to say to me, 'You never made a Vienna roll before?' I says, 'No, I never did.' He didn't believe that I had learned it so quickly. So you see, with me, baking is sort of an inborn trait. That's all there is to it."

"If your family was prosperous in Europe and your father wasn't doing so well in America, why did you decide to come here?"

"It's the same like I told you with my father. I didn't decide. It was decided for me. During the First World War, the czar moved people he considered under suspicion of being in sympathy with Germany to the Crimea. Jews were considered under German influence, so the family was moved to Melatopol in Tabritshiske Gubernye, the Crimea. The house was actually in a *dorf* [village] or at least something in between a village and a town. We had a railroad running through it, which already made it something. The facilities in the town or village was like in any other place—a *brunem,* a well where you got your water from. I remember we used to grow our own cherries and fruit which we ate and used as fillings in the baking. I remember, too, in the bakery we used to make *tsukerkes,* like the gumdrops that you get here. The house was one room with an earthen floor. On the side we had an orchard. I remember also we had stalls like a market so we could sell the bread. This was quite a change for us because in Kovno we had a family house with electricity, running water, and flush toilet even."

THE MIRACLE OF INTERVALE AVENUE

"How long did you stay in Melatopol?"

"We lived in Melatopol for a while. Remember, after the war Russia was still in turmoil with a revolution and then civil war. In 1923 there was a famine and a cholera epidemic in Melatopol. My mother died. So I with my brother and sisters, an aunt, and a large group of kids and grownups traveled around Russia. We went from place to place tracking down relatives. I even returned to Kovno and saw the family home there. Anyway, the HIAS [Hebrew Immigrant Aid Society] came to our help and sent us to Hamburg, where we were treated by German doctors. We were still a whole group of kids with some adults. An aunt came along. You know, in those days we didn't travel with suitcases. When we left Russia, the women who stole across the border with us would wear maybe three or four dresses, one on top of the other. Everything they owned they wore.

"From Hamburg we were sent to Liverpool, then to Normandy, and from there to America. The boat crossing took two weeks."

"Landing here must have been quite a shock."

"No. Not landing. To me the crossing was more of a shock than when I got to America. They gave us food on the boat, meat. And with the meat they gave us wads of what we thought was butter. The *mashgiakh* [supervisor of ritual purity of food] had to explain to us that it was O.K. to eat it because it wasn't real butter, but margarine. In other words, it was kosher to eat with meat."

"That must have been important to you. Your father had been a lamdn. And you were tutored by the Kovner maggid."

"Not really. At that time I didn't only eat kosher because in Melatopol we were starving. We ate whatever we could find. Once we slaughtered a horse and my grandmother cooked horsemeat. That was if we were lucky. Most of the food we ate was animal fodder. We ate corn cobs, which she cooked with a piece of meat. It was a delicious dish. After all, it was accented with hunger and need."

"Did you have a job in Melatopol?"

"I didn't work in the bakery. I just helped out a bit. I sold some baked goods to the soldiers in camp in exchange for sugar. We made *tsukarnyes* [candies] from sugar. I also stole from the army camp some supplies."

"So you became a baker when you came to America?"

"Not right away here either. I did many things before I became a baker. I got here on July 4, 1923. I went to live with my father. He had a home in East New York, Brooklyn. That first week was the hottest time ever. I had nothing to do so I went for a walk in the street, and I saw a buxomy woman walking with a block of ice that she got from across the street, from the Knickerbocker Ice Company. So I went up to her and I asked in

Moishe Sacks inside
his bakery.

Sacks locks up his bakery on Hunts Point Avenue.

On the way home from *shul*, Sacks rests in a local park.

Sacks has called this apartment home for nearly fifty years.

Yiddish, 'Can I lend you a hand?' The woman said, 'No.' But I was insistent. Finally she gave in and I brought the ice to the fourth or fifth floor of the tenement where she lived. The woman gave me a nickel. Another neighbor saw what was going on and offered me a nickel if I would bring her some ice, too. The woman gave me fifteen cents—ten cents for the ice and five cents for me, for my efforts. Sometimes they'd ask me to remove the tray of water inside the icebox and they'd tip me for that, too. Then I began to ask them on my own whether they wanted me to remove the water. The next thing I do is I go to the man working at Knickerbocker. Lucky for me the man is a Jew, and I ask him in Yiddish if he'll give me the ice on account. Now this was after my first trip when my total capital amounted to less than ten cents.

"The man offered to sell me the ice at the wholesale price. He showed me how to cut the ice up. Then I built myself a cart. And pretty soon I was making good money. One day my father asked me if I needed any pocket money. So I stuck my hand into my pocket and pulled out a bundle of dollar bills that I had already pulled in from my new business. I was making as much money as him."

"So you were pretty resourceful. You adapted quickly."

"I adapted because there was no alternative. There was no welfare at that time. And like I told you, my father didn't make that much money as a baker, so I couldn't expect him to take care of me. Besides, in Europe already I had gotten used to fending for myself. Like I told you, in Melatopol things were very hard."

"How long did you stay in the ice business?"

"Not too long because the husband of one of my customers had a business where he used to distribute all kinds of newspapers. One day he offered me a job to distribute to City Line and Far Rockaway. So I began to do that. Eventually I bought a Ford truck. I was making good money—not just from newspapers. You talk about being resourceful. I used to go to the Lower East Side and buy cheap—different kinds of supplies like film and pencils. And I would sell these to the stores. I used to work from one or two in the afternoon until one in the morning. Saturday night I would work right through until the morning. I did this for ten years. I was making good money.

"At that time I had apartments all over the city. I was an eligible bachelor, so the women who ran the rooms that I rented would supply me with a bed, a meal, and sometimes, too, their daughter in marriage if I wanted. The same time I was working I went to high school and then to Brooklyn College. I was so busy I used to pay the lab assistant to write up the experiments for me because I had to go to work.

"Anyway, since we're speaking of going to work, have you had enough

THE MIRACLE OF INTERVALE AVENUE

to eat? You sure? Let me go in back there and get to work on what I got to do."

I pack up my tape recorder and Sacks escorts me to the door. The following week I again accompany Sacks to the bakery. During lunch we talk about the shul. When we finish eating, Sacks seems to be in no hurry for me to leave:

"If you still have questions, we can talk while I work." Sacks puts away the bin of tuna. He places the empty cans and used utensils into a huge gray garbage bin. Then he motions me to follow him into the back of the bakery, his work area. If the front is a holdover from the 1950s, the back might very well be turn-of-the-century: tin ceiling, wooden refrigerators, and thick wooden workbench, made concave by years of rolling and compressing dough. The absence of daylight and the piles of encrusted metal baking pans contribute their share to the overall sense of another time and place. To enter is to feel the presence not of work but of craft.

Sacks dons an apron, opens an ancient-looking wooden refrigerator, and pulls out a huge mound of dough, which he begins to knead. As we talk, he rolls out the dough, cuts it into six-inch squares, and fills each square with apple filling before folding over the diagonals and pinching the ends closed. I decide to resume the discussion we had begun the week before.

"I'd like to know more about how you got to be a baker. So far you've told me only about other work you did, like delivering newspapers."

"When did I start to work as a baker? I was baking then, too. Even though I was doing all these other things, in between going to school and working, I still had something to do with baking. I helped out in my father's place. My father never paid me any wages, mind you. He never had enough. And I was making good money driving the newspaper truck."

"Why did you stop?"

"I was a wild man with the truck. I used to have all kinds of accidents. I had so many accidents that I was finally brought up before the judge. I came there with my books from school and he says, 'We'll have to lock you up for the night.' I says, 'All right. Just send me up a cup of coffee and I'll do my homework.' So the judge says, 'You shouldn't be driving a truck. You have to go to school? Go!' He calls up the newspaper that I delivered and he tells them, 'The nerve you have to have this man drive a truck. Put him in the editorial department. Let him write.' So they did.

"And I learned from the editor of the newspaper, who happened to be a Chinese man at that time. And one of the exercises was to try to teach me Chinese. I also learned to write editorials. Actually I was like a rewrite editor. A reporter used to bring me a story. And there was this much space, so I had to rewrite. They taught me the first thing to do is get the gist of the story in the first two sentences. And then, if there was more space, so you fill in the details. What I learned there, I also made use of here in my work. Today, for example, the most important thing I had to do is to make the apple turnovers. So I already made the apple turnovers. Now I'll make the chocolate cigars.

"I worked at the newspaper for over ten years. You must think I'm a Methuselah. But the trouble with me is just like if I tell you now for twenty years at the Intervale Jewish Center I've been acting rabbi and social director—you heard how I got blamed for not sending someone a get-well card when she was sick—now people may think that what I do in the synagogue is all the work that I do. But I work in here in the bakery congruently. So I worked for ten years on the newspaper. I went to school at the same time. And even so, those weren't the only things I did. I even worked part-time as a mortician. I used to get fifty cents for washing a corpse. And if the person died in an accident, we used to fix him up so he looked good by stuffing cotton in his mouth to push out the cheeks. By the time I got finished with him, the person looked great. That, too, I apply in my baking. You see that showcase over there with all the birthday cakes with fancy decorations and flowers? Well, one cake I made, the helper put a pan on top on the dumbwaiter and pushed in the icing. My boss's wife starts crying, 'The cake is ruined!' Her son says I'll have to take all the icing off and start again. I take a look at it. I get a knife, one of the long ones, and with one fell swoop, less than a second it took me, I cut across the cake and cleaned it off so it looks like that's how it's supposed to look. The roses were so beautiful, they looked like they had been freshly cut.

"Anyway I was telling you that besides doing all these things I also worked part-time as a baker for my father. Not for money, mind you. Sometimes I even gave him money if he ran short. I didn't work full-time as a baker because, like all bakers, my father didn't want me to be a baker. He wanted I should become a doctor or a lawyer and after that a teacher or a civil servant. I had a chance to go to medical school in the Midwest. But I needed five hundred dollars, and my father couldn't lend me the money. He had just remarried and he had two young children. 'Moishe,' he told me, 'you I'm not worried about. You can take care of yourself.'

"The two children, my father had with his last wife. He was much older than her when they got married. That marriage came about because my sister wanted to get married to this woman's brother. The brother had an older sister who was still single, and somehow at the engagement it was decided that my father would marry the sister and my sister would marry her brother. It happened about the same time, so it was almost a double wedding.

"Since I didn't have the money for medical school, I applied to go to

THE MIRACLE OF INTERVALE AVENUE

teaching school. When I went for the test to get in, the woman who examined me for elocution asked where I was born. So I told her, 'Lithuania.' 'Oh, Mr. Sacks,' she says. 'I knew I could trace something in your accent.' In those days if you had an accent, you couldn't be a teacher. So I told her, 'I'll tell you what you could trace. You could trace by my accent that I'm a Jew. And you're an anti-Semite!'

"Then I went to take the exam for letter carrier. There I met another *antesemit*. Only this one was Jewish. I passed all the exams, but you have to be five foot two. So the guy measured me and he made me take off my socks. Then he rams the measuring rod down on my head. With the socks and my hair I was five foot two. Without I was maybe five foot one and a half. So I failed that test. But all that just goes to show you how everything works together. All along I was destined to be a baker. And this is how it happened.

"My father had to swab the ovens. He had to put a big bag on a stick, tie that with a string, and then go inside in those big ovens that they had, and there's a knack to it. That string actually revolves around and cleans the oven. And it cleans the oven so immaculately that you can bake on the bricks. That's a trick that takes bakers years to acquire. To be able to start that thing to swing and keep it swinging. Now, my father in the process of swabbing the oven, the stick broke and the splintered part entered the flesh of his hand. And either he didn't clean it enough or there was a lot of dirt in there, and since he did not bother going to a doctor at the moment, his hand became poisoned, infected, and he was disabled in the work."

"Permanently or temporarily?"

"Temporarily, of course! Permanently disabled for a baker is only when he dies. You had your hands broke and your feet broke. This broken or that broken, but you work. It has nothing to do with being a baker. So he called me in. Naturally loyalty to parents at that time was predominant. I stopped working for the newspaper.

"I could earn good money as a baker, too. Ten dollars a day. Cab drivers I knew were earning that a week. So I decided to continue working in my father's bakery. Besides, it was fated for me to be a baker. Baking is my life. Do you know that I know over three hundred and sixty-six recipes—one for each day of the year? You don't believe me? You're not the only one. I proved it once as a personal *tour de force* for my boss's wife that I could bake a different cake for every day of the year. And all from my head, mind you. I never read a recipe. And I don't only bake Jewish cakes. I know all kinds of German recipes, too, because when I first came in here in 1936, there were still a lot of Germans living here. This used to be a German bakery."

"What brought you to the Bronx?"

"I'M A BAKER, I KNOW VINEGAR"

"I told you that I was working for my father in Brooklyn. The bakery he bought didn't last a year. The Depression was on and he went bankrupt. The problem was that my father was more of a Talmudist than a business-man. So when he went broke, he lost whatever he had. And like a foolish man honoring the old standards, he paid up all of his creditors, even in later years when he got work. He worked and he paid them all. When we closed the bakery I went to work for my current boss's grandfather, who had a bakery in Brooklyn. I worked for him for one day not because he needed us but out of pity for us. Because we were left with absolutely nothing. And with the ten dollars I earned and the ten dollars my father earned, we rented a house. Remember, with the bankruptcy we lost everything. So we had no furniture. We slept on the floor—me, my father, his wife, and their two children."

"You weren't married at the time?"

"No. At the time I wasn't married. I got married in 1936, just before I moved up here. I knew my wife from before, from the *mishpokhe*, the family. We were cousins. Even with all the jobs I used to do, I still managed to go out on a date. So we used to go out together. My father decided we should get married. When he hurt his hand, I told her, 'Lizzy, you come now and work in the bakery with me. Papa got his hand hurt.' The next morning, four or five o'clock, she's there. We're opening the store and Lizzy is there. So my father says, 'What are you doing here?' She says, 'Well, I came down to help Moishe. Moishe told me he's going to work in the bakery.' My father says to her, '*Meydele, du kenst shteyn do, kenst do arbetn. Az du shteyst do* Moishe and you *darfst khasene hobn*' [Little girl, you can stay and work here. Since you're here, Moishe and you should get married]. That's all. It wasn't like a shotgun wedding or something to that effect. My father didn't force me to get married. For the almost thirty years I lived with her, I really loved her. My father just pushed things along.

"I had the wedding in the house. *Geret un geton* [No sooner said than done]. What do you think? They made the *khupe* [canopy] in the house in the living room. All the presents I was promised by the relatives I'm still getting. I'm still waiting. Because most of those people are dead. This one promised me a lamp. The other one promised me a kitchen chair. And the other one promised me a living room set. This one this and that one that. I was a married man. At the time I worked different places as a general baker. I came in at night and whatever had to be done I did. Then the same year I got married, I was offered a job here."

"How did that come about? Weren't you living in Brooklyn?"

"I was. But they unionized this place, the delegate sent me down to work here for a three-day duty—Tuesday, Wednesday, and Thursday. I

THE MIRACLE OF INTERVALE AVENUE

couldn't work the weekends. They were very busy here, but they had good German bakers, expert bakers who were actually much better bakers than I was, and they carried the Saturday and Sunday trade, which was at that time the biggest trade here. At that time, as I told you, mostly Germans and Italians lived in the neighborhood.

"At the time, the three days was considered full time. I was making thirty dollars a week. Thirty dollars a week in those days was equivalent to four hundred dollars now. The other bakers here were only making thirty or thirty-five dollars for six and seven days' work. Since I was the only union baker, I got the union wages of ten dollars a day. Anyway, one day I told the boss that coming here three days a week was pretty hard for me and I would like to move out here and I would like to have an extra day's work. So he called me a communist. To work four days a week and to make forty dollars a week in those days was unheard of. So I had to compromise with him. I told him I'd work the four days for thirty-seven dollars a week. Then he asked me whether I knew how to make challies and stuff. You see, the Jews were starting to move in so he needed Jewish baked goods. I said, 'Definitely, I know.'

"Afterwards, when the war broke out I was slowly promoted to five days, then six days, and during the wartime I worked seven days a week. For seven years straight. Sometimes I worked around the clock. Come home, just two blocks away. Eat. Go into the tub to wash myself and go back again and do it. Seven days a week I worked for seven years straight."

"Why?"

"Why? Because I was young enough. I was strong enough. And I was crazy enough. That's the three things why. Nothing else."

"So why did you stop working seven days straight?"

"First of all, the war was over. Second of all, I had a collapse or heart attack or whatever you want to call it in 1957. From where I'm standing now I fell to the table. I went over with three pans of rolls. They called in the doctor. The doctor told me to stop working and to stop smoking. After a few months of inactivity, I put on so much weight that the doctor told me to take up smoking again. From 1957 till today the pipe still sits on the end table in my living room stuffed with tobacco. I haven't touched it since. As long as I live that pipe is going to sit there because that's a sign to me a doctor's got a nerve to tell you what you're going to die from."

"You don't like doctors?"

"I got nothing against doctors. But those doctors who treated me, every one is dead. I've outlived them all."

"It must have been hard not working as a baker."

"It was. After I got well, I worked at various jobs. I also made out income taxes as an accountant. I was working there like a dog and I didn't like it. Because that was not my work. This is what I like to do. Baking. So I went and asked permission from the doctor to come back. He told me to try it like this. Work two days and stop. At that time I could do what I wanted because it was part my bakery. I was a part owner."

"How did that come about?"

"It came about because I used to work for a man who didn't believe in buying in quantity. So when I needed this ingredient or that, I was always out. It was a nuisance, so I began to buy in quantity myself. We have a huge basement down there, and I could store the bags in the basement. Whatever the bakery needed I would sell to him. Then one day Pearl Harbor happens, and right afterwards rationing goes in. But it doesn't affect me because I wasn't the owner of the bakery. Prices kept going up and something that I bought before for five cents a pound I could sell for a dollar seventy-five a pound. I sold to the other bakers in the area, too. I actually never put any money down on the bakery, but as each new owner came in, I was recognized as a part owner. When my wife was alive, everyone was like mishpokhe. Everyone pitched in. Now I feel more like an outsider. And when I tried to move to Israel ten years ago, I decided to sell my share and I asked the current owner to buy me out for what they would consider a fair price. Anyway, as I was telling you, when I came back to work after I collapsed, I started gradually. For a year I worked two days. Then for a year I worked three days and stopped a day. And then five days a week. And now if I work an eighty-hour week, sixteen hours a day, I don't feel any repercussions. You can make your own assumptions what I had. All further X-rays or cardiograms show that there was no mark, no scar left on the heart."

"How long did it take you to get back into the old routine?"

"Not too long. A year or two. My wife died in 1961. December 2. The sixth Hanukkah *likhtl* [candle]. She had a heart attack. When she died I was already in this groove, although summers when she was alive I worked in the mountains as a hotel baker. This way she could have a little fresh air. I also had a place in Far Rockaway where summers she could go with the kids. I used to go there Friday during the day and work out there all weekend. In between working I still had time to play some poker and the other things I had to do. If I needed any rest it was nothing for me to jump into the ocean, take a swim, then lay down on the sand for about two hours wrapped up in a blanket and go to sleep. Then I'd get up and go to work again."

"Did your wife ever complain that you didn't spend enough time with her?"

"No. I had no complaints from my wife that I wasn't spending enough time with her. If you don't believe me, you can ask anyone who knew me. Though most of them are dead, so they can't say anything bad about me even if they wanted to. I would work a full day at the bakery and sometimes even more, sometimes thirty-six or forty-eight hours straight. But even when we started dating and I worked nights for the newspaper and went to school, if we had something on, I was there. All she had to do was tell me in advance. Saturday nights we used to play poker. In those days I wasn't *shomer shabes* [observant of the Sabbath], and I would work all day Saturday in the bakery. At night we would go to the poker game with friends. We would play all night and into Sunday, then Sunday evening I would be back in the bakery."

"It sounds like quite a life."

"I enjoyed living. But at the same time, baking is a certain pleasure to me. People may consider it work. Not to me. Not when I see the finished product from raw material. These danish look almost alike to you? When I see the product afterwards, passable to be sold because I turned the tray this way to the hotter part of the oven or that way to the colder part, I get pleasure from it. I enjoy this work."

"With the money you were making, I'm surprised you never considered investing in some property."

"You mean I should buy one of those burned-out buildings?"

"No, no. I mean before the area declined."

"So who says I never considered? Even with all the work I was doing, there was always more I thought I could do. Before my wife died, I thought of buying some buildings. I had the money, and as I told you, I was already doing enough jobs, so one more really wouldn't matter. But my wife was against it. She wanted to leave the area. Also she preferred to give someone else the headache. What did she need to sit outside the building and give someone the pleasure of complaining that this needs fixing or that needs fixing? Then when she died, twenty years ago, I was in shock for years and in no condition to consider buying anything. I remember at that time I used to go on long walks from Hunts Point to Flushing Meadows and other places, too. Just recently I tried to walk along Fordham Road. I had to turn back because it was too dangerous."

"You live in Fort Apache and you find Fordham too dangerous? Isn't it supposed to be a much safer area than Hunts Point?"

"Does that surprise you? Here it's not dangerous for me and there it is? Well, it's true. Here I'm known. There I'm a target. Here I'm used to people and they're used to me. Here people know me as 'Mister Sacks.' 'Mister' they call me. Even a bum on the street asking me for a dime calls me 'Grandpa.' If I moved someplace else they'd just say, 'Get away, old man!'"

"I'M A BAKER, I KNOW VINEGAR"

"When did the neighborhood change?"

"You think it's all of a sudden that black people and Spanish people started living here? Even when I moved here in 1936 there were black families living across the street from me. People tended to keep their distance from them, too. You know why? Not because they were black but because they were upper class—professionals and civil servants, and we were simple working-class people. So people were a little bit in awe of them."

"But there were really very few Spanish or black people in the area then."

"Yes. Most of the Spanish people moved here in the 1950s. Manny, the guy who owns my building, his father was a middle-class Puerto Rican who bought Titelbaum's, the grocery store on my street. Titelbaum sold it because Jews were moving away and he had trouble making a living. Manny's father expanded it. He set up a take-out deli counter. But he was shot during the 1960s in a holdup. It had something to do with some kind of gang activity, although I don't know the whole story. Anyway, besides my building, Manny owns the liquor store, the pizza parlor, a billiard club, and Titelbaum's. He's like his father—a middle-class Puerto Rican. By the way, he married a Jewish girl. He even gives me money sometimes for the shul."

"You must have found the transition of the area from a Jewish to a Puerto Rican one hard."

"Not really. The influx of Spanish people into the area never bothered me. I got along very well with them."

"Do you find them noisy?"

"No. Only when they had dances outside sometimes. Or when they have more than one family in an apartment. Sometimes the music bothers me because I listen mostly to classical music. I remember one time I decided I would get even. I opened wide all my windows and turned every radio in the house on full blast. The neighbors all wanted to know what kind of music that was."

"And when there were gangs in the area they never bothered you?"

"The gangs never gave me any trouble. They all know who I am. Not too long ago I was in the subway and a gang of kids comes in. They were looking to mug somebody. And one of them says, 'Leave him alone! That's Moish from the bakery.' The few times I was mugged, the people who did it were not people I knew. Once I was mugged going into my building. Someone was waiting for me. He put a knife to my throat. Thank God a woman came in just in the knick of time and screamed. So he ran away. Another time I was on the way to the bank. I was carrying my usual shopping bag where I keep all my main possessions, including my bank book. When he mugged me I gave him what I had in my pocket, it was maybe a couple of dollars. He took my shopping bag and threw it into the garbage can. As soon as he left I picked up my bag and I went into the bank to make the deposit. The last time I was mugged was this past year. I was going from the bakery to my house. Three kids jumped me from behind a car. One held his hands over my eyes. Another put his hands into my pocket and took out my wallet. Before I had a chance to ask what's going on, they were gone. Aside from a sore arm where they held me, the only problem was that I had to spend time at the bank the next day canceling my credit cards. And when I went to Social Security to get a new card, the first thing the guy asks me is, 'Do you have any identification?' So I try to explain to him that the reason why I'm here is because that, along with everything else I had, was stolen. He still insisted I had to have some piece of identification. And that's not the only funny part to the story. When the cop came to fill out the report, he asked me how much money I lost. I said, 'It must have been about seventeen or eighteen dollars.' So he says, 'O.K. I'll put you down for *khay*.' [The Hebrew letters stand for the number 18. Since the word means "life," the figure or a multiple of it is a traditional sum for gifts.] Aside from the trouble with the Social Security, the only lingering trouble I had was that my arm was a little stiff for a couple of weeks where they grabbed me. But you see, that was my fault, not theirs. If I had been younger, my arm would be more flexible, so it would have offered them less resistance."

"What about when they had all the fires in the late 1960s and early 1970s? Didn't you feel threatened?"

"You mean the night the lights went out? It didn't affect me. Stores on either side of me were broken into and looted. But the bakery wasn't touched."

"How come?"

"For two reasons. One was because Murray Ellman and a couple of other cops from the 41st Precinct stood outside with shotguns. One even stood with his gun cocked and dared the looters to come for him. He was just itching to get at them. But even without the cops, I don't think the bakery was in any danger. You see, the leader of the looters was a young black fellow. I knew him since he was a little boy. He grew up on Faile Street near my house. He was a very smart boy, too. I think he had an I.Q. of a genius. He worked for me sometimes in the bakery. I would tell him a recipe once and he would remember it. This boy told the looters, 'Leave the bakery alone. Mr. Sacks is in there.' So the bakery kept on going even during the riots. Eventually, he ended up in Dannemore penitentiary. I don't think for murder, but something close to it."

"So you never considered leaving the area?"

"I considered. I told you, ten years ago I decided to move to Israel. I wanted to join a kibbutz. So I tried out being a baker there. I remember I decided to make apple strudel. Now, this kibbutz had the most up-to-date machines. But when I looked around for the canned apples, everybody started to laugh. 'The apples are in the orchard,' they said. Some of the women went out to get some apples and they peeled and cored them. It was just like my grandfather's bakery in Russia. Everything was fine. Until they came to the papers, which is my old trouble. The same as I got here with the Social Security. There's a little thing that they have on the papers—age. Or maybe it was that I asked them whether they take care of a person after a certain age. 'Sure,' they tell me. 'But what do you have to worry about it? Definitely we take care of you after you retire. But what the hell are you talking about retiring? You have to worry about that? You're still in your forties! By the time you retire you'll have given us twenty years.' 'Boytchik,' I says, 'it doesn't work that way. Here's my age. Here's my Social Security.' He's looking at me and he says, 'You're working?' I says, 'Sure, I'm working. I'm working in a bakery here yet.' He showed me afterwards people who are younger than me but so downtrodden by their age that they were actually semi-invalids that the kibbutz was taking care of. So naturally they didn't believe my age. Then my sister who was with me told them, 'What do you have to worry about? This man never wants to retire.'

"But like I'm telling you, things didn't work out for me in Israel because I couldn't find a place for me to work. I even went to one bakery in Jerusalem and offered to pay the owner to let me work. He says he can't do that. I ask him why not. He says, 'If you work here and I pay you, so we know that I'm the boss and you're the worker. But if you work here and you pay me, then how are we supposed to know who is the boss and who is the worker?' "

"So you stay in the area, in part, because you have a bakery where you can work despite your age."

"I stay because here I'm a big fish in a small pond. It's better than being a big fish in the ocean. Also I'm known here. I'm respected. There's the shul and the bakery. It's baking that keeps me alive. I've never heard of anyone dying from baking, only from not baking."

"Dying from not baking? I don't understand."

"My father died from not baking. His wife died when she was sixty-six. He was in his eighties and she died three years before him. She was his last wife and she was the longest wife he ever lived with. He loved her. He just died from a broken heart. He refused to do anything. Up to the day that she was alive he worked in the bakery so that I couldn't keep up with him. I worked in Rockaway with him, he as a bread baker and I as a cake baker. He used to pick up a two-hundred-pound bag of corn bread, and if I didn't give it fast enough to him, he took it himself. He was over eighty. He was only about four years, comparatively speaking, older than I am now. And when she died, forget about it. He stopped baking. He had his own apartment. He had a shul there. He had everything there. But the moment she got sick, he stopped. He stopped working. My sister took him in and fixed up an apartment for him in Queens. He had a beautiful apartment. To this day it's still there. She's waiting for me to retire there."

"Is that why you've never considered remarrying? Because you associate remarriage with your father's death?"

"Let's say it's a good thing Freud isn't around here. You see, my mother died when I was still young. So from then already I learned not to put too much trust in a woman because she may one day not be there. Then, when my wife died, it sort of confirmed what I already felt. Besides all that, I wouldn't consider remarrying because I'm married to the bakery. To my job. This is all I need. If I married a younger woman and she'd want to spend time together and I wouldn't have the time, it wouldn't be fair to her. And don't think there haven't been any offers. When I was in Israel I went to the religious section of Jerusalem. As soon as they found out I was a widowed American, they all had daughters they wanted to marry me to."

"So you have no plans to remarry?"

"I wouldn't say I have no plans. Let's just say I have no immediate plans. After I retire, then maybe I'll get remarried."

"You don't envy how your father's life ended?"

"No."

"Because he died poor?"

"He didn't die poor. He wasn't rich, but he wasn't poor either. Listen, my father was from the old school. He believed in paying off all of his debts. Remember, when we went bankrupt there were a lot of people he owed money. But he lived to pay them all back. Legally, he didn't have to do that. But even with all that he still left enough money in his will for not only his grandchildren but even for his great-great-grandchildren. My father left a very funny will. He left nothing to the children. His entire estate he left so that every grandchild—my sons, my sons' sons, their sons—at every birthday they get a check from Grandpa, from Great-Grandpa, from Great-Great-Grandpa. They get a ten-dollar check for their birthday. They never saw him, but they still get. He didn't die a poor man. He died a smart man. He left a legacy for himself that lasted for generations. Now, that's immortality."

"Would you like that same kind of immortality yourself?"

"I don't know whether I'll be able to have that kind of immortality because the tax system has changed since then. My immortality is in my baked goods. I told you, when I die someone will come in here, smell the

danish, and remember that I used to bake them. Or they'll remember me
from a wedding cake or somethng I once made them. The fancy decorations that it had. Some of the cakes I even keep pictures of. I got one right
here in my bag."

Sacks rifles through a plastic shopping bag on top of his workbench and
takes out a pile of papers held together with a rubber band. He removes
the elastic and flips through the pile until he comes to a color snapshot.
"This is a picture of the *bar mitzvah* cake I made for my grandson in
Virginia. I worked on this cake for ten days. It even has an open Torah
scroll with Hebrew writing on it. You can even read that it's from the
parshe of his bar mitzvah. I made that from a combination of chocolate,
glucose, and honey. I was so afraid that something would happen to the
cake that I even bought a separate ticket for it on the plane so I could put
it on the seat beside me. The travel agent had the ticket made out so that
one was for me and the other was for Mrs. Sacks. When I got onto the
plane, the stewardess wanted to put the box in the rack up front. I told
her, 'No, I'm putting it on the seat beside me.' She said, 'No. That seat is
for Mrs. Sacks.' So I told her, 'There's no such thing. The seat is for my
cake.' So I put the cake on the seat and they all came over to see it. 'Oh,
my! It's so beautiful!' They couldn't get over it."

"So baking gives you the chance to impress people with your skills as an
artist?"

"Not just as an artist. You can do it in a practical way, too. When I was
in Virginia, I took my son and his wife out for dinner. I ordered a bottle of
wine with dinner. So the wine steward brings the wine and he goes
through the whole ceremony. He pours a little and he lets me smell the
cork. I smell the wine and I make a face and say, 'This smells just like
vinegar. It's no good. Take it back.' The waiter is flustered. He smells it,
then he, too, makes a face and sends it back. It creates a whole commo-
tion. The next bottle arrives, again he goes through the whole ceremony
with the cork. I taste it and this time there's no problem. So my daughter-
in-law says to me, 'Dad, I didn't know you were such an expert on wine.'
'I'm not,' I said. 'I'm an expert on cake. I'm a baker, I know vinegar.'

"Look, Jack, I'm getting tired, so if you have no more questions I'll let
you out. It's late and I have to get ready to go home. We can talk some
more another time."

As I packed up my tape recorder Sacks prepared a box of cookies and
danish to hold me over until our next meeting.

We talked many times during the five years I visited the Intervale
Community. Throughout our discussions, there always emerged that
sense of creative resilience and self-assurance that first became evident to

me in the story about opera fudge. Toward the end of my study, Sacks encountered a heavy blow to the self-contained world he had created for himself. The owner of the bakery, determined to retire and unable to find a buyer, abandoned the business, leaving Sacks and its various employees without a place to ply their craft. Although Sacks had anticipated the event for at least two years before it happened, he still found it difficult to separate himself from his place of work of nearly fifty years. He still had a key to the store, and on weekends after shul he would walk to the bakery and sit there, reflecting on his life. I joined him sometimes and listened to his musings on how he would spend the rest of his days.

"Now that I have so much time on my hands, I'm thinking maybe I'll become a writer. The only thing is I can't figure out what to write about."

Sacks's interest in a new career was only half-hearted. The truth was that he was waiting for someone to buy the bakery. His attitude was wait and see. He didn't have to wait too long. Eventually the business was purchased by two Venezuelan-born bakers. The new owners were only too glad to have him work for them. Not only was he still, approaching eighty, capable of doing the work of several men, but his association with the place drew in hundreds of loyal customers from the Hunts Point Market who had missed the old Jewish bakery. Still, despite their need for one another, the relationship between Sacks and the owners was stormy. On the surface, the cause for disagreement was the owners' desire to attract a Spanish clientele, while Sacks was determined to keep the old Jewish customers. Whose style would predominate? Underneath the tension, however, lay another reason for the conflict, stemming from Sacks's temperamental nature. Moreover, Sacks's feistiness had long been his *modus operandi* at the bakery. In part, it was an artist's prerogative. But in part, too, feistiness was a personal rebellion against the tyranny of fate, a protest against the helplessness of aging. Despite advanced age, Sacks's angry outbursts had the effect of cowering not only uncooperative helpers, but even the very owners of the bakery. It was his way of asserting control.

One Saturday on our way toward the bakery for lunch after shul, I asked Sacks how he liked working once again.

"Things are going O.K. I already had a good fight with them this week."

"So it's just like the old days."

"Just like the old days. Only now there's a different accent to what we fight about. Like what happened on Thursday. The owners and my helpers were all in the back yapping away in Spanish, and I couldn't understand a thing they said. I didn't know if what they were saying was important, like something had happened outside that needed attention, or they were just talking. So I asked that around me they should speak in English. They said it's a free country and they could speak Spanish if they wanted to. So I said that's true. But it's a free country for me, too. So whenever they speak to me, I'm going to answer them in Yiddish. They kept coming to me and I kept giving them back answers in Yiddish. Some of the Jewish customers who were in the store heard what was going on. They heard me talking Yiddish and they thought it was the funniest thing they ever heard. Even the new boss's uncle, who speaks Yiddish fluently, got a charge out of what was going on. This went on all day long. Finally they agreed that around me they would speak English. I told them, 'Look, you can speak Spanish as much as you want, but when it has something to do with the baking and it concerns me, speak in English so I can understand, too.' "

"Don't you think that there might be ways to handle things without fighting with people? Aren't you tired of the aggravation it causes? Most of the time it's probably not even worth it."

"I don't agree with you. For life to continue there has to be a conflict. When you're too passive, you get nowhere. The moment you acquire such a solution to the problems of life, you stop living it, you're putting a damper on your life. Some of the most juicy things in life are fights."

"Well," I respond, trying to firm up my argument, "I don't mean all fights, of course. I'm just saying that not all fights are worthwhile."

"How can you evaluate a fight?" Sacks counters. "You can't evaluate a fight. A friend of mine died from a heart attack during a fight over a two-cent bottle deposit. He used to lose hundreds of dollars at a time when we played cards together. I used to bluff him out." It seems to me that Sacks has given me some ammunition. Not realizing that it's really bait, I use it. "But you see, that's my point. Why drop dead from a heart attack for a two-cent deposit?"

"It was a good fight. It cost him his life, so it was a good fight."

"For two cents?"

"No! The fight was not for the two cents. The fight was because his whole business and everything he was worth would amount to nothing if some young whippersnapper has the gall to tell him that his word that he bought the bottle at that store is no good. Look, he died fighting. His life was worthwhile. What difference does it make if a person is killed in a hijacking or he dies in a fight over a bottle deposit? The result is still the same. If a fight costs a man his life, it was a good fight. You can't figure on the two cents. A fight is a very important part of a man. You can't put no value on a fight. Absolutely not. Besides, when a man gets older and he reaches the autumn or the winter of his life, he needs some offense to get the adrenaline going. So there's nothing like a good fight to stimulate the body. If you're too passive, then you become like a vegetable. I like a good fight. It's sort of a way to tell myself I'm still alive."

· 3 ·

"THAT'S THE SHUL
I DON'T GO TO"

It is Saturday morning. Moishe Sacks pivots his head away from the Ark to scan the congregation. "How many we got here?" he asks.

"Nine," someone answers.

Sacks takes a quick count to determine whether all of the regulars have arrived, adds the names of two others who have informed him during the week that they will not be present, then instructs one of the men to open the Ark containing the Torah scrolls.

"We got a minyan. We got nine, so we'll open the Ark and God can stand in for the tenth." Sacks's voice betrays a sense of triumph. Several days earlier, on the Jewish holiday of Shavuot, only six men had been present, not enough to constitute a minyan even with God's help. At the time, Sacks had apparently felt doubly cheated. He believes that the continued existence of the Intervale minyan is guaranteed by God; and without the minyan, the priestly blessings to ensure the well-being of the congregation could not be made.

Determined to right a wrong, Sacks turns to Malachi and Mordechai, seated just behind him, and asks: "Do you want to *dukhn* [recite priestly blessings]?" The two *kohanim* (priests) look at each other, uncertain how to answer. Mordechai waits for his father to speak first.

"It's shabes!" Malachi finally responds, sounding bewildered.

"I know it's shabes." Sacks retorts. "But this week was a holy day and you couldn't make the blessings because we didn't have a minyan. Now we got a minyan. Do you want to do it now?"

"You're supposed to do it on the holiday, not on shabes," Malachi insists. "The only time you make the blessings on shabes is on Yom Kippur. Yom Kippur is a bigger holiday even than shabes."

"Look," Sacks responds. "It's up to you. I'm saying you can do it if you want to."

Mordechai, who has been silent until now, suddenly joins the discussion. "Come to think of it, I was once in a synagogue in Brooklyn somewhere, a Sephardic synagogue. And they made the blessings on shabes. I didn't think the Ashkenazim do it, though."

"That's right," Malachi confirms, responding to his son's uncertainty. "Ashkenazim don't make the blessings on shabes. Kasidim [Malachi pronounces the gutteral kh sound of Hasidim as a hard k sound] don't do it either."

"All right," Sacks concedes, sounding disappointed. "It's up to you. If you don't want to do it, then let's just finish the service."

During the kiddush following the service, we discuss the issue of whether or not one can chant the priestly blessings on shabes. Sacks responds to Mordechai's continuing uncertainty with a tactful reprimand:

"There's a story I read about a famous rabbi in Safed. One day he says to his students, 'Let's all go down to Jerusalem and go pray at the Western Wall of the Temple.' Anyway, one of his followers, a young man, objects that he can't go right away. He first needs a few minutes to go tell his wife. The rabbi suddenly becomes very disappointed and he says, 'Never mind. We can't go now. You see, had we all decided at that moment to go to Jerusalem, our spontaneity alone would have brought down Messiah. Now we'll just have to wait until the right moment comes again.' You see, Mordechai, had we all agreed at that moment to make the blessings, we might have brought the Messiah down."

Mordechai seems a little distressed by Sacks's story. "I'm sorry, Mr. Sacks. I just didn't know what to tell you. Ashkenazim don't do it on shabes. Sephardim do. I figured we do things here the Ashkenazic way."

Sacks realizes he may have gone too far in reprimanding Mordechai. Concerned about Mordechai's feelings, Sacks closes the discussion by poking fun at the makeshift way things are done at the Intervale Jewish Center.

"What's the matter with you, Mordechai? Don't you know already that we don't go by the Sephardic way or by the Ashkenazic way? This is the South Bronx. Here we go by the Intervale Jewish Center's way."

What Sacks actually meant was, "Here we go by Moishe Sacks's way."

THE MIRACLE OF INTERVALE AVENUE

In its current composition, the Intervale minyan is virtually an invention of Sacks's imagination. There are times, though, when even Sacks must bow to a determination greater than his own, namely, that of Malachi Parkes, a strict follower of mainline Orthodox Judaism.

Although Sacks is seen by anyone even remotely connected with the Intervale Jewish Center as its leader, or "rabbi," on Saturday he shares the helm with Malachi, the congregation's "cantor." (Malachi hesitates to use the term himself since he has no formal training in liturgical singing.) Indeed, in matters of ritual practice, Sacks generally defers to Malachi, by far the more observant of the two. Unlike Sacks, Malachi plays it by the book, reflecting the firm religious training he received when he first came to this country from Abyssinia.

A Falasha Jew, Malachi emigrated in his youth, and he remembers little about the land where he was raised. But he can describe synagogues that were built high up on hills, where the air was so thin it was hard to breathe. Some even remind him of the Intervale Jewish Center because, like it, they were built of stone and were dug into the ground. Malachi left Abyssinia with his father. At the time, Emperor Selassie was harassing the Falasha, and those who could began to seek new homes in more hospitable countries. Malachi arrived here on a merchant ship. Like other immigrants, he was greeted by a representative of the Hebrew Immigrant Aid Society, who introduced him to a rabbi at International House. The rabbi had a major impact on Malachi's life. He instructed Malachi in American Orthodox Judaism, and he introduced him to his future wife, a strictly Orthodox Yemenite Jew. Before coming to this country she had lived in Morocco and worked in France as a schoolteacher and later in England, where she learned Yiddish. Mordechai, the offspring of that union, was raised in an atmosphere of utmost piety. He attended the Salanter Yeshiva, and even now, years after he graduated, he wears the garb of the ultra-Orthodox. While Malachi, Mordechai's father, retains simultaneously an identity of a Falasha and an Orthodox American Jew, Mordechai's primary identity is that of a yeshiva bokher. Even his speech exhibits the curious blend of the vernacular and Yiddish, a typical trait of yeshiva graduates. Malachi, exhibiting pride mixed with mild rebuke, refers to Mordechai as the "Kasid" because he spends so much time in Williamsburg, a hasidic neighborhood in Brooklyn. "If Mordechai were able to, if his hair weren't curly, he would grow *peyes* [sidelocks]."

As an Orthodox Jew, Malachi believes that religious laws, fully obeyed, bring God's grace upon the congregation. "Every morning during the High Holy Days, Mordechai blows the *shofar* [ram's horn] in the living room of our apartment," he says. "I tell everyone in the building that it brings them good luck. That's why ours is the only building on the street that's still standing. All the others, they got burned or got destroyed. But our building is still standing."

A humble man, Malachi tries to blend in rather than stand out. Religion for him is a way of assuming his place among the generations and of living out his remaining years with a sense of dignity and inner peace.

Unlike Malachi, Sacks is determined to leave his mark. Religion is a weapon that he brandishes to ward off nagging fears of oblivion. For him the continued existence of the Intervale minyan is a personal triumph in a struggle with mortality. Although he insists that God alone assures the survival of the minyan, he realizes that God may at times have other things to attend to; so Sacks keeps a constant vigil on the comings and goings of congregants, always hopeful that with some coaxing, a casual visitor might develop into something more.

For Sacks, the ability to maintain a congregation represents the fulfillment of a thwarted dream to be a teacher or a rabbi. Although he is not ordained, he has *smikha* (ordination) of a sort, as he jokingly claimed when the synagogue received a brochure from Gamblers Anonymous marked "Attn: Moishe Sacks, Rabbi, Intervale Jewish Center." A more serious claim to rabbinical ordination derives from the comment of a rabbi friend whom he sees at the annual banquet of the Union of Orthodox Rabbis: "You know, Moish," the man insists, "you're more of a rabbi than a lot of other people at this table even with their ordination, because of all of them, you're the only one with a congregation."

Like his rabbinical ordination, Sacks's congregation is very much his own creation. Of the original members of the congregation who were present before Sacks arrived some twenty years ago, none are left. Congregants arrived for reasons of their own and stayed in large measure because of Sacks's encouragement. The relationship is reciprocal. For just as they are his congregation, he is their rabbi.

Whereas Malachi is resigned to fulfilling God's commandments, Sacks actively innovates, using his fertile imagination to twist and turn and on occasion invent religious law to accommodate the needs of an aging congregation. In Sacks's view, "*Halokhe* [religious law] is like a rubber band. You can stretch it and bend it, just so long as you don't break it."

Sacks is well versed in rabbinic law, and he knows the ins and outs of permissible behavior. Sometimes he goes a little beyond the limits of normative Judaism, intuiting adjudications that lack any precedent in rabbinic jurisprudence. One April 16, for example, the day after income tax is due, there were only six men in the congregation for the Sabbath service—four short of the ten needed for the minyan. Sacks suggested that since it was April 16, it might be possible to consider the minyan complete: "Five of the men are over sixty-five. And if you're over sixty-

THE MIRACLE OF INTERVALE AVENUE

five, you get a double tax deduction, which means you're counted as two people. So, if you're two people in the eyes of the IRS, you probably count as two people in the eyes of God." Sacks was overruled by Malachi.

This frequent tug-of-war between them has a playful, almost gamelike quality to it. Each is respectful of the other. Malachi knows that Sacks's charisma attracts new members to the congregation, thereby enabling the shul to survive; Sacks knows that Malachi's piety gives the congregation a kind of dignity that offsets many indiscretions that take place in the house of worship. Each is aware, too, that underneath their differences lies a basic commitment to the same ideal, the preservation of the only living trace of Judaism in the South Bronx. Out of that common commitment has emerged a very deep trust between them.

The contrast between Malachi and Sacks stems, in part, from two distinct sets of experiences and different approaches to Orthodox practice. But there is another difference here, which has to do with the nature of the community in which they live and lies at the base of their religious devotion. For both men, religious observance provides a crucial link with the world they shared with their spouses—a very different world for each of the two men. When mentioning his wife, Malachi always describes her fierce piety. Sacks, speaking about his wife, describes a very different woman, one who was very much a part of the neighborhood:

"Twenty years ago, when my wife was still alive, she was a diabetic and I had to watch her. I had a home out in Rockaway. And when I didn't watch her she would go to Howard Johnson's and order 'The Kitchen Sink.' It was every ice-cream flavor they have. For her it was pure poison. I came home and I had to rush her to the hospital. She was so sick the *khevre mishnayes* [religious study group] I belonged to had to come over to recite *tehilim* [psalms]. There's a church opposite my home. Years ago, they would play bingo there, just like they do today. My wife used to play regularly, and one day she hit the jackpot. So I would make a contribution when they asked me to, just as if I belonged. When my wife was sick, I told the priest and he came up with a group of nuns. They lit candles and said prayers. My wife was on the critical list. I saw her that night and I told her, 'I'll see you tomorrow.' 'Do you think I'll be all right?' she asked. 'Are you kidding?' I tell her. 'With all this help, how could you not be?' "

Behavior, too, can be an act of commemoration. The contrast between Sacks's adventurous liberalism and Malachi's cautious conservatism inside the synagogue extends to their attitudes toward the surrounding neighborhood. Although Malachi and Mordechai are black and one would think that their color would give them a measure of safety in the neighborhood, in fact they feel anything but secure. They avoid leaving the apartment unattended for any length of time despite their good relations with others

in the building, particularly with an elderly black Jew on the ground floor
who sits by his living room window and watches everyone entering and
leaving the building. Mordechai usually hurries home after services while
his father enjoys the kiddush. Each house-sits on alternate Sundays while
the other joins the brunch at Intervale or sponsored trips to suburban
synagogues.

Mordechai has frequently warned me to be careful walking in the area:
"The muggers know the old people don't have any money, so they don't
bother them. But they don't know you, so they assume you've got money.
You're a target."

Mordechai carefully places all the money he carries in his shoe in case
he gets held up. Both father and son avoid streets they believe to be
dangerous and, on some they do take, stay as close as possible to the
center of the road to avoid possible ambush by muggers lurking in dark
alleys.

Both also spend considerable time outside the neighborhood. They
frequently attend morning services in Pelham, where Mordechai shops
for kosher products no longer available in the South Bronx. Malachi, too,
often gets upset at the "hoodlums," kids who hang out in the park adjacent to his apartment with their radios blasting disco music. "All night,
they go thumpity-thump, thumpity-thump," he complains. "You can't tell
them nothing because you never know who has a gun." Although the two
are friendly with local merchants and others in their building, while
walking with them, one is constantly reminded of the dangers posed by
the unknown, particularly by groups of youths.

In some ways, the two lead the lives of recluses. Their four-room
apartment is sparsely furnished. The former dining room has a miniature
Ark in which they store several tiny printed Torahs, as well as phylacteries and prayer shawls. A small *mizrekh* (ornament marking the East,
toward which Jews pray) hangs on one wall of the blue-painted room lined
with chairs. The room with the uncomfortable-looking chairs looks like a
place to sit *shiva*, the seven days of mourning. The blue paint and bare
floors intensify the gloom. This is the room where they pray, but it is also
the room where Malachi's wife did her sewing. Her sewing form is still
there. As Malachi explains: "When my wife was dying, she asked me not
to give away her clothes. So I kept them. They're all in this closet.
Everything else I gave away, the furniture, everything. But the clothes I
kept." The room is a shrine; its sparseness highlights the centrality of
prayer and mourning in the house.

Sacks's home is a shrine, too. Besides the personal possessions of family
members and those of a close friend who lived there several years ago, the
rooms are filled with newspaper clippings and correspondence related to

THE MIRACLE OF INTERVALE AVENUE

the Intervale Jewish Center. Whereas Malachi's sanctuary alternates between the home and the synagogue, Sacks's sanctuary is spread out, divided among several "safe" spots—the home, the synagogue, his workplace, the bakery, and a local park where he spends considerable time. He is outgoing, and his tendency is to include an ever-widening circle of people within his orbit. The strategy he pursues inside the shul is no different from the strategy he pursues outside on the street. As a result, Intervale has come to resemble somewhat the streets of its constituency.

Over the years, Sacks has expanded Intervale's congregation by deliberately keeping an open mind as to who qualifies for membership. Sacks's view is that anyone who calls himself a Jew is welcome. Sacks's position may belie an effort to reconcile practical considerations and bizarre situations. One occurred some time ago when a local "street person" decided to "join" the shul. Sacks tells the story as if it were the most natural thing in the world to arrive one day for services and find that someone had entered the building through a window and literally moved in. When Sacks related the incident to me, I asked him why he did not have the intruder removed. Sacks replied with his own peculiar sense of logic, "Because he would simply have broken in again. This way, with someone living in the shul, the place would have around-the-clock protection from vandals." Partly in jest, I asked Sacks whether the man was included in the minyan. Sacks hesitated for a moment, unable to remember one way or another. At first he said the man was not included. Later he corrected himself: "Actually, the man was included. Malachi referred him to a rabbi, where he studied to convert and was told by the rabbi that if he were accepted by a congregation as a Jew, he could be considered a Jew. I presented him before Intervale's congregation, and the man was included in the minyan. Unfortunately for us, the man turned out to be a psychopath. One Saturday we arrived in shul, and when we opened the Torah we discovered that it had been desecrated with human manure. Then, when we went to get the other two Torahs, we found that they, too, had been desecrated. The man denied that he had anything to do with it. He insisted someone must have broken in while he was out. Not long afterwards, he was arrested for murder or attempted murder. I think he tried to kill his father or his father-in-law. He went to jail. And aside from occasional letters from the jail's rabbi, that is the last we've heard from him."

Despite that incident, non-Jews are not discouraged from attending services. Sundays, a frail-looking, squeaky-voiced black woman, widely reputed to be a former madam, attends the brunch and sits through the review of the parshe. She makes contributions to the shul and even has Sacks say memorial prayers for friends and relatives. A second non-Jewish woman, a southern-born white Baptist, attends too. She chooses to avoid the black Baptist church near her apartment. "They're not my people. These are my people," she says, pointing to the others at the Intervale congregation. Although she is interested in the service, particularly the Sunday review of the Torah, her identification with Intervale is a matter of race rather than religion. The black woman, though, virtually considers herself a Jew. She frequently attends holiday services and sometimes makes rather substantial contributions to the shul. Sacks has a simple explanation for her behavior: "She needs some form of religious expression, so she comes here and she gets it here."

Through his job in the bakery, Sacks sooner or later comes into contact with almost everyone who lives and works in Hunts Point, from the producer of the Paul Newman film *Fort Apache* to the girls in the Hunts Point whores' market. If the person has any connection to Judaism, Sacks actively solicits him as a member of the Intervale minyan. Two blocks from Intervale, up the hill toward Jennings Street, stands a black synagogue that has been struggling to remain alive for the past several years. Sacks has repeatedly tried to get the congregants to attend Intervale, so far with little or no success. Individuals come now and then. But most live outside the area, and there is little motivation to return for the sake of a shul other than their own.

Sacks also has a way of finding the Jewish element in the least likely places. Some of his openness stems from earlier experiences, resulting in part from the fact that the Hunts Point area of the Bronx, though largely Jewish, was never entirely Jewish. Germans, Irish, and Italians lived there before Jews arrived, and some remain there even today. Sacks's bakery, for example, was a German bakery when he began to work there in 1937. His fellow bakers were German, and from them he developed an extensive repertoire of German wares, from breads to elaborate cakes and cookies. Some of these find their way into the Sunday brunch at Intervale despite the fact that the only Germans currently in the area dwell not in houses or apartments but inside Sacks's mind as fond, almost tangible memories. Among them is Louis Horn, who worked with Sacks in the bakery and acted as *shabes goy* (a non-Jew who performs essential tasks that Jews are forbidden to do on the Sabbath) in the neighborhood. "The man used to do everything," Sacks recalls, "from turning on the lights on shabes to filling in for the minyan. Once I walked into shul and I see Louis Horn sitting there. I asked him what he's doing there. So he tells me, 'I'm waiting just in case they need me.' He meant for the minyan." A few years later, at Temple Beth Elohim, the synagogue Sacks attended before coming to Intervale, Sacks's son Arthur and some of his friends who were on the football team sang in the choir. "In fact, two of them weren't even

THE MIRACLE OF INTERVALE AVENUE

Jewish," says Sacks. "So they weren't counted in the prayers, only their voices were. When the shul closed, these two non-Jews wept louder than anybody else."

Sacks's openness to non-Jews contains a curious blend of the practical and the mystical. On Saturdays, I usually walk with him from shul to the bakery. Sacks is cautious about changes in the contour of the road or sidewalk lest an unwary footstep cause a fall and injury. But even such precaution does not preclude casting a sharp eye on the social landscape. One Saturday, about a block from the shul, Sacks recognizes an old, haggard-looking black man. Sacks greets him and asks how his friend, "the one-legged guy," is doing. The man responds: "My friend is O.K., but I'm not. I just got out of the hospital. I have diabetes, and I still feel very weak." Sacks, in his typically optimistic way, assures the man that he looks pretty good, then turns to me to confirm his assessment. On cue, I agree. Continuing on our walk, Sacks says to me: "I told him he looks good. But he really looks pretty bad."

"Who are these people?" I ask. "And how did you meet them?"

"I know them because they used to sit on the stoop of an abandoned building. This was when the shul was getting vandalized all the time, and every day almost I was getting calls to go with the police to see the condition of the shul. I would pass them by, and they would say *shalom* to me. A man who says shalom is at least ninety percent Jewish. When the weather got a little colder, I invited them into the shul to warm up and have some refreshments, both for the spirit and the body. Some wine and some cake. This way I figured they would tell their friends that Jews aren't such bad people and that no one should do anything to the shul. So instead of having a hundred break-ins, I had maybe fifty. One of the women would tell me off for letting what she called the 'riff-raff' into the shul. Maybe they are riff-raff. But the ten percent that is riff-raff is balanced by the ninety percent of them that is Jewish."

Other examples abound. Summertime, the bakery is closed for a two-week annual vacation. Having no work to do, Sacks spends his weekdays in a small public square on Southern Boulevard and Hunts Point Avenue and reads Jewish novels, popular science magazines, or *Reader's Digest*. Behind him a group of blacks in their mid- to late thirties hang around and shoot craps, using the metal frame of a subway entrance as a backstop. The players know him, and Sacks sometimes listens in on their conversations. "Once I overheard one of the players use the Yiddish term *shokl* for shaking the dice," he recalls. "So the man must be a Jew."

Sacks is often in contact with individuals who ask him to perform certain services connected to Jewish ritual: "There's a Puerto Rican owner of a store next to the bakery. He gives me money each year for the *yortsayt* [anniversary of death] of his father-in-law. The man apparently married into a Jewish family, his wife must be Jewish. Maybe he'll also join the Intervale Jewish Center."

Sacks has the peculiar belief that there are Jews hidden within every nook and cranny of the Hunts Point area. Their Judaism is dormant but will emerge in the course of time. They are, for Sacks, a reservoir of people whose fate is very much bound up with the continued existence of the Intervale Jewish Center. All of them are prospective members. They appear among the congregants as they are needed and as they themselves need the shul. One man, a gentleman in his nineties, drops into the bakery from time to time. Sacks has been trying to persuade him to join the minyan. The man refuses to consider doing so, saying, "Synagogues are for old people. You see these? [He points to his mouth.] I still got my original teeth. And you see these? [He points to his eyes.] I don't need glasses. So long as I got my teeth and I don't need glasses, I'm not old and I'm not going to shul!"

One Yom Kippur a young man dressed in dirty work clothes, his breath smelling from beer, walked into the shul and stood just behind the other men. I handed him a prayer book and invited him to join us, but he refused.

"You got a minyan here?" he asked.

"No," I responded, realizing only then that he meant no harm.

"What time you blow shofar?" he asked.

"About eight P.M.," I replied.

"O.K., I'll be back in the evening with some people. You'll have a minyan."

Later that evening he returned wearing a suit, accompanied by another man who was also dressed up. "I'm sorry. I promised to bring a whole bunch of people. But only my cousin was available." The two were sufficient; another visitor had arrived during the afternoon. The *Neilah* service marking the end of Yom Kippur was conducted with a minyan.

One case of a congregant emerging to shore up a depleted minyan is that of Juba Abraham Rashim. For two years Rashim had been a periodic visitor to the Intervale Jewish Center, dropping by from time to time, generally when services were nearly over. He came to see Mrs. Miroff. According to her, he disliked the "bums" who hang out inside her tailor shop, so he preferred to visit her in shul.

At the time when Rashim first began coming, Horowitz, a short man in his late seventies who spoke very little and so remained one of the more enigmatic people I found at Intervale, was still a regular member of the congregation. He would sit opposite Mr. Flisser, Mr. Abraham, me, and Mr. Kaplan, facing us at the same table. Although he rarely spoke, he was

THE MIRACLE OF INTERVALE AVENUE

affable and communicated through the residue of what must once have been a charming personality. Indeed, he was known as a lady's man. Saturdays he would accompany Rose Cutler to shul, then back to the projects where they live on Tinton Avenue, two subway stops from Intervale. The two would watch television together, then he would fall asleep. Rose believed that Harold, or "Herry" as she called him, wanted to marry her. But she, still loyal to her handsome husband who passed away more than two decades ago, preferred courtship to marriage. Eventually, Horowitz entered a home for the aged. His decision was rather sudden. Rose felt abandoned, and the minyan was missing one man: the home Horowitz had entered was Orthodox and frowned upon residents traveling on the Sabbath. Although he had promised to commute by bus to attend the Sunday brunches, he never did.

Ever since I have known Sacks, he has held firmly to the belief that God protects the minyan. Someone will always come along to take the place of a congregant who moves away or dies. At about the same time Horowitz entered the home, Rashim changed from an occasional visitor to a regular congregant.

Rashim's reception at Intervale was pretty much straightforward. No one questioned his motives, nor for that matter his pedigree. Rashim was not the first black person to join the congregation. Malachi, the cantor, and his son Mordechai are both black. Lena Michaels and her mother are black Jews from the Caribbean and had been regular congregants for many years. Deborah, Lena's cousin, is also from the Islands, though in recent years she had visited the shul only sporadically after moving some distance away. Her nephews, Yohab and Seth, one a yeshiva student, the other just past bar mitzvah, would join her on occasion, and the presence of both was heralded by the congregation—by Sacks in particular—as an infusion of young blood into an aged congregation.

There were others who attended sporadically, as Rashim had at first. One elderly black man, an accomplished musician, would stop by on Saturdays when not on tour. He was counted in the minyan although he refused to be called to the Torah, always claiming not to feel well. In shul he usually chewed a large wad of gum, which he placed behind his ear during the kiddush. Another who dropped in once was a slightly scruffy though nice-looking young man in dungarees and denim jacket. He stopped by, seeing the door open; he was curious, never having been inside a shul before. The young man was handed a *yarmulke* (skullcap) and a *khumesh* (Hebrew Bible) and shown where to follow along in English. Clearly not Jewish, and making no claim to being so either, he was not included in the minyan.

On the surface, therefore, there is little that is extraordinary about

Rashim, certainly not in the context of the Intervale Jewish Center. Yet Rashim is in fact very different from the other blacks, both sporadic visitors and regular congregants, particularly so because of Rashim's peculiar beliefs regarding his connection to Judaism.

Rashim claims neither to have Falasha ancestry nor to have converted to Judaism. I once asked Rashim whether any member of his family had ever converted. He replied, "Let me put it this way. I have to put it the way I understand it now rather than then. Now, my awareness of my identity in terms of my people I've recognized from three to four years old. I'm just that type of individual. I'm the misfit. I'm the sheep out of the fold.

"I came from a place in South Carolina, a place called Saint Helena's Island. Here is a place where my people, which is still the case today, they are Jews. But the only services that is known, as you know in the South, is Christianity. Any part of the South is Christian. If you're a Jew, you're isolated. Even Jews from Europe. There is no synagogue, yet there are Jews there. They're isolated. So when you speak of going to church, you go to a Baptist church where there's singing, there's praying. They are people who maintain their African customs and culture. So this is that combination of religious ceremonies and rites that you have there. But my grandmother, she came from a family of kohens [priests]. When I go up to the Torah, the reader says, 'Kohen,' right?

"Now, you ask me about my grandparents, whether they're converts. I don't know whether they're converts or whether they came here and some just did not accept the Christian thing that was put down their throat. See, you first have to remember that Christianity is not an African religion. It's not the black man's. This was given to them. So I say, now who is the Christian? Me or you? No. Who is the convert? Now, where are you saying I'm a convert to Judaism? I say, I was converted to Christianity. Now, who was doing the converting? Me or you? These things have to be dealt with."

Rashim meant those words as a challenge to me as an anthropologist. It ought to be my responsibility to reveal the truth about his African background and justify his claim to Jewish descent. Indeed, Rashim's belief in the connection between American blacks and ancient Israelites contributed to a certain insensitivity on his part to the strictures of Orthodox practice. As an original Jew, he felt fully justified in determining for himself when and if he was deviating from accepted Jewish practice.

Rashim's differentness stems not from the merits of his claim to Judaism but from his being torn between two worlds. He wears a purple and yellow knit skullcap, the kind that has become fashionable among certain groups of American blacks. In shul he wears a large and very elegant

THE MIRACLE OF INTERVALE AVENUE

beige cotton *talis* (prayer shawl) with deep black stripes which he carries
inside a jet-black velvet sack with a large gold Star of David embroidered
on the front, matching, in size and contrast with its background, the gold
Star of David that hangs by a chain around his neck and rests boldly on his
dark chest. By birth he is an American black from the South. In spirit he
is both an African and a Jew.

Rashim is now in his late forties. He lives by himself in an apartment on
the Grand Concourse, a once-fashionable upper-middle-class Bronx
neighborhood. Most of the Concourse Jews have long since gone and
been replaced by poorer black and Puerto Rican families. Weekends
Rashim drives his beat-up blue-gray station wagon to the Intervale Jewish
Center.

Rashim learned about the center as a fieldworker for the West Bronx
Jewish Community Council. His job was to seek out isolated Jews and
provide them with vital social services. As he tells it, he loved his work
but gradually found himself alienated from his boss, who he felt resented
a black man's seeing the underside of white society. This, together with
the extraordinary rapport Rashim established with clients, injured his
boss's pride. "So for a while we had quite a battle going," Rashim says.
"And the people who lived in that neighborhood, they would come, then
go back. They would call and ask for me, and I'd make a special appointment to be there. And at times he would send me out just to keep me
from seeing them. So it was quite a struggle. I used to go and sit down and
tell Mrs. Miroff about it. And she would say, 'Don't worry about it. Don't
worry about it. You got to keep going.' You know, at times it would really
hurt me because of his ignorance, his limitations."

Elsie Miroff is a warm but willful octogenarian. She and Rashim became close friends. Rashim offered her transportation to doctors, and in
return he received encouragement and the affection of a woman known
throughout the neighborhood as "Mom." As a regular congregant at the
Intervale Jewish Center, "Mom" shares the responsibility of drumming
up new congregants, and she did what she could to get Rashim to attend.
Being black and somewhat suspect in regard to religious pedigree,
Rashim encountered various difficulties at synagogues he attended before
he came to Intervale. For a while he attended Rabbi Matthew's synagogue in Harlem, a well-known congregation of black Jews, and he was
very much in awe of the congregation's leader: "As much as you would
take, he would give it. But I wouldn't take because I found what he had to
give very powerful. He's the kind of person you have to pronounce the
word exactly. The *khof* and *khet*. I mean they had to be exactly. And if
you're reading and you make like three mistakes, that was it. You're just
cut off automatically. But if you had the will to receive what he had to

give, he'd give it to you. And he always predicted I would be a very good
Jewish leader. 'Because of the fact,' he said, 'you're hard to learn.' And it
has been his practice that anybody that is hard to learn, when they do get
it, they're usually better than the guys who just come and learn."

Rashim's problems at Rabbi Matthew's were not restricted to learning.
The congregation consisted mainly of Islanders (blacks from the Caribbean), and, according to Rashim, Islanders tend to see American blacks
"through the eyes of their masters" (English colonials). But what really
irked the wrath of the other congregants was Rashim's closeness to Rabbi
Matthew, with whom Rashim believes he had "a lot in common spiritu-
ally." "It caused a lot of jealousy," he says. "So when he died I just
couldn't afford to stay, because all the animosity that gathered while he
was alive started pouring out. So that's when I left and came to the
Bronx."

Rashim's path to Intervale was somewhat convoluted, with regular visits to various synagogues nearer to his home on the Grand Concourse: "I
see a synagogue across the street and I say, maybe I'll go. I'll get up one
day in the morning and decide that's where I want to go. In spite of the
experience. In spite of the way I am received. And if I don't have the
feeling to return, I don't return. But I'll go once anyhow. H.I. [a syna-
gogue] is two blocks from where I live. And I've been attending [services]
there for some time." Rashim interrupts the story to describe the rabbi
and congregation of the shul he had attended previously in the Bronx,
which had been very much to his liking: "It was a type of spiritual vibra-
tion that I've never found anywhere. Who you are, what you look like,
never entered into anybody's mind. For some reason they closed the
synagogue down. Because I guess the bookkeeper was making a lot of
money. You know the big salaries that they give out. It's one thing to this
day I haven't figured out, why the salaries that they give out. So they
were forced to close. And that's when I went five blocks down. Naturally,
some of the members went to Y.I., which is on the Concourse a block
away. And a lot went to H.I., which is five blocks away. So I went to H.I.
because when I went to Y.I., I found this very strong wave of prejudice.
The first time I walked in, I walked in with my talis and *tefillin* [phylacter-
ies] and everything. A gentleman met me at the door and he went around
and took up an offering and he gave it to me. 'Isn't that what you want?' he
said. I looked at him and laughed. And then I took the offering and I put it
in the box where you drop coins into for charity. And I looked at everybody, and one gentleman who recognized me walked over and told him,
'This is Rashim!'

"But even prior to that I've gone on by and they look at you like you're
not welcome here. So rather than making other people restless, I just

THE MIRACLE OF INTERVALE AVENUE

withdrew myself and I started going to H.I., where they were friendly. But the rabbi, what's his name, Rabbi N., he's still there. He always had this attitude that I found at Y.I. I would sing and he would resent it. But the members at the time would overpower him. When I'd get ready to do something, he would try to call somebody to prevent me doing it. And . . . all right. I allowed these things to happen. But what nipped it was on January 1, 1979. I can never forget this because it was one of the coldest days in New York City. And I went into the synagogue to make a minyan in a *mayrev* service, an evening service. And it was really cold. And when I walked into the synagogue there was about eight people. So they was glad I was there to make the ninth. And they opened the Ark. And he was sitting in the front reading. Now, I had been attending here for over a year, all the services. My *brokhe* [honor] was taking the Torah out and putting it back into the Ark. But all the time this larceny was in his heart and mind—which I read, of course—that in fact he didn't know whether I was a Jew and I had never proved to him that I was a Jew. And I looked around at all the others, the smiles. W. was a friend who came from the other synagogue. So I looked at them and I shook everybody's hand and I said, 'Tell the rabbi'—and I said it loud enough for him to hear—'that if he checked his history, and he goes back far enough, he'll discover that I was the only [real] Jew in the synagogue.' And I left. And since then several of them have called me and asked me to come back. And I should come and serve. But . . . there is a Talmudic law, that if you enter a house and you find it not worthy, then shake the dust off your garments, draw your peace unto you, and never enter. So taking it from that point of view, I've told several of the members, and they don't even have a minyan now. You know, they're not even as good as Intervale—a big fancy synagogue. But the curse is there. So I cannot, knowing what I know, reenter as long—and I told this to W. this week—as long as Rabbi What's-His-Name is there. I can't go back as long as he's there."

When "Mom" met Rashim he was an ideal candidate for the Intervale minyan. He no longer felt welcome at other synagogues he had attended. He was divorced—estranged from his family and very much in need of a place to belong. With Mom's encouragement he would drop in at Intervale from time to time. Then, facing extended unemployment, and feeling he could be of some value to people, he became a regular member. Rashim explained his reasons for attending: "In the Orthodox idea of service, you give the sacrifice and service. I feel that in Intervale I offer the combination at one time. Because it is a sacrifice going to Intervale and *that* I find the service. Intervale is, you know, cold as hell. It's freezing. So the greatest sacrifice a person can give is himself. So it is a sacrifice in being cold for an hour, even if it's thirty minutes, in order to

Sacks reads from the Torah on Simkhat Torah while Malachi Parkes checks his reading in the *khumesh*.

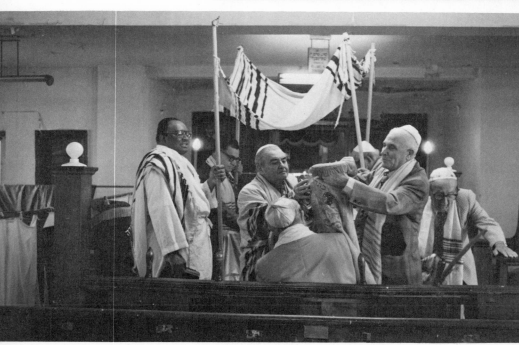

A new congregant helps to cover the Torah after the Simkhat Torah reading.

Mordecai Parkes
regularly chants the
haftorah on *Shabes*.

(*Overleaf*) Malachi chats
with Lucy after Sunday
morning prayers.

Dave huddles by one of
the few working radiators
in the hallway of the
Intervale Jewish Center.

THE MIRACLE OF INTERVALE AVENUE

hold the service. It's not only doing a sacrifice, it's giving energy through encouragement to those who feel the need to serve only this way. That they shouldn't be discouraged. That they should continue in something that is worthy until such time as they pray for the return of the Messiah. Somebody will come with a greater offering, a greater sacrifice, and pay to maybe paint the place and fix it up and renew it. As the new Temple built on the ashes of the old, it will continue to go on. So that's mainly my personal purpose in being there."

In a congregation consisting largely of the elderly, eccentric behavior comes very close to being normative behavior. No one questioned Rashim's motives, nor for that matter his pedigree. Even Rashim's way of mispronouncing words like *Torah*, which he reads as "Taro" while chanting the benedictions for the reading of the Torah, was not unusual. Malachi, the cantor, has his own rather strange and, I assume, Abyssinian pronunciation. Dave Greenstein, who died two years after I began attending services at Intervale, was completely illiterate. When he was called to the Torah, he would simply mumble the blessings in an improvised Ashkenazic mumbo-jumbo. And the fact that Rashim drives to shul on the Sabbath never raised a word of criticism. Despite the Orthodox affiliation, the congregation imposes no code of conduct on its members outside the shul and is tolerant inside as well. Mr. Abraham drives to shul. I ride the subway. And Dave, in addition to his repertoire of lewd remarks and gestures, draws signs in shul. The Intervale Jewish Center is nominally Orthodox. But, in the words of one congregant, referring to the fact that congregants regularly visit other synagogues asking for spare prayer books and other religious paraphernalia, "Denominationally we are whatever prayer books we manage to get."

Although codes of orthodoxy are not imposed, others in the shul are stricter in their observance. Rose Cutler, before she broke her hip and was forced to move in with a daughter in Queens and subsequently to a nursing home in the Bronx, would sit outside the shul on warm sunny days and watch disparagingly as Dave, Sam, and others violated the rules concerning work on the Sabbath. She would click her tongue and refer to Intervale as *"di komunistishe shul"* (the communist synagogue). Malachi stands in front of the Ark praying with his back to the congregation, thereby protecting his view from various indiscretions that are part and parcel of normal behavior at the Intervale Jewish Center. Sacks abides by a liberal orthodoxy, leaving people to do as they please. For the most part he keeps a blind eye to the congregation's behavior and is not bothered by violations of the Orthodox code. Although he gets a kick out of one congregant's joke about the cost of a mashgiakh—"The one with two eyes is one price; the guy with only one eye is double"—there is nothing

"THAT'S THE SHUL I DON'T GO TO"

cynical about his liberal outlook. What may seem to the outside observer as religious indiscretion on the part of individual congregants frequently has, in Sacks's view, some higher religious meaning. After all, each congregant is an integral part of the miracle.

In other congregations Rashim might have stood out sufficiently to provoke a challenge on the part of more strictly Orthodox members. Not so at Intervale, at least not initially. From the standpoint of my research, Rashim at first seemed like a minor character. Neither old nor a resident of the area, he seemed too much an aberration to be useful as a subject for study. Although I thought that his differentness might make him a good informant (anthropologists frequently find their chief informants among the more marginal members of a community), my talks with him were disappointing. At the same time, I could not place his reasons for attending in the same category as those of most of the other members of the congregation. It was precisely Rashim's lack of a handle on the community that led him to commit a faux pas with deep repercussions for him and his relationships with the various members of the community. Although at the time I was very much concerned that Rashim's indiscretions might adversely affect the future of the congregation, the incident not only posed no real threat to the congregation, it revealed facets of the community that until then I had neither seen nor understood, and led to a change in my perspective from static portraiture to the narration of dynamic tension between fundamentally different views on Judaism.

Observing the strains and tensions that sometimes erupt in small societies, the anthropologist Victor Turner developed a model for examining conflicts and their resolution.[1] According to Turner, these "social dramas" characteristically have four phases: (1) They begin with a disruption or breach in the norms that govern social relations between two parties. (2) The conflict rapidly spreads to include a larger segment of the population and does so by dovetailing with preexisting divisions. (3) An attempt is made to mediate the conflict through redressive action. (4) The matter is either resolved or simmers beneath the surface until an irreparable breach is recognized and the two segments split apart, forming their own separate communities. Social dramas are common in any social interaction. Although the four-phase structure that Turner outlined is rarely discernible to the actors, little effort is needed for an observer to see it. Moreover, the model helps to untangle a thickly knotted line of events. I shall use it here to examine the conflict that arose over Rashim's participation in the Intervale minyan.

Every few weeks Hatzilu, a Long Island–based relief organization for the Jewish elderly in ghetto areas, arranges an outing to a suburban host congregation. The Intervale congregation swells to several times its nor-

THE MIRACLE OF INTERVALE AVENUE

mal size whenever it is scheduled, attracting isolated individuals from various parts of the Bronx. Each synagogue affiliated with the organization hosts one outing a year. Since most host communities have participated for several years, congregants are familiar with the day's food and activities long before they arrive. They rate the affair in comparison with the previous year's food and with that provided by other synagogues. They know which outings are worth attending and which promise only meager fare. Some communities go to great lengths to make their guests feel comfortable and cater to their every whim. At one outing, the president of the host congregation announced that if anyone needed help going to the bathroom, he should raise a hand and someone would come to escort him. Leaning over to Sacks, I jokingly mentioned I was considering availing myself of the service. No sooner had I uttered the words than a host took me by the arm and whisked me to the nearest lavatory, pushed the door open for me, and left only after I assured him I was quite capable of doing the rest myself.

Entertainment is a regular part of each outing, and, as with the food, quality varies considerably. Day-school children are featured performers at some, although almost all communities manage to include them somewhere in the afternoon's activities. At one synagogue, the cantor's daughter, who was trying out for the lead role in the Broadway play *Annie,* sang the song "Tomorrow" several times, repeating it each time a member of the audience screamed "Encore!" One congregation's drama group performed songs from the play *Guys and Dolls,* while another, fully costumed, performed a medley of Broadway hits, including "Get Me to the Shul on Time" and "If I Were a Rich Man."

Besides home-grown entertainment, some congregations hire musicians, generally of the caliber found at modest bar mitzvahs and weddings. The host communities also take care to include their guests in the entertainment. If there are services before the meal, Sacks is asked to officiate, while Dave, Intervale's "trickster"/*kaddish*-sayer, is asked to recite the mourner's prayer. Even when there are no services, Sacks is asked to say a few words toward the end of the outing. He always thanks the host congregation, comments on the *mitzvah* (good deed) of bringing grandchildren and grandparents together, and somewhere along the line throws in a highly condensed summary of the parshe of the week, skillfully using some aspect of the afternoon's activities as a cue. Other members of the congregation are encouraged to perform too; most have a set repertoire that they repeat with or without their peers' consent. One woman gets up and sings "I Don't Know Why You Love Me Like You Do." A woman in the audience calls out, "I don't know why either, so shut up and sit down!" A third woman, a Polish refugee who lived in

"THAT'S THE SHUL I DON'T GO TO"

Israel for many years, sings "Hava Nagila" and "Sim Shalom," then proceeds to fire off a slew of jokes in Yiddish to which no one, save me, pays much attention. Excluded till the end of one outing, she took the microphone as everyone was about to leave and had people stand while she sang "Hatikvah." At other outings, she is permitted to sing one song, then reluctantly hands back the microphone to the master of ceremonies.

When Rashim is asked to sing at an outing, he is a welcome departure from the usual entertainment. Summoned to the stage by the master of ceremonies with the fanfare of a night-club act at a Catskill hotel, Rashim, a professional performer, continues with the same pizzazz:

"Good evening, everyone. [It's actually early afternoon.] And I'm enjoying myself immensely. This is my first time being here. And I want to first of all thank you for having me. I would like to do two numbers for you if I may, if I have enough time. The first number is what has come to be known as a Negro spiritual. All right? This Negro spiritual is entitled 'Go Down, Moses.' And I want you to first of all understand that the black people in this country were also, as you know, in slavery similar to as it was in Egypt in the days of Moses. And because they identified with that beautiful story of Moses, one of the things my ancestors were not allowed to do was to speak the language which was known to them. They were cut off from all culture. So the biblical story was one that they could sing in the fields, in their work while doing slavery. So I want you to share this Negro spiritual with me please, 'Go down, Moses.' "

Rashim sings a cappella. His baritone voice is thunderous and slow, resonating with authority. The audience is hushed, and he is in no hurry to let go. During the performance, Mrs. Miroff glows. We bump into each other as I wander about the room looking for a suitable spot for photographs. "You see," she says. "I believed in him and I was right." At the end of the song, the audience breaks into wild applause. Pleased by the response, Rashim steps down from the stage.

On the ride back to the Bronx, Rashim is quiet, but his face displays the glow of triumph. Moving to the empty seat beside him, I ask if he has ever tried to establish a professional career. He explains that he uses his talents sparingly, among the right people and in the right atmosphere. He mentions a rift he had with a promoter who tried to present him as a Muslim. The identity did not suit him, and he stopped singing professionally. He feels comfortable among Intervale's congregants, so he is willing to sing.

Rashim apparently did not suspect the irony lurking beneath the surface of his words. He was too caught up in the success of his performance to pay much attention to Mordechai, seated just behind us, silent and sulking. When I approached Mordechai to find out what the matter was,

THE MIRACLE OF INTERVALE AVENUE

he related his objection to Rashim's singing gospel songs: "Ashkenazic people are the finest people in the world. Long before there was any such thing as integration, I was able to attend a yeshiva and never felt any prejudice. But what makes me mad is the charge some people make that black rabbis are illiterate or that Christian practices are included in the service. If they look at him [Rashim], they'll think they're right." Mordechai's fear that his religious pedigree might be questioned may very well stem from experience. Whatever the cause, Rashim's performance was the source of profound discomfort for Mordechai, and he was determined to set things straight.

The Saturday following Rashim's performance, I arrived at the Intervale Jewish Center to find Rashim pacing the hallway, apparently unwilling to enter the synagogue. Since one of the few working radiators is located in the hall, it's not unusual to find individual congregants huddled over the warm coils, joining the service only when their presence is vital for certain prayers. I assumed Rashim was there for that reason, so I said *gut shabes* (Good Sabbath) to him and headed for the entrance to the main room. Rashim beckoned me over. He wanted to talk before I entered.

"You're not going to believe what just happened," he said.

"What happened?" I asked, aware even by the tone of his voice that something was wrong.

"I came into the shul and went over to shake hands with Malachi and Mordechai, but they would not shake my hand. They just told me to get away, that I'm not wanted here. 'Go to your Christian friends. You're no Jew,' they said."

Rashim was very upset by the rebuff. He continued pacing as we spoke, and his voice had a slight tremor to it. I asked him whether he had any explanation for such bizarre behavior, figuring that he would mention Mordechai's feelings about gospel songs. Rashim mentioned nothing of the kind. He was certain that the cause lay squarely with Mordechai's jealousy. There may have been at least a grain of truth to it. At the outing, the only sour note was Mordechai's dour expression while Rashim sang. Perhaps Mordechai was envious of Rashim's taking the spotlight. Like Rashim, Mordechai has a rich, thunderous voice, but he never trained for a professional career. Perhaps another source of conflict was Rashim's having recently attached himself to Mordechai's father, Malachi. Although Rashim did not sit with Malachi, he would often approach him during prayers that are recited while standing, and he would hover just off the side while Malachi stood on the *bima* (platform) keeping tabs on Sacks's reading of the Torah. Malachi would point out to Rashim where to read in the text and advise him on appropriate ritual behavior.

Malachi had not heard Rashim's performance since it was his turn to guard the apartment. Malachi knew about Rashim's triumph only through Mordechai's apparently none-too-favorable account.

I had arrived during a hiatus in the service before the Torah is removed from the Ark. I was the ninth man. In accordance with Intervale's practice, we would proceed as if the minyan were complete. The door of the Ark is left slightly ajar and the *shekhine* (Divine Spirit) is invited to complete the minyan. Without Rashim, the number would drop to eight. The benedictions for the *aliyas* (calls to the Torah), the *kaddish* (mourner's prayer), and some responsive prayers could not be recited. In a congregation consisting largely of elderly people, the elimination of the kaddish is a serious matter. Just as serious for the morale of the congregation is the failure to obtain a minyan. Although this would not be the first time a minyan was not assembled, if Rashim were permanently excluded, the chances of assembling a minyan in the future looked grim. Moreover, the absence of the minyan signals the inevitable end of the congregation.

Malachi and Mordechai had already witnessed the closing of half a dozen other synagogues in the neighborhood, so they were quite aware of what was at stake. Of all the congregants, they are the most devout. Indeed, they are the only truly Orthodox members of the congregation. But they are also the only members whose religious pedigrees might ever be questioned.

The task of settling the dispute became, as such matters invariably do at Intervale, the responsibility of Moishe Sacks. Sacks was faced with a serious dilemma: whether to rule in favor of Rashim or of Mordechai and Malachi. As in any social group, there is a hierarchy of status at Intervale. Mordechai and Malachi have attended services without fail for years. Both father and son act as *baal tefile* (prayer leader) and cantor, and they lend the congregation a semblance of order and observance that no one else can match. As a practical consideration, they are far more valuable to the congregation than Rashim. Moreover, Sacks owes a special debt to Malachi. When Malachi first came to Intervale in 1972, he had no desire to play the role he currently does in the synagogue's service. As he explains:

"It was Sacks's idea for me to become baal tefile. My intention was to move. When things got tight, I wanted to move out of here. I had no intention of being baal tefile. But on account of all the fires, most of the remaining Jewish families just left. The ones that were left were too old. You're not supposed to even read the Torah when you're old 'cause you make too many mistakes. You don't see so good. Even Sacks makes too many mistakes. Reading the Torah, that's something for a younger man. So one day Sacks says to me, 'You know, Malachi, we're going to have to close the shul down.' I says, 'Why?' He says, 'I can't do the job myself.' He still had a minyan, but he had nobody to come up and lead the prayers. Mordechai and me had plans to move out west, to California. But it's that shul. The shul keeps us here because Sacks says, 'As long as you stay here, Mr. Parkes, I won't move. Don't you leave, because if you do I got to close this place. You help me out. I can only have a minyan just as long as you stay.' We would have been out after my wife died.' "

Although throwing Rashim out would pacify Malachi and Mordechai, as a solution it was a Pandora's box of problems that might significantly jeopardize the membership of the congregation. No one other than Sacks and me knew anything about Rashim's background; no one ever asked and most likely no one cared. The African sound of his name and the commingling of Jewish and African traits were never even cause for discussion. Intervale is a congregation based on tolerance. The behavior of the congregants is rarely seen as threatening, no matter how aberrant it may be from the strictures of orthodoxy. Yet on closer inspection, aberrant behavior is permissible only in certain parts of the shul. And in effect, there exists at Intervale a division of territory. One part is ruled by Malachi, the other by Sacks.

Sacks, Malachi, and Mordechai sit between the bima and the Ark. One could call this area, using the framework of the anthropologist Erving Goffman, a "front region." In a front region, a group displays its ideal self to outsiders. Conversely it relegates the non-ideal or what we sometimes consider the real side of itself backstage.[2] Despite the general laxness of ritual observance at Intervale, the front region is a space where ritual practice must conform to strict orthodoxy. The space is governed by Malachi and Mordechai, and even Sacks acknowledges their hegemony here, particularly on questions of ritual practice. If someone enters the space to get a talis from the stand on the platform in front of the Ark or to open and close the door of the Ark, Malachi will tell the person to stand still during certain prayers, and after their completion he explains proper behavior. At the same time, the other members of the congregation who are seated behind the bima may be entirely out of step with the service; they sit while they should be standing or talk while they are supposed to be fully absorbed in silent meditation.

Three-quarters of the shul's floor space is located from the back of the bima to the hallway. The area is a ritual "backstage" where practice is in accordance with personal need. It tends to be casual, in direct opposition to the formality of the front region. When Bloch, a man in his mid-forties, attended the synagogue, he would sit two rows behind the bima, generally alone but sometimes joined by Hy, who, like him, works in the area but lives elsewhere. Bloch is Orthodox but as manager of a department store, he cannot choose his own hours and must commute to the Bronx to work on Saturdays. In spirit he is aligned with the formal orthodoxy of Mordechai and Malachi, but in practice he violates the Sabbath by working and commuting to the Bronx. So he sits by himself in a kind of halfway world between the Orthodox and the non-Orthodox.

The bulk of the congregation—Mr. Flisser, Mr. Abraham, Mr. Kaplan, and myself—occupies one bench several rows behind and to the right of the bima. Mr. Kaplan pays close attention to the prayers, and he sits separate from us, all the way at the other end of the bench. The rest of us are not Orthodox, and we engage almost conspiratorially in frequent banter during the service. Prayer for us runs a close second to conversation. Sacks is quite aware of this, and he uses the aliyas as a way to break up overly heated discussions. Malachi does not know what goes on since he never ventures over to us, and Mordechai visits only for a moment or two, to exchange the customary handshake and greeting *yasher koyekh* after he sings the *haftorah*.

Between our bench and the entrance to the shul is a second level of backstage, a sort of off-offstage. It provides a second *mekhitse* (partition) without a wall or curtain. Before she died, Pauline would occupy the bench behind us. She preferred to sit away from the other women and closer to the men, partly because of her argumentative nature, which invariably brought her into conflict with one woman or another, and also because she did pay careful attention to the parshe. By following closely in the khumesh and by sitting closer to the front, she was demonstrating her Orthodox inclinations. Sometimes the space was occupied by a stranger who would venture into the synagogue. Not yet a regular congregant, he need not choose a place to sit in accordance with his level of orthodoxy. Dave, Intervale's prankster, never occupied a seat. He roamed about the backstage region, either cutting up the cake for the kiddush or joking with the women seated in the last row next to the entrance, or across the waist-high curtain that ritually divides the men's from the women's section. If a stranger was present, particularly a young woman, Dave spent a good part of the service entertaining the newcomer with his repertoire of pranks and lewd remarks.

When Horowitz left, Rashim moved from the row behind us to the same table where I sit with Mr. Flisser, Mr. Abraham, and Mr. Kaplan, but facing us, with his back to the Ark, just as Horowitz used to sit. His joining us seemed to be his way of indicating that he was no longer an outsider and he was making a commitment to be a member of the minyan. As such, the ambiguity of his identity—the combination African/Jew—posed no problem. Given our own ritual waywardness, none of us could point an accusing finger at Rashim. Indeed, there really was not much in his behavior for us

THE MIRACLE OF INTERVALE AVENUE

to question. Rashim's problems began when he moved from the backstage and highly permissive area of the shul to the front region dominated by the highly restrictive orthodoxy of Malachi and Mordechai. And particularly because Rashim saw himself as an African Jew, his behavior threatened the self-definition of two leading members of the congregation who also defined themselves as African Jews. Rashim had to choose between different sets of identities if he wanted to remain in the front region. Ambiguous behavior could be tolerated only backstage.

By chasing Rashim out, Mordechai and Malachi in effect were posing a challenge to Sacks's leadership, particularly in regard to questions of ritual propriety. Sacks had stretched the bounds too far and they were pulling them back in, forcing him to take some action and define a proper code of behavior. Of course, the challenge was presented with particular force because it came not from white members of the congregation but from black members. Rashim was accustomed to handling challenges from authority by denying their legitimacy and insisting that they were motivated by prejudice. Malachi and Mordechai would be difficult targets for such an accusation. Moreover, they were not claiming that Rashim was not a Jew (as a non-Jew he could do as he pleased), but rather that he had not acted like a Jew. It was the behavior and not the man that had been rejected. Fortunately for Intervale, the specificity of the accusation suggested the most suitable route of resolution.

The objection that Malachi and Mordechai raised to Rashim's behavior also posed a challenge to Sacks. The two were expressing their displeasure over the bad demeanor of a fellow congregant who had embarrassed them by flaunting his non-Jewishness in a public setting. Moreover, that public setting had as its audience white middle-class Jews, the very people whom they would expect to have very little sense of the special conditions under which the Intervale Jewish Center operates, and consequently very little sympathy. The fact that the larger Jewish world outside the South Bronx is considerably less Orthodox than Intervale is not something that Malachi and Mordechai would fully understand, since their primary affiliation with Jews outside the South Bronx is with Hasidim in Brooklyn and Orthodox Jews in Pelham Parkway. Given such points of reference, it is little wonder that Rashim's behavior threatened them.

Rashim's behavior cast a shadow on the balance of power between Sacks and Malachi. At the same time, it threatened to expose, and thereby subvert, the peculiar mechanisms of *makhn zikh nisht visndik* (pretending not to know) what goes on backstage, which enabled the minyan to continue even with a strange and distinctly un-Orthodox crew.

In the past, Sacks's willingness to turn a blind eye to individual congregants' indiscretions went a long way toward keeping people in the minyan. But the case involving Rashim had gone right to the core of the congregation's worldview, touching a raw nerve in its sense of self. At the same time, the controversy involved a matter of proper deference to Malachi. Despite Sacks's greater familiarity with rabbinic texts, he recognizes Malachi's greater piety and on questions of ritual defers to Malachi before making any decisions. Sacks is a great innovator. His Judaism is as much his own invention as it is a sacred tradition passed down to him. But there are bounds beyond which he cannot step, and those bounds are set by Malachi as a representative of mainstream Judaism.

Sacks may very well have thought of a solution to the conflict right from the outset, but without deferring to Malachi, he would have jeopardized the respectful relationship the two men have with each other. Malachi is a proud and very dignified man. Rashim is equally proud. A decision or resolution could not be imposed on either one of them. It would have to emerge from a more subtle form of agreement that would allow both to save face.

A crucial element on Sacks's side was time. The service was running increasingly late, and no one else had arrived to fill in for the tenth man. The longer that remained the case, the clearer it became that Rashim is an indispensable part of the congregation without whom the Intervale Jewish Center was truly in danger of closing. Yet the disagreement among Rashim, Mordechai, and Malachi could not be solved so easily. Malachi is a stubborn man; so is Rashim. And Mordechai, as his father would subsequently admit, was deeply influenced by his mother's religious upbringing and is therefore totally unyielding except to his father. Sacks realized that the fine points of the conflict were not resolvable, at least not immediately. Yet, despite what seemed to me like a very grave conflict, he appeared peculiarly calm. Knowing Sacks, I had expected him to arrive at some resolution based upon an interpretation of rabbinic commentary. But knowing Malachi as well as he does, Sacks would not risk imposing a resolution based upon Sacks's own halakhic innovation. Sacks had a more subtle plan. A week after the conflict was settled, he revealed his strategy to me:

"Reading Kissinger's memoirs, I learned the basics of shuttle diplomacy. The first thing Kissinger did was, before getting both parties to sit down together in the same room, he had to get them to agree that a room is a room. In this case I had to find out whether there was anything that all the parties would agree upon."

The issue had to be addressed not to the congregation at large but to those who had raised or might raise an objection to Rashim's inclusion. Sam, Dave, Mr. Flisser, Mr. Abraham, Mr. Kaplan, and I were not central parties to the dispute. We sat some distance away from the bima

THE MIRACLE OF INTERVALE AVENUE

and did what we were told. We never argued in favor of one or another form of procedure. In other ritual matters, we abided by the decisions made by Sacks or by Malachi. Bloch alone posed a possible problem since he was a stickler for orthodoxy. But Bloch had only a minimal stake in the community. He lived on Long Island and attended holiday services at a synagogue near his home. For him, Intervale was a convenient Saturday waystation rather than a permanent sanctuary. Besides, since he did not observe the Sabbath strictly, he was in no position to impose his orthodoxy on anyone. (He subsequently took a new position that allowed him to be shomer shabes.) So Bloch presented no more of a problem than the other occupants of the backstage region of the shul. The spotlight remained on the original parties to the dispute.

With the central characters isolated, a technique emerged to facilitate a resolution to the conflict. During the discussion, Rashim remained in the hallway, where I had found him when I arrived. Mordechai sat in his usual spot with his back to the bima. He and Rashim were separated like fighters retired to their respective corners. Round two would be fought by other members of their teams. Indeed, the negotiating was done by Sacks and Malachi, both of whom stood facing each other on the bima, one standing for Rashim, the other for Mordechai. And whereas neither Rashim nor Mordechai had any compelling desire to resolve their differences, sibling rivalry and avocational jealousy reinforcing their mutual antipathy, Sacks and Malachi had every reason in the world to find a resolution, including friendship, mutual respect, and the shared experience of widowerhood. Despite their opposite characters—Sacks's inventiveness and Malachi's conservativism—each saw a part of himself in the other. Indeed, the presence of the other allowed each man to articulate a sensibility that might otherwise prove harmful to the shul and its special character: Sacks might innovate too far; Malachi might impose too rigid a religious observance.

To arrive at a basic understanding so that the opposing parties could sit down together, Sacks had to determine what the fundamental dispute was. In this case it was whether or not Rashim is a Jew. Sacks posed the question to each member of the congregation in turn. Sacks knew perfectly well that on this particular issue, the main characters in the dispute would be the least likely people to raise any objections. For Malachi and Mordechai, blackness and Judaism are not mutually exclusive. Also, Malachi had known and respected Rabbi Matthew, so Rashim's connection to the man placed him in good standing.

Sacks asked Malachi whether he had any objections to Rashim aside from his behavior at the outing. Malachi insisted that the only bone of contention was Rashim's behavior at that time. He then asked Bloch whether he had any objections. Bloch had none. Like Malachi, Bloch had not actually witnessed the performance. "O.K. The thing is settled," Sacks announced, then turned to me. "If the man is a Jew, he has a right to pray in a shul. Go tell Rashim to come inside. We now have nine men. Let's take the Torah out and read the parshe."

The issue was nominally settled, but it remained far from fully resolved. After chanting the haftorah, Mordechai regularly shakes hands with all the male members of the congregation, beginning with those closest to the bima, then walking over to where I sit with most of the other men. This time he shook hands with each of us but cold-shouldered Rashim. At the end of the service, during the singing of the prayer *adon olam*, Malachi gradually, and in time to the singing, made his way from where he stood in front of the Ark toward the rear. The other men fell into line behind him, forming a snake line, single file, with Sacks at the tail end. When Malachi extended his hand to Rashim, Rashim brushed it off.

The following week I asked Sacks whether he intended to mediate the conflict further. Sacks insisted that he had already done all there was to do. "You see," he said, "it's like the guy who tries to break through the ice on a river in the middle of winter. He can chop and chop, but as much as he chops through, it still manages to freeze over. But if he waits until spring, the ice will thaw on its own. So it's just a matter of time." I am still waiting to see the thaw.

The following week, Malachi apologized to Rashim, explaining that he knew only secondhand what had happened. Rashim and Malachi resumed the relationship that had been developing earlier, although periodic rifts later put an end to it. Rashim still complains to me on occasion that Malachi is a fanatic and will not listen to reason. Malachi complains that Rashim is "just like those others [Negroes]. They think they know everything. They don't want to learn. You got to learn. When I came here, I didn't know nothing. I had to listen. That's how I learned." The relationship between Mordechai and Rashim remains hostile and silent. Mordechai still makes a point of not shaking Rashim's hand, and Rashim refers to Mordechai in none-too-friendly terms. In Sacks's words, "There remains between them a sort of lukewarm hostility."

Despite continuing friction, Sacks's tact did create a partial solution. If the feuding parties are not friends, at least Rashim's membership in the congregation is tolerated. Indeed, two months later, Rashim decided to sing once again. Only this time it was in shul during the kiddush.

"I have something special for the kaddish," Rashim announces.

"You mean kiddush," Kaplan corrects him, chuckling at the common error of substituting one word for the other.

"Kiddush, I mean," Rashim corrects himself. Rashim stands up and sings a Negro spiritual. While he sings, Sacks and Bloch look at each other uncomfortably. Bloch gets up to leave, whispering to Sacks, "He was right the first time. It is a kaddish." Malachi, surprisingly, seems unaware of any transgression of synagogue propriety. His only concern is after Rashim finishes, when people begin to applaud. Grasping Rashim's hands, he admonishes, "You're not supposed to clap your hands on the Sabbath." Mordechai had left as soon as Rashim announced his intention to sing. Although Rashim had potentially made a more serious breach in the congregation's norms by performing Christian folk liturgy during a Saturday service, the incident did not generate a conflict similar to that caused by his Long Island performance. Bloch and Mordechai, the two most likely to object, expressed their disapproval by leaving. These were private statements not intended to provoke a group response. Although Sacks later acknowledged to me that he did not feel that Rashim ought to sing such songs in shul, he decided against reprimanding Rashim this time: "If he does it again, I'll have to tell him not to." Whether or not Sacks would really be prepared to say something in the future I do not know. In this particular case, since there was no publicly acknowledged breach, Sacks felt no need to intervene.

In comparing the two performances I am struck by the difference between public and private domains of propriety. In the performance on Long Island, Mordechai felt particularly threatened by the behavior of another black Jew in a white Jewish setting. The redressive action was necessary to protect his identity as an Orthodox Jew. The conflict had to be made public in order for Mordechai to publicly state his orthodoxy. The breach in the synagogue service, when Rashim was temporarily excluded, had the quality of what anthropologist Barbara Myerhoff refers to as a "definitional ceremony." Myerhoff uses the term to explain the occurrence of certain types of social dramas. Belief systems are complex and never fully systematized. Under normal conditions, contradictory beliefs are held without posing a threat to the overall system; in crises, the contradictions become manifest and may require smoothing over.[3]

In this particular case, there are two elements requiring definition. On the one hand, the self-definition of Mordechai as a black Jew, intent on making a clear distinction between the identities of authentic black Jews and self-styled black Jews; on the other hand, the self-definition of the congregation as a group open to all. The first instance required an exacerbation of an existing conflict. It proved not to be totally resolvable since any solution would have required Mordechai to become less of an Orthodox Jew, Rashim less of an American black. Neither one would make that sacrifice. But the scale of the conflict was such that it could be more or less swept under the rug: Rashim lacked allies, and without allies revolutions are not made.[4] In the second instance, the ideological differences between Mordechai and Rashim resonate in the views of Malachi and Sacks. One has an exclusive view: "To be a Jew you got to act like a Jew." The other has an inclusive view: "Anyone who calls himself a Jew is a Jew." The confirmation of Rashim as a member of the congregation spoke to a third principle, a common link between the two positions: no Jew can be turned away from a Jewish congregation. Indeed, it is only as a member of the congregation that Malachi and others could exert pressure on Rashim to behave in accordance with congregational norms.

What is most apparent to the outside observer but not to the participants was Sacks's use of sleight of hand to achieve the resolution. By emphasizing a principle that no one would dispute, Sacks managed to relegate the opposing arguments to secondary positions in the face of a stronger, more enduring one. Neither Mordechai nor Rashim changed as a result of the confrontation, and in that sense each could derive a sense of moral victory. But since the congregation defined itself as one that is open to anyone calling himself a Jew, the ultimate victor in the conflict was Sacks. Indeed, the resolution was a vote of confidence for a policy he had been pursuing all along.

So the minyan continues week after week. But its success rests on the latitude permitted in defining group boundaries. Consequently, Intervale resembles more and more the streets of its constituency. And the likelihood, as Sacks, Mrs. Miroff, and others readily admit, is that it will continue to resemble them even more as time goes by. For Mordechai and Malachi, such changes may create dangerous divergences from orthodoxy, particularly from the kind practiced by their Orthodox friends in Pelham or among Hasidim in Williamsburg. It represents to them the inevitable failure of the Intervale Jewish Center and forewarns of their departure from the area, a departure held in check by their commitment to Sacks to stay as long as he does.

For Sacks, though, the changes are merely grist for the mill. The more congregants stem from untraditional backgrounds, the greater his determination to stretch the bounds of religious law and, where need be, invent his own traditions. To him, the Intervale Jewish Center is a holy place. And as a holy place it sanctifies all who enter, Jew and non-Jew alike. Rashim's true identity is of significance to God alone. Noah, after all, was not a Jew, yet it is through his righteousness that we are blessed with life. Indeed, the story of Noah has particular relevance at the Intervale Jewish Center: were it not for the commentary of Rashi [the great medieval scholar] on parshe Noah, the synagogue might long ago have lost one of its last footholds on life. Sacks considers the minyan complete with only nine men. I once asked him about the halakhic justification for

THE MIRACLE OF INTERVALE AVENUE

it. After explaining to me that the Ark is left slightly ajar as an invitation to God to stand in for the tenth man, Sacks proceeded to explain Rashi's interpretation of the reasoning behind the number ten:

"We know that ten men are needed for a minyan because when God told Abraham that He was going to destroy Sodom on account of all the evil that took place there, Abraham asked whether He would do it if He could find fifty righteous men in the city. God said He would not. So Abraham asked if He would do it if there were forty-five righteous people inside. Again God said no. And forty? Again no. They went on like this all the way down to ten. When God said that He would not destroy Sodom if ten righteous men could be found, Abraham realized he could ask no more and he walked away. So we know that ten men are enough to save the world."

"That explains why ten are needed," I interrupt. "But you make the minyan with nine, claiming that God stands in for the tenth. Why not try to figure it with eight?"

Sacks motions with his fingers for me to be patient. "We can't do that, and I was about to explain to you why. At the time of the Flood, there were eight righteous people. Noah, his wife, their three sons, and their wives. So there were altogether eight righteous people, and they weren't enough to save the world. We know from Abraham that ten is enough. And from Noah that eight is not enough. Nine, we don't know. So if we don't know, we can always hope that it's enough and God will hear our prayers."

There is another association to parshe Noah which I make without prodding from Sacks. There is something awesome, almost Godlike in the ferocity of the devastation of the South Bronx. For that reason, Intervale seems all the more like Noah's ark. It is home to people and animals. The superintendent of a nearby building has transformed the rubble-strewn lot adjacent to the synagogue into a garden with tomato plants and pens for raising roosters. The plants have a hard time in the untilled soil. But the roosters, which fare much better, he sends to a brother in Puerto Rico, where they apparently command a very good price. As he explains, "American cocks are very popular in Puerto Rico."

All summer long the cocks multiply. From a lonely cock-a-doodle-doo grows a chorus of young voices, audible inside the shul and not infrequently in time with a responsive prayer or amen. The cocks are not included in the minyan, although congregants sometimes joke about the timing of their crowing. Nor do they count the rats that periodically make an appearance, despite Dave's insistence that they are Jewish. And they do not count the flies, despite Sacks's assurance that they are the *nishomes* (souls) of dead congregants. Nor do they count Christians in the minyan, although they do on occasion make a *misheberakh* (prayer for good health) for Christian friends or family members who may be in need of a little help from above. Then again, they have not yet reached the point where their inclusion would be absolutely necessary for the continued existence of the minyan. One winter, when for a number of weeks only eight men appeared for services, Sacks began to search for a rationale for conducting a full service even without the quorum. He referred once again to the story of Noah to back up his belief that women should be included in the minyan: "Rashi counted Noah's wife and Noah's sons' wives among the eight righteous people, so there is good reason to count women among the ten Jews needed for a quorum." Bearing in mind that the situation was temporary and a break in the cold weather would return the missing congregants, Sacks would do little more than muse on the problem. "I'll have to take this up with Malachi. But I'll wait until it's necessary. Right now I still got the minyan just with the men." A serious departure from ritual law could wait until the need was truly urgent.

Months after open hostility between Rashim and Mordechai ceased, the two still related to each other with cold indifference. I began to wonder whether the ice would ever thaw, as Sacks had predicted. On shabes, after Mordechai chants the haftorah, he comes over to where I sit next to Mr. Flisser, Mr. Abraham, Rashim, and Mr. Kaplan. He shakes hands with each of us. I try to push Mordechai's outstretched hand toward Rashim, but to no avail; Mordechai does not want peace. Deciding to take a more direct approach, I sit down next to Mordechai in front of the bima, and I ask whether he wants to end the conflict with Rashim. His answer is a resounding no. I try to press the matter, but Sacks, though reading the Torah, overhears the conversation and calls me for an aliya. It is his way of informing me to leave well enough alone and not to interfere. Perhaps he is afraid that by pushing the issue, I may accidentally subvert the technique he had used to resolve the conflict. Or perhaps he simply realized that the conflict does not pose a threat to the continued existence of the shul. Mordechai and Malachi have accepted Rashim's inclusion in the minyan, and Rashim continues as a regular congregant. The combination of Malachi's kindly disposition and Rashim's isolation precluded any of the more serious and long-lasting consequences. The conflict between Rashim and Mordechai was a flesh wound rather than a mortal blow. What it ultimately revealed is the truth of Victor Turner's assertion that even small societies contain within them discordancies that give social life an emerging, ever-changing character.[5] This fluid quality is crucial to the survival of the Intervale Jewish Center. It enables the minyan to survive and it helps the congregation assert its vitality in the face of an aging membership. Little wonder, then, that Sacks felt such profound disap-

THE MIRACLE OF INTERVALE AVENUE

pointment at Malachi's refusal to dukhn on Saturday. The spontaneity that symbolizes life was overruled by a rigidity that threatens to overwhelm the congregation. Little wonder, too, why Sacks was relatively calm in the face of the irresolvable conflict between Rashim and Mordechai: for Sacks, conflict is a sign of life. Nor is he the only congregant who realizes that.

One shabes, watching Rashim and Mordechai cold-shoulder each other on the bima, I turn to Mr. Abraham and ask him, "Do you think the two will ever settle their difference?"

"Never!"

"Why never?" I ask, bewildered by the certainty of his statement.

"Because Jews are that way."

"What do you mean, Jews are that way?"

"Jews are that way. Have you ever heard of a shul without a conflict? This guy doesn't speak to that guy. It happens all the time. It reminds me of a story about a guy who is shipwrecked on a desert island. Years later a boat comes along and rescues him. So this guy shows the boat's captain around the compound that he built. First he shows him his house. Then he shows him the stable. And finally he shows him the shul. So the captain asks, 'If this is your shul, then what's that over there?' 'Oh, that?' the guy answers. 'That's the shul I *don't* go to.' "

·4·

REBBE AND GODFATHER

Sabbath services are over. The nine men and three women seated at separate tables are using white plastic forks to scoop up sliced pieces of citrus fruit from Styrofoam bowls. Next to a half-empty bottle of sweet kosher wine, a pile of clear plastic cups sits unused. Dave has saved them from last week's kiddush. Finding traces of old food and wine in them, most congregants forgo the liquid refreshments. "Is Weissman from Hatzilu coming tomorrow?" Mr. Kaplan asks, his mouth full of fruit. While waiting for Sacks to reply, Mr. Kaplan's hands sweep across the table to grab hold of the remaining pieces of cake, which he dangles one at a time in front of his mouth. A moment later, some room cleared inside, his jaws open wide and the cake disappears behind sealed lips.

"Weissman's supposed to come?" Mordechai asks, mistaking Kaplan's question for a statement of fact.

"I don't know whether Weissman is coming or not coming," Sacks responds while spearing the remaining chick peas on his plate. "If he comes, he's more than welcome. He told me that he *may* come but he's not sure. I know he has some clothes to give out if anybody needs it. Anyway, we'll be here. And we'll have the regular Sunday brunch. If he comes, we'll be here to greet him." Sacks tilts back his head to drain the last drops of whiskey from his cup. A baker all his life, he is less bothered by the traces of old cake in the plastic cups, and he manages to find one that is clean enough to use. The shot of Dewar's is a weekly indulgence, both a reminder of younger days, when a fifth of Scotch was a daily reward for his awesome work pace, and a taunting of medical experts who advised that alcohol might aggravate a diabetic condition. Sacks takes special pride in having already outlived quite a few medical experts.

"He promised last week to come," Kaplan comments. "But he didn't show. The least he could have done was to call and say he's not coming."

"Mr. Kaplan," Sacks replies, "he couldn't come last week because of the snowstorm. There was no way he could get here."

"Unless he has reindeer," Mr. Abraham suggests.

"And he doesn't have reindeer," Sacks confirms.

"So you think he'll be here tomorrow?" Kaplan asks again.

"If he comes, he comes," Sacks responds. "Otherwise, we'll have the usual brunch and I'll go over the parshe like I always do."

The following morning Weissman arrives with boxes of secondhand clothes. Rashim helps him deposit them in the front part of the shul near the Ark. Congregants busy themselves sifting through the bundles and trying on individual items of clothing. Dave is wearing several different sports jackets, one on top of the other. Lucy is clutching clothing both for herself and for Sam, her husband. One woman approaches Weissman and asks for a new winter coat. Another woman, looking much too frail to live in such a neighborhood, asks for a new pair of shoes. Weissman promises to do what he can. Mr. Kaplan approaches me, holding up a heavy gray cotton work shirt. "Jack, whenever they give out clothes, you never take anything. But this you have to take. It even has your name on it." Kaplan shows me the red-embroidered lettering over the breast pocket spelling the name Jack. I take the shirt. Kaplan heads back to hunt for more treasure, and I wander over to see if there are pants to match the shirt.

Neither Sacks nor Mrs. Miroff look for clothing. They are givers rather than takers. Sacks and Weissman discuss the repairs being made to the shul and the plans for future outings to Long Island. Sacks tries to get Weissman to sit down and enjoy the brunch and dvar Torah (interpretation of the Torah). Already overcommitted, Weissman declines: "I promised my bride of thirty-five years I would be home by noon," he explains. "It's five minutes to twelve already."

"So sit down," Sacks insists. "You've still got five minutes." Weissman appreciates the humor but leaves nevertheless.

Although Sacks encourages visitors to stay for the brunch and dvar Torah, few members of charitable organizations will do so. Sometimes they leave before Sacks begins. Often they arrive later and interrupt the narrative. Too busy to wait until Sacks finishes, they make their an-

THE MIRACLE OF INTERVALE AVENUE

nouncements of forthcoming events or distribute food and clothing. Sometimes there is time left after they leave to resume the review of the parshe. Often there is no one left to hear it. When clothing or care packages are given out, most congregants take their booty and leave. One organization in particular would show up each week with a cadre of youthful volunteers of both sexes who would huddle around a separate table. The dvar Torah was a remote event to them; they were there as actors rather than audience. Once they had played their parts, they faded into the background, reentering through gossip the world of their peers. In general, benefactors to the shul know very little about the place. For the most part they see it as an object of charitable work, a needy place occupied by indigent Jews. If the people weren't needy, why else would they be there? As an anthropologist I am perhaps overly intolerant of those who are not interested in the ways of life of people quite different from themselves. Or perhaps the extent of my involvement at Intervale has colored my vision, forcing me to see things through Sacks's eyes. For him there must be reciprocity between giver and taker. Indeed, it is his extraordinary ability to see reciprocation where others would not that allows him to act the role of broker for the Intervale community, protecting their interests and defending their pride before various Jewish relief organizations. Reciprocity, as I shall show in the next chapter, in Sacks's view even characterizes the congregation's relationship to God.

Reciprocity is the most striking pattern of behavior among the Intervale congregation. It pervades every aspect of their relationship with the local non-Jewish population as a whole and with individual neighbors in particular. Moreover, it suggests one of the prime reasons they as elderly people choose to remain in the area. Here they are needed; that sense of usefulness gives them leverage in their dealings with others. Although most congregants have children who would like them to move in with them, few are willing to forfeit the status they have accrued in their present environment. Even those who could well afford to live elsewhere are reluctant to move. Many congregants have spent years saving. They are at the age where material comforts are less satisfying than the knowledge that they are able to leave sizable inheritances for their children and grandchildren. As the saying goes, "When a parent gives to a child, the child is happy and the parent is happy. When the child gives to a parent, both weep." Sacks, for example, retains considerable admiration for his father's ability to provide annual gifts of money to his various grandchildren years after his death. Viewing their savings as capital with which they ingratiate themselves with children and secure their relationships to grandchildren, congregants have added reason for shunning homes for the aged.

REBBE AND GODFATHER

One Saturday, Rose Cutler wobbles about the table near the entrance to the shul, frantically scanning the floor. She begins to hunt through her bundles, using both hands to grab hold of the contents, drops her cane, then waddles back to her seat. She announces that she has lost something, but however much I rephrase my questions, she is unable to describe what that something is. I notice a green thermos cover underneath the table. I reach under the table, pick it up, and hand it to her. "Is that what you lost?"

"Yeah, daht's it. Tenks Got nobody took it." Rose hasn't noticed that her cane has fallen. So I pick that up too and hand it to her. She turns around, then heads back up the stairs, clutching the banister to elevate her body ever so cautiously from one step to the next.

Rose's eyesight has been deteriorating. One day during the summer I see her seemingly dressed for the beach, in sun hat and dark glasses, wobbling down the middle of the road on her way to shul. Joining her, I ask why she doesn't keep to the sidewalk. She replies, "The sun doesn't go there because of the buildings. It's dark. So I don't see so good. The sidewalk is bumpy, so I'm afraid I'll fall down. The street is sunny. I can see."

Prompted in part by poor eyesight and in part by the defection of Horowitz, who has entered a home for the aged, Rose, too, is thinking of entering a home. Sacks has heard of her intention and one Sunday, just before the brunch and dvar Torah, when congregants generally hand Sacks small contributions for the shul, Rose approaches with a donation and he asks her about it point blank: "What's this I hear that you're thinking of going into a home? You continue the way you are. It keeps you up and keeps you alive. You want to enter a home because you want to be with Mr. Horowitz." Rose denies the statement.

Sacks continues on a new line of attack. "Look, personally I don't think you're ready for a home."

"Or is a home ready for her?" Mr. Abraham pipes in.

"A home is for younger people than me," Rose counters.

"I know, I know, I know," Sacks admits. "Why don't you get a woman's service?"

"No."

"Why not?"

"You got to pay for the girl. I don't got no money."

"And another thing. If you go into a home, whatever you own goes to the home. In other words, all of your bank books. All your money, your Social Security. They will become the owners."

"He [Horowitz] paid twelve thousand dollars," Rose confirms, then adds, "but I won't have to pay that."

"What will you pay?"

"Social Security. That's all."

"And what will you do with the rest of the money? Hide it? In your pocket?"

"I don't have to. I have grandchildren."

"Let me explain something to you, Mrs. Cutler. The money which you are now giving away, your children are not allowed to accept."

"But I'm not giving it away. When I die, I will. Maybe I'll die? I'm already over ninety."

"Mrs. Cutler, I must explain to you how the law works. The law works that you cannot give your money to your children during the last year before you enter a home. If you gave the money to your children, they must return it. They have to give it back to the home if the home takes you in. That is the law. The law is that if you want to do something like that, you must do it two or three years before you enter a home."

"Before I go and die?"

"No! You're never going to die, Mrs. Cutler." Rose laughs. "Before you enter a home, you must see what your financial situation is. Ask a lawyer."

"Herry [Mr. Horowitz] paid all that. He gets the Social Security. You see, the children say to me, 'Mama, take the money. [They say] I need the money. But I don't got that much money. I got a few hundred dollars. That's money?"

"That's not money." Sacks agrees. "If it's only a few hundred dollars, they'll let you keep it. But if it amounts to the thousands, which you should only have in good health . . ."

"All right. I'll try [to continue as I do now]. Where is the receipt?"

"Now you're talking. How are you going to make donations and ask me for receipts if you're in the home?"

"Next week there'll be a party [brunch] here?"

"Sure, Mrs. Cutler. Just like today."

"So I'll again give a few dollars. I don't have much money. I gave to my grandchild."

Although all congregants reserve the bulk of their assets for the inheritance they will leave to children or other family members, the ability to reciprocate with peers signifies the very independence they cherish and contributes, too, to their sense of self-esteem.[1] Congregants experience, therefore, a constant tug-of-war between the need to show their independence and enhance their self-esteem through acts of reciprocity and the desire to amass wealth to leave as an inheritance. One joins them into a community, the other divides them into separate families.

One Sunday morning, before the brunch, Mr. Abraham, Mr. Kaplan, and Rashim surround Sacks. They have divided among themselves Sacks's copy of the Sunday *Daily News*. One looks at the comics, the other the advertisements, while the third reads the news. Individual congregants approach to make donations. Mrs. Tipple, a non-Jewish black woman, hands Sacks a ten-dollar check inside a crumpled, stained envelope. Sacks opens the envelope and removes the check. Mrs. Tipple asks for the envelope back. Martha Beaumont, a Southern Baptist woman who attends fairly regularly, approaches and gives him a three-dollar check. Sacks pleads with her not to give it to him until she is certain she has enough money in the account. "It costs me more this way than if you didn't give me anything in the first place." Martha assures him there is money in the bank to cover it.

Mr. Flisser is next. "How much do I owe, Mr. Flisser?" Sacks asks.

"Two dollars. Did you see I put in the toilet deodorizers?"

"I saw, Mr. Flisser. As soon as I saw them, I knew you were back on the job. I hope you had a good vacation." Flisser and his wife Betty spend summers in a bungalow in the Catskill Mountains. His annual return in the fall marks a renewal of the minyan's vitality. Flisser has installed one of the deodorizers in the Ark, figuring it would neutralize the musty smell inside. Sacks gives him two dollars plus three five-dollar bills. When Flisser walks away, Sacks explains:

"The two dollars is what I owe him for those things he bought for the shul. The fifteen dollars is for a monthly payment, like the twenty dollars I give Dave each month. Apparently he needs it, and this way he shouldn't feel that Dave gets and he doesn't. So you see, despite everything we are growing. Our staff and payroll are increasing all the time. You know, here we have the miracle of Hanukkah in reverse. I give Flisser various jobs. He has to buy different things we need for the shul, like the toilet deodorizers or the light bulbs. Well, the entire time he was away, all the bulbs of the menorah were O.K. Now that he's back, three of them are out. So they, too, know that Flisser's back on the job."

Rashim is waiting impatiently. He is holding a ten-dollar bill that Malachi, who had to leave early, gave him to give to Sacks. Sacks takes it and hands him a receipt. Sacks and Mr. Abraham discuss a document Sacks received relating to a now-defunct synagogue in the area that is liquidating its assets. Dora, who now lives near Bronx Park, is a member and should receive title to her husband's grave and her own plot next to it. Sacks asks Mr. Abraham to look over the legal forms to see that everything is O.K. Mr. Abraham reads the document, then comments, "They're distributing their assets to the members. If she's a member, she'll get a grave or something."

"That's quite a prize," someone comments jokingly.

THE MIRACLE OF INTERVALE AVENUE

"Well, listen," Mr. Abraham replies, "if you don't have a grave, it can be an embarrassing situation." He pauses for a moment, then adds, "It smells."

I hand Sacks a five-dollar bill as a donation. Sacks puzzles over what category of donation it is (memorial prayers, call to the Torah, commemoration of a death, etc.), then checks off the appropriate box on the receipt. "Thank you very much," Sacks tells me as he gives me a receipt and a handshake. "I wish you should come in here for the next hundred and twenty years."

"And we should all be here to greet you," Mr. Abraham adds.

"Well, that's asking—" Mr. Abraham cuts Sacks off to ask whether Sacks has another receipt. Mr. Abraham then pulls out a hundred-dollar traveler's check. He is donating it for the prayer Sacks recited for him while he was in the hospital. He has since recovered, and today is his first day back.

"For that amount you should get a speedy recovery," Sacks comments.

"It's cheap at that price," Mr. Abraham replies.

Kaplan tries to get Sacks's attention. Up to now he has been sitting at the same table, though at the extreme end, away from the other men, studying the weekly Torah reading. "Mr. Kaplan"—Sacks recognizes him—"what have you got to say?"

"I owe you money. And when I remember to bring it, I'll bring it down."

"That'll be nice," Mr. Abraham comments. "You can't buy any soup for that, you know."

"Mr. Kaplan," Sacks responds, "I am so worried, you see my hair immediately turned gray."

"I noticed," Kaplan replies.

"And various other colors," Mr. Abraham joins in.

"I'm worried about my ability not to remember. I mean to remember!" Kaplan replies.

"Well, that is an important thing," Sacks agrees.

Mr. Abraham pores over the legal document.

"Who is the person you're going to explain this to?"

"Dora Durst," Sacks replies.

"Where's Dora?" Mr. Abraham asks.

"She's not here."

"It's hard to explain to her under those conditions."

"You never knew we do the impossible here, Mr. Abraham? It takes a little longer, but we do it. I'm going to get her telephone number and I'll call her right up." Sacks deputizes the men sitting nearby to watch over the money he has collected, while he heads over to the phone. He tries his best to reassure Dora that there is no danger of losing the burial plots. When he returns to his seat, Mrs. Freedman, a former neighborhood resident who visits the shul from time to time, hands Sacks a ten-dollar bill. Sacks makes out a receipt, and without her prompting, he puts a tick next to the category "memorial prayers." "You've got a pretty good memory," Mrs. Freedman comments.

Fanny, who is waiting in line to make a donation, joins the discussion: "Well, he should know. He's done it so often."

"You should always be like that," Mrs. Freedman comments.

"How long can it be?" Sacks asks. "Moses they gave till a hundred and twenty. I'm reaching that age."

"Now they're living after a hundred," Mrs. Freedman advises reassuringly. "Anyway, they didn't know how to count then."

"They didn't know how to count?" Sacks asks. Fanny Greenstein is nudging from behind. Sacks accepts a five-dollar bill from her. "That donation, Mrs. Greenstein, is for . . . ?"

"For everything. My mother. My husband . . ." Fanny usually has a slew of names needing special prayers during Saturday services. She scrupulously avoids taking more than her share of food during the Sunday brunches, and she contributes by taking home the plastic silverware to wash. Her one indulgence is hoarding the prayers to help sick relations or to commemorate the dead, a habit for which other congregants sometimes criticize her. Sacks draws an arrow pointing to each category. "I don't need a slip," Fanny says.

"I need it," Sacks informs her, handing her between two fingers the folded slip of paper together with a handshake. Sacks then hunts through the bundles he has brought with him, looking for a challah he has promised to bring her. When he finds it, Fanny puts it into her shopping bag and goes to join the other women already seated at the table.

Despite the desire to amass wealth for inheritances—a hedge against mortality—the congregants' very survival in the South Bronx depends upon their individual abilities to establish relations of reciprocal trust both among themselves and with the surrounding population. Even the most miserly congregant has such relationships. Indeed, private acts of reciprocity frequently have their impact upon the overall well-being of the shul. Mrs. Miroff's close relationship with the "bums" who hang around her tailor shop and "freelance" (their term for a combination of odd jobs and stealing) at the Hunts Point market is the primary source of fruit and vegetables for Intervale's Saturday kiddush. She provides them with shelter and hot meals; they, too, feel compelled to reciprocate:

"Can I get you something today, Mrs. Miroff?" asks one husky man. "Maybe some apples or oranges?"

"No," she replies. "You brought me that yesterday. Do you carry string beans?"

Mr. Abraham is the one person who knows exactly what Mrs. Miroff contributes to the kiddush. Each Saturday he drives to her apartment on his way to Intervale from his home in Queens and honks his horn. Pushing aside the white lace curtains, she signals to him from her bedroom window that she is on her way downstairs.

Mrs. Miroff is grateful for the rides. Eager to repay the favor, she frequently mends his clothes. Then, when Mr. Abraham's wife broke her hip and needed his constant assistance, he began to bring her with him to shul on Saturdays: he would pop inside for a little while either to pray or to partake in the kiddush, while she waited in the car, unable to climb downstairs. Mrs. Miroff felt obliged to leave the shul and keep Mrs. Abraham company, although she regretted missing parts of the service. She was particularly worried that Mr. Abraham might ask her to stay in her shop on Saturdays and look after his wife while he went to shul. If he did, she would have to tell him no. "How can a person be so cheap?" she asked me one day, referring to herself. "After all he did, for me to say no. How can I do that?" Mrs. Miroff enjoys attending services partly because it gives her the chance to display herself as a gracious hostess by preparing the chick peas or slicing up the fruit for the kiddush, and partly because of Sacks: "I love to hear that man pray."

For years now, Mrs. Miroff has been in love with him. Every day she waits faithfully in her shop until 5:15 when he drops by for a moment on his way home from work. He generally leaves her a bag of rolls and muffins, most of which she uses to make sandwiches for the "bums." When he leaves, she sends her companion, Nelly, to escort him across the street. Sacks and Mrs. Miroff continually disagree about who is doing whom the favor. When Sacks's bakery closes for the annual three-week vacation, Mrs. Miroff complains to me that she is losing weight. "I'm used to his rolls. That's all I can eat." Though Sacks was within earshot when she made that remark, she was reluctant to say it directly to him, as if to do so would transform a compliment into a request and obligation.

Mrs. Miroff would like to marry Sacks. She bitterly complains that he has no interest in any formal attachment: "If he wants me, he's got to do it legal. I don't do nothing without the paper. After all, I'm a grandmother. I got to set an example to my granddaughter."

But Sacks dismisses any possibility of marriage with Mrs. Miroff: "She's older than me. Anyway, I am married to the bakery."

Despite Sacks's standoffishness, Mrs. Miroff believes that her love is not entirely unrequited. She frequently asks me whether Sacks mentions her name in our discussions. I tell her yes. She wants more details, and I desperately search for words that will neither wound nor lie. I tell her that of course he likes her. She then quotes me as "the one who told me that Sacks loves me."

One Sunday Mrs. Miroff arrives in shul and immediately informs Sacks that her daughter Florence will be arriving shortly to drive her to her (Mrs. Miroff's) son's home on Long Island. Mrs. Miroff then complains about Louise, Nelly's mother, who has asked her to bring her a challah. Nelly is Mrs. Miroff's black "daughter." She is in her early forties, slightly retarded, and very much in need of supervision. The two became friends at the time of Mrs. Miroff's husband's death over twenty years ago. Nelly had just moved into the neighborhood, and Mrs. Miroff enjoyed the young woman's companionship. Later, when Nelly's mother left the area to take a job as a domestic, she left Nelly in Mrs. Miroff's care. The two are now constant companions. Nelly spends much of her time in Mrs. Miroff's shop, and she accompanies her to shul, waiting patiently for the kiddush or Sunday brunch. She also accompanies the congregation on the outings to Long Island. Although Mrs. Miroff refuses Nelly's request to accompany her to church, the relationship is not entirely one-sided. Besides companionship, Mrs. Miroff enjoys the security of "being seen next to a black face" whenever she leaves her block. In addition, Nelly's eyesight is considerably better than Mrs. Miroff's; without her assistance, Mrs. Miroff would not be able to use public transportation. Resentful toward Louise for abandoning Nelly, Mrs. Miroff feels quite put out by having to carry around the challah for her. Sacks hands Mrs. Miroff a second package. This one is for Lena, who isn't feeling well and will not be in shul. Since it is Sacks who asks her to carry the package, Mrs. Miroff does not complain.

Florence arrives and is greeted at the door by Dave Lentin, Intervale's eccentric caretaker. Sacks pays him a modest stipend to sweep the stairs and to open and close the shul on weekends, and at no additional charge Dave has thrown into the bargain the role of greeting new arrivals. Dave's appearance takes a little getting used to. His teeth are visibly rotting, his chest is sunken, giving his torso a distinctly concave shape, and his clothes are quite different from the drab, muted colors worn by the others. Dave was a sign painter, and his love for flair and color shows up in his blue hounds-tooth jacket worn together with a red polka dot tie and green polyester pants. Dave extends his hand to Florence: "Press the flesh! How's your love life, Florence?"

"Pretty good. How's yours?" Florence, a chip off the old block, is unfazed by Dave's bawdiness. Mrs. Miroff calls her "the new Mom" and admires her daughter's fearlessness in dealing with the neighborhood's various unsavory types. Florence, a rather large, personable, and, like her mother, outspoken woman, teaches in a primary school around the corner from her mother's apartment. Before Dave can answer, Florence spots her mother carrying several shopping bags of food. She becomes irate. "Ma, what's the matter with you? Why can't you stay home one day with a humidifier? You have to come here and carry around so much stuff?"

Sacks overhears the argument. He is busy filling out receipts for the small donations congregants are making. He takes a moment off to tell Florence off. "Leave her alone and don't interfere with old people. They do what they do because it's good for them." Florence walks over to Sacks, says hello, and explains that she's here to take her mother for the day. They look at one another like old rivals, more caught up in the pleasure of battle than the lust for victory. Sacks wishes Mrs. Miroff an enjoyable day and tells her not to wait for him in the store because he may stay very late at the bakery. Mrs. Miroff counters by advising Sacks not to look for her tonight because she'll be home late from her son's house. A draw. Neither one owes the other anything.

Besides Mrs. Miroff's bums, acquaintances of other congregants are also useful for the shul. Mrs. Darginsky's friend Ramon, an extremely good-natured, middle-aged, middle-class Puerto Rican electrician, provides not only needed electrical repairs but, on occasion, ritual objects such as a menorah when he sees one in a junk shop waiting to be rescued and restored. Sacks reciprocates in part with money, although Ramon undercharges for his services, and in part through the offer of a prayer for his health. When Ramon explained to Sacks that he was about to enter the hospital for surgery, Sacks told him not to worry: "Next Saturday I'll make a *refue shleyma* for you. We'll say a prayer for your good health. Do you have a Jewish name?" Sacks asks half-jokingly, puzzling over how to find a biblical equivalent for *Ramon*.

"My Jewish name?" Ramon asks, a little bewildered. "Do I have a Jewish name? You know, come to think of it, I used to work for a Jewish guy and he always called me Sonny. Is that my Jewish name?"

Not long afterward, Ramon sold his business and went to work for the city as an electrical inspector. One Saturday, a year later, Ramon appeared in shul and took a seat next to the other men. Dave brought him a yarmulke and a talis, both of which he donned, and a prayer book, which he opened and tried to read. Realizing that he would be bewildered by an indecipherable script, I began to make conversation with him: "How's it going? Do you like your new job?"

"My job is fine. It's me that's not fine."

"What's the matter?"

"My health is no good. I got cancer." Just then Sacks called me to the

REBBE AND GODFATHER

Torah, and I related to him what Ramon had just told me. Sacks turned to Ramon and asked him to come up to the bima. He asked about his health and then explained to Ramon that he would make him a prayer for a speedy recovery. When Sacks finished reciting the prayer, Ramon's eyes welled up with tears. He hugged Sacks and kissed him on both cheeks. He then removed the talis and left the shul. He had gotten what he had come for.

Sacks's close relationship with the 41st Precinct is a boon to the shul, offering protection to both the building and the congregation. Indeed, Sacks himself is frequently chauffeured to his bakery in a squad car just after midnight. In return, patrolmen on the beat are invited in for hot coffee and fresh danish. Retirement parties at the precinct generally include a large cake decorated with the precinct's logo—a fort pierced by arrows and the words "Fort Apache" at the bottom—made by Sacks.

But even the most unequal form of charity, the outings to Long Island sponsored by Hatzilu, provides an opportunity for Sacks and others to practice a form of reciprocity. Dave letters a sign in Yiddish thanking the hosts for the afternoon; several congregants, mostly women, perform Yiddish songs. Sacks, in particular, eagerly anticipates the chance to do his part. He is a gracious guest and remembers to convey a sense of gratitude for the day's event. At the Midway Jewish Center, the president introduces Sacks: "I would like to say a few words about Mr. Sacks. He doesn't like it because he's going to be very embarrassed. You know, Mr. Sacks is like the modern Moses because he is leading his people, he is staying with his people because of his heart, not because of his pocketbook."

Sacks walks to the front and takes the microphone: "Ladies and gentlemen. With the introduction I should stop while I'm ahead and sit down. Unfortunately I can't do that. I have to say a few words. And therefore you'll have to listen to me whether you want to or not. And that brings me as usual to the [Torah] portion of this week that we read Saturday. It starts off with Moses telling the people what they should do.

"Ladies and gentlemen, we are told at the beginning of the parshe that Moses told the people what to do. But he starts off in telling them that the Sabbath cannot be desecrated—that they must observe the Sabbath. And there is a *midrash* [commentary] that tells us that there are things given to the Jewish people; if they deserve them, they keep them. For example, Erets Yisroel [the land of Israel], the Migdash [the Temple], and the Kingdom of David. They did not deserve them and therefore they lost them. But there are things given to the people such as the Torah and the *kohanes* [priests] and shabes that God gave us out of love. And those things, whether we like to or whether we deserve it, we get to keep them. Now I would like to add one more thing to those

THE MIRACLE OF INTERVALE AVENUE

things that we get whether we deserve it or we don't. And that thing is Hatzilu. Whether you deserve it or you don't deserve it, this is a thing that you get, a thing that is given to you from love. A thing that transcends all necessities of life. A thing that is given from one heart to another and that you keep."

The gracious, almost obsequious quality of Sacks's speech is very much in contrast to his forthrightness in demanding help or money from relief organizations. Indeed, Sacks can be rather blunt when an organization does not deliver as promised.

Just before the *yizkor* (memorial) service for the Jewish holiday of Shavuot, Sacks gives a short sermon to Intervale's congregation on the theme of promising without delivering: "Everybody tells me, 'You need to repair the wall from the break-in? Don't worry. I have a brother-in-law who lives in Long Island who knows someone who can donate half a gallon of paint and a few brushes.' 'You need the alarm fixed?' the Shomrim Society tells me. 'Don't worry. We'll take care of it after yizkor.' Hatzilu promises to fix the floor. Another group is going to install a new heater. I can assure you, ladies and gentlemen, a year from now they'll still be promising."

Whatever Sacks may say, the shul is very dependent on outside contributions. The yizkor appeals net no more than a couple of hundred dollars. The speech, therefore, has the quality of a typical synagogue "Kol Nidre appeal"—the annual call for donations that have become so much a part of American Jewish synagogue life. Indeed, not having one would be an admission of the moribund state of the congregation in the same way that the absence of an itinerant *shnorrer* (beggar) signals a minyan's imminent demise.[2] At the same time Sacks's appeal is an assessment of the fact that, to some degree, the congregation as a whole and congregants as individuals survive as much by their own wits as through the help of any outside organization.

Only one organization has ever been singled out for special criticism, largely because of its erratic behavior which has become a part of Intervale's folklore. During one kiddush, less than a week after the organization borrowed the shul to run an activity for another community of elderly Bronx Jews while the Intervale group was on a Hatzilu-sponsored outing, Sacks and Mr. Abraham gripe about the poor condition in which the group left the shul. Some tablecloths are missing. So are some prayer books. And the curtains separating the men's and the women's sections are gone. Mrs. Miroff joins the conversation:

"My son Leonard is working on a deal to sell computers. He thinks they'll close the deal today. If he does, I'll buy new curtains."

"Mrs. Miroff," Sacks admonishes in the usual curt manner he uses with her, "don't promise anything. You can think it, but don't say it just in case you decide not to."

"I can't say a thing that I want to? I don't got to listen to you. What's the matter with you? I'm not supposed to say something if I want?" Mrs. Miroff walks away in a huff.

Sacks ignores her. He continues speaking to Mr. Abraham. "I let them [the relief organization] do what they want in the shul, figuring on the couple of hundred dollars I'll get from them."

"What couple of hundred dollars? Have you gotten anything from them yet?"

"Sure, I have. And there's a story here, too." Sacks chuckles, realizing he is about to confirm his friend's assessment. "They gave me a check for two hundred dollars, and I went to the bank to deposit it. The check comes back marked 'Insufficient Funds.' So I redeposit it, and it comes back again. The third time I bring it to the teller and he asks me whether I want to pay the bounce fee in advance. So I laugh and tell him no. Then he tells me O.K., but if it bounces again I better not bring it again because there's no more room on the back to stamp 'Insufficient Funds.' "

"It sounds to me," Mr. Abraham remarks, "that instead of paper this guy uses checks made out of Uniroyal rubber."

Sacks's attitude stems from his role as broker for the congregation: he welcomes any group or individual that may be of some use to the shul. Nor does Sacks's opportunism go unnoticed, particularly since relief organizations are sometimes at loggerheads over their respective turf. To each group he plays a role of needy recipient that is completely out of character with his own role of provider within the community.

Indeed, the humble tone of Sacks's thank-you speeches at the Hatzilu outings is so uncharacteristic of this proud "I-don't-need-nobody" sort of man that I can only consider it as a kind of game in which Sacks is acting a part.[3] As broker for the congregation, Sacks delivers to the host congregation the principal element that justifies their expenditure of time and money, namely the presentation of a face of neediness on the part of the Intervale congregation.

Of course, most congregants are more than happy to play along. They bring shopping bags to store away second helpings. Some even bring plastic containers for nonsolid food. Individual congregants have been known to take the very tablecloth on which the food was served or the silverware with which they ate. Even those who pride themselves on their unwillingness to take charity in general demonstrate no such scruples at the outings. Mrs. Miroff, for example, always takes home extra portions, though not for her own consumption; she distributes them later to the street people who live on her block.

THE MIRACLE OF INTERVALE AVENUE

At the end of the outing, when care packages are given out to each person as they enter the bus to go back to the Bronx, they all accept. I alone do not take. My refusal invariably generates criticism from the other congregants.

"Didn't you get a package?"

"Take a package. Go tell them you didn't get a package!"

"What's the matter with you? Look, there's gefilte fish inside. There's borsht. Take one!"

"I don't need," I reply, hoping somehow to get them off the topic. "I can get those things at the grocery store near my house."

"Huh? What do you mean you can *get* it?" one man asks rather caustically. "You can buy it, right? Is that what you mean?"

"Yeah," I reply sheepishly.

"Well," he responds. "This is free. There's a slight difference there. If you know what I mean."

Curious to know what Sacks thinks about the interaction with charitable organizations, I decide to use our walk to the bakery to ask him whether the people who organize the outings really assume that their guests are the needy and deserving poor. Sacks feels they know that's not entirely true. "Although some of the organizers might think that to be the case," he says, "the more sophisticated among them realize that in today's world, with Social Security, no one is starving. Also, Jews being what they are, even if a man was paid three cents a day, he lived on two and still managed somehow to put away one as savings."

"So you mean to tell me that you don't find accepting charity in any way undignified?" I ask. Sacks responds without a moment's thought: "No. First of all, they're not giving it because people are starving. They're doing it because the people in the Bronx rarely get the chance to go to an affair with food and entertainment. So this breaks the monotony of their lives. Besides, I don't think that I'm getting charity. I am just giving the people a chance to show their generosity. In other words, they're benefiting from the act as well as we do. That's number one. And if the person who gives and the person who receives could be on both sides of the demarcation line, there is no such thing as you feeling undignified."

Sacks and I continue our walk. I become silent; I am looking for another way to pose the question. Before I find it, Sacks picks up where he left off. He is about to resort to his main line of attack—rabbinic lore. "We have stories about professional beggars. One story is told where a beggar comes to see Rabbi Gamliel and he asked him for some food. Rabbi Gamliel asked the beggar, 'What do you want to eat?' And the guy said, 'Well, I'm used to having ducks, fat geese, wine, and everything.' Rabbi Gamliel replies, 'Well, my fare is just simple beans. I'm a poor man and I

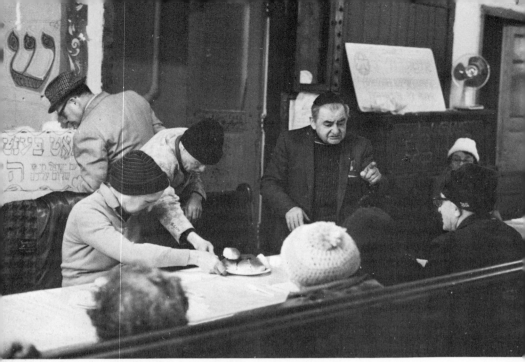

As rebbe and godfather of Intervale, Sacks provides the
food for the Sunday morning brunch.

Elsie Miroff, a central member of the congregation,
displays a piece of costume jewelry that Sacks has just
distributed.

Dave draws a welcoming sign of *shalom*.

haven't got it. So I can't give it to you.' And the story continues, just at that point his sister sent them over a fat goose for lunch—to the rabbi— sent them over wine, sent them over everything. And then the beggar said, 'Well, you see, I wasn't asking you. I was asking God for it. God provided me with this. Your sister's giving over my fare.' The rabbi realized that the beggar was telling the truth. He gave him over the whole deal. He said, 'God's taking care of you.' Now, that beggar didn't feel as if he's asking for charity. He was asking for the fare that he was accustomed to getting from God. You can see that with the Intervale group when they go out to Long Island. They go out to a place where they'll serve them tuna fish or salad, and they'll stick their nose up because that's their regular fare. When they're taken out, they want something special like a chicken dinner with all the fixings on it. And they love it. That's what they want. And they don't feel like they're asking too much because that's what's coming to them."

Despite the esteem all congregants have for Sacks, he is no saint. Much like Moses, his biblical namesake, Sacks's tolerance for the complaints of the congregation falters on occasion. One Sunday just before we mount the bus on our way to a Hatzilu-sponsored outing, I watch him suddenly stop his usual distribution of bundles of bread and cake and angrily put everything back into his shopping bags. When the crowd of demanding congregants realize that he has no intention of resuming the food distribution, they leave the shul. Sacks and Dave prepare to lock up and take their seats on the bus. I follow them to the door, then take a seat next to Sacks. When the bus gets going I ask him what happened.

"I'm up to my neck with these people," he answers. "Lucy says I'm cheap because I don't bring enough raisin cake. This one says the rolls are too hard. What do I need this for? These people have so much nerve. The Westchester Reform Temple makes them every year a *seder* for Passover. Word got around somehow that the temple would this year have their members make the meal themselves because the cost of the caterer that usually makes it is getting too high. When people got wind of it they became worried that the food might not be up to par."

"Which people?" I ask.

"These people. These shnorrers here! So I'm fed up." Sacks is quiet for a while. He takes a roll out of his shopping bag and offers it to me. I decline. Congregants have already told me that the temple we are going to usually puts on a very nice affair so I'm reluctant to spoil my appetite. Sacks chews on the roll. Not even the anticipation of a catered luncheon can induce him to deny himself the pleasure of eating his own baked goods. The taste of the bread seems to affect his mood. The anger disappears, and he resumes the conversation on a more lighthearted note:

THE MIRACLE OF INTERVALE AVENUE

"As usual, I suppose I'll relent. And next week they'll again get their bundles. You know, it reminds me of something. The other week they took us on a trip to a temple in Long Island. The rabbi was telling me that the synagogue has several different committees and each one fights with the other over which committee should get how much of the budget. So I told the rabbi that we got no such problem. Here at the Intervale Jewish Center we're all agreed that we all should get."

Sacks's humor notwithstanding, there is some disagreement as to who should get and how. Certain individuals are noted for their deftness at hoarding, and their activities are carefully monitored by other congregants. Those who repeatedly take more than the allotted share are labeled "shnorrers." In Yiddish the word has a fairly neutral connotation, in part because professional shnorrers or beggars were very much a part of Ashkenazic culture. They were sometimes déclassé individuals who would make the rounds of synagogues, often showing a letter from a rabbinic authority as proof of their past and present status, and solicit alms. In American usage, though, a shnorrer is not a beggar but a freeloader, a cheat. When congregants use the term, they mean someone who takes from the larger group. There are various ways in which this is done. The most common is to stash away extra portions of communal food. At the Sunday brunch, plates of cake or rolls are passed from one end of the table to the other, and along the way, one or two individuals manage to remove various items and put them into plastic shopping bags held between their legs, hidden from view underneath the table. All kinds of food can be stashed away. Cake disappears from the table as fast as it is served. Cream cheese and jelly pose no obstacle at all: a determined hoarder can sandwich the cheese between paper plates while the jelly goes into one paper cup tucked into a second. Even soup and coffee disappear, since individuals come armed with empty jars. Occasionally certain individuals become targets for vicious verbal attacks. They have been spotted taking more than their fair share. The viciousness of the attacks is striking, an indication of the degree of disapproval for behavior that threatens the moral order of the community. The logic of these people's lives weighs in favor of reciprocity; it is what distinguishes them from what they most fear—dependency. Shnorring is a crime in this community because of the need congregants have to disassociate themselves from what time itself will inevitably make them be—helpless and needy.[4]

But the righteous condemnation of shnorring has other qualities to it, too. It is a way of striking out at others who appropriate what is meant for general distribution. The food at the brunch is a gift. "One man's gift," the saying goes, "must not be another man's capital."[5] Moreover, those who hoard are saving their own resources and, in one case at least, without just cause. They are acquiring at the expense of the group. As I suggested earlier, they are acquiring immortality by enlarging an inheritance and depriving others of theirs. But despite the monitoring, conflicts rarely escalate beyond confrontations between individuals; public accusations are relegated to the domain of gossip.

Monitoring through gossip also serves the purpose of humbling those who act too proud. During one summer early in my study, I would spend time during Saturday services with Rose, who would sit outside the shul and sunbathe. Rose was not a popular member of the congregation. Well into her nineties, she seemed to have a secret formula for survival, and it made some of the younger women envious. Perhaps they sensed that they would never acquire the same number of years, or perhaps they merely resented her good luck with men. Lucy and others became indignant at the amount of time I spent with her. One Saturday, Lucy twice came outside and politely told me to join the other men. The third time she ordered me to go inside. I obeyed. As I headed toward my seat, I could hear her comment to Sam, "That Rose is always looking for a man." Rose's relationship with Mr. Horowitz was also a bone of contention between her and the other women. After Horowitz entered a home, Lena would sometimes egg Rose on about Horowitz's indifference to her: "Some women told me they saw Horowitz the other day. 'You should see how good he looks,' they said. 'He enjoys himself there. He looks terrific.' They live in the West Bronx in some apartments there not far from where he is." Rose is obviously hurt by Lena's bit of news.

"I got a letter from him once," Rose responds. "He probably has women there. I wasn't married to him. He just used to come over on shabes and I would give him lunch and he would go home. I had to make myself lunch anyway, so why not make him something, too? Sometimes he brought me bread. I always gave him the money for the bread. I'm ninety years old. I had a very good husband. *Er iz geven a sheyner* [He was handsome]."

"Yeah," Lena confirms, "your husband was good-looking. I remember him. But still, the least Horowitz could do is give you a call sometimes."

This friendly advice was tinged with cruelty. It underscored the fact that it isn't just enemies who make accusations against each other; friends do it, too. The Intervale Jewish Center is a community based on necessity rather than choice. Outsiders may notice the group identity, the traits they share in common; they, however, see themselves quite differently. They are individuals. As one man put it, objecting to my photographing him inside the shul, "I don't want to be seen next to that herd." Fanny and Rose, for example, live in the same project. They escort one another to shul and they regularly do each other favors. One Saturday I overhear the two women talking. Fanny mentions that the time for the unveiling of her husband's tombstone is approaching, but her cousins who usually drive her to the cemetery are not well and may not be able to attend the ceremony:

"One has a heart condition, the other has some illness, so I don't know who is going to take me," says Fanny.

Rose is fed up with Fanny's whining. "What are you complaining about? They're suffering? I'm suffering. You should see my side. It's all red. I got to sleep with the heating pad. I wake up, it's all red. So you don't got no children. You got no luck. Look how my children helped you. How many times my daughter gave you a cup of coffee or a sandwich."

"Yeah," Fanny responds sarcastically. "Once she gave me a cup of tea." Fanny lifts her hand to straighten her blouse. Rose, mistaking Fanny's sudden hand movement for a sign of imminent aggression, lifts her arm to protect her face from the threatened blow.

Vulnerable, often lonely, and for the most part reluctant to see themselves in each other, they sometimes misinterpret even friendly words. One Father's Day, Sacks serves a large cake in honor of the occasion. As he serves, he wishes everyone "A happy Father's Day—to everybody, the women, too." One man wishes a woman standing next to him a happy Father's Day, too. Offended by the remark, she barks back, "You're no father! What are you wishing a happy Father's Day for?"

"Neither are you," he replies. "But I can still wish you a happy Father's Day." Neither of them had living children, and for each the other was a painful reminder of something missing in their lives. Built into their need of each other is a need to deny that very dependency.[6]

The shul is the link that joins congregants to each other. For most it is a vehicle for meeting certain obligations: the living to commemorate the dead; the healthy to pray for the ill; the old to thank God for a new generation.[7] But the shul is not sufficient to make a community out of these people: without Sacks's ability to elevate their individual eccentricities onto a religious plane, conflict and mutual mistrust would have long ago prevailed, leaving these cantankerous, independent individuals without a still-functioning Jewish center. Sacks gives congregants a sense of meaning, order, and purpose in their lives. His leadership role here shows a curious blend of the pragmatic and the mystical, suggesting a cross between a mafioso godfather and a hasidic *rebbe*. As godfather, Sacks protects the congregation. He sees that their needs are attended to by Jewish relief organizations, and he takes care of those who need additional food or money. As rebbe, he tends to their spiritual needs and provides a mythical framework within which even seemingly erratic behavior can be infused with meaning. Moreover, it is the rebbe who forms the

REBBE AND GODFATHER

group into a community, seeing perhaps through his own imaginings 'a. unity where others would fail to. I use the word "imagining" rather than "imagination" in order to distinguish the act of shaping reality through creative thought from the act of fleeing reality through make-believe. Sacks makes others believe in his imaginings, and so the physical world around him literally begins to resemble the world as he conceives it. Herein lies the nature of his charisma: he convinces others of the realness of his imaginings. Sacks has given congregants a sense that by staying in the Bronx and participating in the shul, they are partaking in something so extraordinary that it resonates with the miracles witnessed by their biblical forebears. I shall discuss this at greater length in the next chapter. Here let us look at Sacks's role as spiritual leader of the congregation.

One of Sacks's primary tasks at Intervale is to make sure that the proper rituals are performed to commemorate deceased family members of congregants. Indeed. Sacks's role as eulogizer and overseer of funerary rites extends beyond Intervale's congregation. Although Sacks is contemptuous of his employers' methods of running the bakery and is frequently at odds with them for it, when Evelyn, the boss's wife, died, the family insisted that Sacks deliver the eulogy. He prides himself on having been able "to make the eulogy without covering up Evelyn's bad side so as to make her unrecognizable, but still leaving not a dry eye in the crowd."

But style alone does not make Sacks's eulogies popular. More important is his familiarity with the deceased. In an age when officiating clergy at funerals usually have had very little contact with the deceased or their families, Sacks's eulogies are like a throwback to another time.

Beyond guaranteeing the dead a proper Jewish burial, Sacks is also called upon to counsel the living, particularly the surviving spouses of recently deceased congregants. Barry and Helene were a relatively young couple (mid- to late forties) who would come to shul usually on those Sundays when the congregation was taken on outings to Long Island. Both were slightly retarded and received disability pensions. Barry had never managed to hold down a job and had long since given up looking for work. Then Helene, who was quite obese, died suddenly of a heart attack. The following Saturday Barry was in shul and Sacks hoped to make a regular Saturday congregant out of him. Though promising to come more often, Barry did so only once or twice. Sacks kept me informed on Barry's whereabouts, for a while at least still expecting him to join the minyan. One Saturday, as Sacks and I walk toward the bakery for lunch, he describes his most recent encounter with "the young man":

"He came to the store yesterday. Apparently he wanted to talk to somebody. It's finally starting to hit him that his wife is dead, and he was feeling depressed. So I sat with him for about half an hour. He talked to me about the last few days before his wife died. How he tried to keep her legs up to help the circulation. The main problem he has now is that he doesn't know what to eat because he doesn't know how to cook for himself. His wife used to cook for him chicken in a certain way, and that's what he likes to eat. He says he has chicken frozen in the icebox. Dorothy, who lives across from him in the same building, doesn't want to help him. I'll ask her to show him how to cook the chicken. I tried to help him overcome his mood. I told him the best thing is to clean up the home just for the physical exercise. And if that's too much for him right now, then he should move the TV. Once he moves it, he'll have to move the other furniture to fit. Then, while he watches a program, he'll have to move the TV again, and again he'll have to move the furniture. He'll get so tired from all that, that he'll feel a little better emotionally."

I asked Sacks whether Barry felt better after the conversation. He answered, "He felt better in the sense that when he came in he was a hundred percent depressed and when he left he was eighty percent. You see, I would make a pretty good psychotherapist."

One woman, Shirley, came to Sacks terribly distraught over the death of her cat. Rather than bury it, she had simply put the corpse into the garbage as friends had advised her. Later she felt as if she had violated a sacred trust and wanted to know what Jewish law says about burying pets. Her friends brought her to Intervale, insisting that Sacks would have the answer for her. Sacks assured the woman that she had done nothing wrong: "A pet serves a purely utilitarian purpose of allowing its owner to express feelings of love. When the animal dies, so does its function. The best thing you can do is to get a new pet to replace the old one." The woman was grateful for Sacks's assurance that she had done what was proper by disposing of the cat without burial.

Just as all congregants make contributions in honor of a dead relative, many come to have prayers said for the ill. Poor all her life and with a sick husband in recent years, Fanny is frequently in need of help from her family. She uses prayers as a way of reciprocating: "My brother-in-law and sister were very kind to me. So now they're not well and I have Sacks say a prayer for them. I give him a few dollars for the shul."

Mrs. Miroff, too, has Sacks recite prayers for members of her family. "That's my job," she says.

Hy Bohrer, who owns a store on Southern Boulevard, became a fairly regular congregant out of a desire to help out a sick friend. "You know, at first I didn't want to go to shul," he says. "But Bloch [who also works on Southern Boulevard] said, 'Come. You've got to see this place.' When I got there, I was so taken with the place that it kept pulling me back. At that time I had a guy who used to trim my windows for me. He was a young man. But he had cancer and the doctors gave him only a month to live. When I came here and I was called to the bima, I said a prayer for him. And then each time I came I had a prayer said for him. You know, the guy now passed away. But he lived a year and a half. And I believe that my prayers had something to do with it."

When I mentioned Hy's story to Sacks, he had a surprisingly rational response: "It helps because you believe in it." The statement underlines the deep ambivalence of much of Sacks's beliefs. He alternates between his sense of having direct communion with God through the shul (the rebbe) and a purely rational, rather prosaic assessment of the importance of the shul in the lives of the congregants (the godfather). Nor is there a clearly drawn line between these two points of view. One Saturday, after Sidney Flisser has recited the blessings over the Torah, his wife, Betty, approaches the bima and asks Sacks to recite a prayer asking God to find a job for her unemployed son-in-law. Sacks does so by changing several words in the usual benediction for good health. He is rather pleased with himself, as if he has hoodwinked a congregant into believing that help is on the way while finagling God through a sleight of hand into fulfilling the somewhat altered request of the usual prayer.

Several weeks later, it is my turn to ask Sacks to use his pull. A friend is very ill, and during my aliya I ask for a special prayer for the friend's health. Sacks asks me for the Hebrew name of the woman and her mother. Her name we can improvise based on the English name. But for the mother's name, I don't have a clue. The problem has a simple solution: Sacks telescopes the woman's genealogy to the matriarch Sarah and prays to God in the name of a daughter of Sarah—*bat Soreh*. Later we discuss the nature of the friend's ailment, and I mention the name of a prominent rebbe who was also asked to recite a prayer. "I'll bet," Sacks comments, obviously rather pleased with himself, "that the rebbe didn't have to make up a Jewish name."

"Well, I'm pretty sure he didn't have to," I agree. "I guess that's your specialty—improvising. It reminds me of the prayer you said for Betty's son-in-law."

"Listen. Let me tell you something. The prayer worked. He got a job. Or I should say he got a temporary job." Sacks reflects for a while on the implications of his statement, then tries to assure me that the prayer I asked him to recite will be of some help, too. "I don't know whether your friend will be cured. But the prayer will help. At least your friend will feel better. She won't be in as much pain, let's put it that way. However long she has to live, she'll be able to enjoy it. The pain won't be unbearable."

Hoodwinking is pretty much common behavior at Intervale. As I shall show in the chapter "Maybe It's Brodsky," it has a good deal to do with the cat-and-mouse game old people feel they are playing with death. Religion is one of the many devices they turn to, to try to cheat death: since congregants take the prayers quite seriously, Sacks frequently finds himself on the receiving end of someone else's attempt to finagle. Before they leave the bima, Sacks often double-checks congregants to make sure the prayer for their good health was recited. Sam typically responds to Sacks's question with, "I really don't remember, Moish. I don't think you said it." Each time, Sacks repeats the prayer, knowing full well that Sam's memory is fine but that Sam, not in the best of health and wanting special consideration, could use a double dose of Sacks's pull with God. Congregants consider Sacks a personal intercessor with God, and they are particularly comforted by his approach to ritual; he knows his religion and he knows them.

A year before her death, Lena asks Sacks to say a prayer for the speedy recovery of two acquaintances. Sacks recites the prayer in between readings of the Torah. As he does so, Lena timidly approaches the bima and listens. Later, she thanks Sacks for the prayer, then adds, "I was expecting more. Somehow I didn't think it would be so short."

"I made you the proper prayer," Sacks responds. "If the person believes in it, it will work. Anyway, I did do more. I made you two prayers like you asked. I could have done them both together, but I made them separate. So I did do more. If you're not satisfied, then just give half."

"How much should I give?" Lena asks.

"Lena, sit down here. I'm going to tell you something. And I know Jack loves to hear a joke, so he'll listen too. At a Long Island synagogue for the Kol Nidre appeal, they read aloud the names of the membership list alphabetically, and each one announces how much they intend to contribute. When it came to Epstein each year, he would say, 'I give nothing!' Finally they decided not to call out his name. When he doesn't hear his name called, Epstein protests and asks, 'Why didn't you call my name?' 'Because every year you refuse.' The *gabbai* [sexton] tells him. 'All right. Who gave the largest contribution this year?' Epstein asks. 'Gold did. He pledged five hundred dollars,' the gabbai tells him. So Epstein yells out, 'I pledge six hundred!' Collecting the money is another story. Months later they take him to court and the judge rules in favor of the shul. Next year during the Kol Nidre appeal, they again skip Epstein's name, and again he protests and asks who gave the most this year. 'Gold did,' the gabbai tells him. 'Every year he pledges five hundred dollars.' 'Then I pledge six hundred!' Epstein announces. The whole congregation is silent. Everyone is embarrassed and no one knows what to do next. So the gabbai tells him, 'We're sorry, but you promised that last year, and to get

REBBE AND GODFATHER

you to pay we had to take you to court.' 'All right,' Epstein answers, 'this year I pledge six hundred dollars plus court costs.'

"So Lena, you see, you can give whatever you want just as long as you give. But it should be more than ten cents." Uncertain whether Lena fully understands his point, Sacks adds a second anecdote, this time a more personal one. Sacks typically counsels by citing a similar experience of his own. "You know, that reminds me of another story, a true story. I used to go every year to a United Jewish Appeal event with my uncle. We were placed at a table with people who give five thousand and ten thousand dollars. When they called out my name, I meekly called out, 'A hundred dollars.' My uncle leans over to me and whispers, 'It's O.K., Moishe. At least from you they'll collect.' "

The frequent jokes typify the ease and familiarity with which ritual is conducted at the Intervale Jewish Center. But they also point to the peculiar personality of Sacks, who generates a sense of intimacy and comfort in dealing with the otherwise awesome world of the sacred.

Despite the brokerage role he plays for the congregation vis-à-vis ritual obligations, Sacks's special genius at the Intervale Jewish Center has to do with mediating less on a personal level than on a higher religious plane: Sacks the godfather becomes Sacks the rebbe. Indeed, by finding sacred meanings in mundane actions, Sacks manages to weave a sacred tapestry out of some highly eccentric though colorful individual threads. The tapestry is really a story, and it is the height of achievement of an imagining mind. In subsequent chapters I shall examine the rich sources for Sacks's storytelling—both traditional Jewish lore and his own personal struggles. But first let us look at some of the raw material Sacks has to work with, the colorful individual threads within the Intervale Jewish Center.

It is Saturday after kiddush. Dave has his coat buttoned, and his cane hangs loosely hooked around one arm. He is waiting for us to leave. Sacks heads to the rear of the shul, puts away his talis, puts on his coat, and takes a firm grip on his plastic shopping bag that contains most of his worldly valuables. Sacks looks around the room and notices that two windows are still slightly open. Sam opened them earlier, claiming that his doctors advise him to get plenty of fresh air because of his respiratory condition. Ever since the doctors' recommendation, Sam opens the windows inside the shul even on the coldest days, then huddles next to a radiator to keep warm. What ensues is a scene out of Keystone Kops. Mr. Abraham usually follows close behind and shuts the windows that Sam has opened.

Sam is a gambler. At the beginning of each month, while he still has money from his Social Security check, he spends Saturdays at the track. Realizing that Sam will not be present, Sacks maintains a high degree of certainty that the absence is only temporary. "God is on our side," Sacks declares. "He makes sure that when Sam goes to the track, he loses it right away. By the second week of the month Sam is back in shul." On the afternoons when Sam goes to Poe Park off the Grand Concourse to play cards, Sacks insists that he take along extra pieces of cake from the kiddush to distribute to his friends. Sacks's generosity has ulterior motives: Sam's friends will come to expect the cake and urge Sam to attend services before the card game. This is typical Sacks strategy. He makes a similar gift to Hy, the nearby storeowner, who leaves the kiddush each week with a plate of cake for his salesgirls. For me, Sacks has a regular supply of chocolate babka. I am expected to indulge my addiction, as tribute both to a master baker and an arch-finagler. The more of it I eat, the greater the reassurance that I will continue to attend services.

Sacks is more than simply being tolerant toward Sam: he believes that Sam has a special relationship with God. Sam is a carpenter by trade, and he sometimes brings his tools to shul and makes various repairs. Although Sam will not hesitate to hammer a nail or drill a hole on shabes, Sacks is quick to explain the hidden piety of the religious violation: "You think he's violating shabes? He's not. Sam is very knowledgeable in the Hebrew prayers. He can daven like any Jew. But to him it's more satisfying to say, 'Look, God. I am fixing the abode that you live in. I'm putting a nail into the *aren kodesh*' [Ark]. That's his form of prayer."

Sam's behavior may be unusual, but it rarely disturbs other members of the congregation. Only when he uses his talis to wipe his hands do people make disparaging comments. Dave, though, is far more controversial and at the same time far more central to the congregation than Sam. Whereas Sam is merely eccentric, Dave's uniqueness takes on the quality of the trickster, a clownlike figure.

Dave Lentin is the only member of the congregation who was raised in the Bronx. He is a bachelor, now well into his seventies, who lived with his mother until her death in 1963. Dave is notoriously irreverent and takes great delight in mocking the sanctity of ritual. Whereas congregants have learned to ignore Dave's antics, first-time visitors are often shocked by his behavior. At one Hatzilu outing, a young woman greets Dave and asks if she can take his coat, promising to return with a check number. Dave tells her not to bother: "If a rat pops out, you'll know it's mine." Later, when the meal is over, another young woman asks if she can get him anything.

"Oh, yes. I'd like a chicken," he says.

"You're too late for that. The food's already gone."

"I don't mean *that* kind of chicken. I mean *this* kind." Dave uses his hands to draw in the air the figure of a curvacious woman.

REBBE AND GODFATHER

When visitors admire his hand-painted signs on the shul's walls, Dave usually tells them about his plans to cover the cracked ceiling with a mural of Adam and Eve. "The only thing is I'm not sure whether to do it with or without the leaf." Genitals are a frequent theme in Dave's monologues. He repeatedly decries the fact that his penis is too small, using its size as an explanation for his having cut the pieces of cake for the kiddush into tiny portions. Or he laments the fact that there are no young "chickens" (*shiksas*, or non-Jewish women) around, only "old hens—their openings are so big, if you try anything you're liable to fall in."

Why the preoccupation with shiksas? "Jewish girls are born with zippers. No touching the merchandise. First you got to sign on the dotted line." This is an apparent reference to an ill-fated love affair earlier in life.

Dave seldom tempers his irreverence. Agitated by Sacks's willingness to let non-Jews attend services (he apparently had a spat with one non-Jewish woman), Dave began referring to the shul as a church. "The shul is across the street. Pretty soon I'll get myself a robe and a collar, then a shiksa, and I'll go into competition with this place." Reversals are an integral part of Dave's machinations. He states his age each successive year as seventeen, twenty-seven, thirty-seven—reversals of the actual numbers. He transposes Jews and Puerto Ricans, rabbis and priests, Hebrew and Spanish: "*Buenos días*—that's Hebrew for 'Good day.' " *David Lentin* he often pronounces as *David Lentín* "because I'm really Puerto Rican." In fact, even time has a tendency to reverse itself. Observing the fact that more and more buildings are being dismantled and local Puerto Ricans are raising roosters on the rubble-strewn lots, Dave comments, "Maybe the area is going backwards altogether. Soon it will be the way it used to be. First they'll bring back the trolleys. Then there won't be any buildings left. It'll just be farms, and there'll be goats and cows and chickens." Even the recitation of the kaddish, his trademark, is subject to reversal. Before he heads to the front of the shul to recite the prayer, he debates whether to recite the kaddish or the Lord's Prayer. Lamenting the sorry state the shul was in after a series of break-ins and vandalism, he suggested, "Maybe we should say kaddish for the shul. Or maybe the problem is that I say the kaddish too much and that's what causes the break-ins." On another occasion, at the senior citizens' center, Dave began to recite the kaddish for the Puerto Rican director: "You see, now you won't die. The kaddish you say only after you die, not before." There are sexual reversals too. Complaining to a doctor that his penis is shriveling, he asks whether he is gradually "turning into a woman. My stomach keeps growling too. Maybe I'm pregnant or something. I'll become famous."

Visual and verbal puns are also prominent in Dave's repertoire. Pumping a hand while shaking hands reminds him of a water pump, and Dave

THE MIRACLE OF INTERVALE AVENUE

invariably checks to see if a stream of water emerges from the groin. "Playing pool" is his euphemism for masturbation. To Puerto Ricans curious about the Hebrew characters he constantly draws, Dave explains that the Hebrew letter *shin*, for example "isn't a letter at all. It's really just three men in a boat." In regard to verbal puns, Dave's mind is equally fertile. Reflecting on the Aramaic word *hamevorekh* in the kaddish, Dave asks, "Could you tell me something? How come if this is supposed to be kosher, they have ham here? *H-a-m*—hamevorekh—you see, there's ham in there." Often he changes the traditional Hebrew congratulatory phrase *yasher koyekh* to the somewhat homonymal name Jascha Heifetz. Sometimes, in a particularly creative mood he elaborates on the connection between J. C. Penney and Jesus Christ: "When Jesus comes down here, he's got to do something to earn a living. So he has a business—J. C. Penney. Why else do you think they call it J.C.?" Both Jesus and the domain of death are favorite themes of Dave's. Both, of course, are taboo topics, particularly because Dave has a tendency to flaunt them in the least appropriate contexts. "You know, me and Jesus is like this," Dave says, crossing his fingers. "I tell all the Puerto Ricans at the center, any time they want to speak to him, they should just come to me. Why not? Jesus was a Jew. He was a rabbi. The Last Supper was a seder. I tell them that I go upstairs to talk to him. I've already got an apartment waiting for me. You know, you got to fill out an application. First you go to the moon and then they see whether you go upstairs or downstairs. The only thing is you got to be careful because when you go upstairs, you shouldn't go alone or you're liable to get mugged by a junkie. People get upset when I talk. Especially when I start to talk dirty. But I just tell them to go read the Bible. It's all in there."

Related, perhaps, to an underlying concern with illness and death, Dave is quite preoccupied with anality. Early on in my research I learned that asking Dave how he feels may result in a good deal more information than I care to hear:

"I had dinner last week at an Italian friend's house. The food was so spicy that I got acid. I wasn't feeling well. I couldn't move my bowels. So I went to the doctor and he gave me a barium enema. You know what a barium enema is? The stuff is still in my stomach. I can't go to the bathroom. It's too dry. I have to squeeze, and that's no good because it gives you hemorrhoids. So I have to go back to the doctor. Only I tell him, 'No enemas, please!' Besides that, I have a sciatic back. They give you a shot of opium or something like it at the hospital, but it only lasts a couple of hours. Sometimes it's so painful all I can do is go home and sit still. I'm going tomorrow for a doctor's appointment. Aside from that I feel fine."

For the most part, Dave's anal obsessions focus on rats. He talks about them a great deal, seeing them in part as representatives of the devil and in part as personal friends. Rats do not figure, for example, among the creatures he recites the kaddish for: "You see, I say the kaddish over and over so as not to forget it. If I see a dead animal, I say the kaddish. Or even a dead tree, I say it. Look, their branches are pointing up to God like they're praying. The only thing I won't say kaddish for is for dead rats. They belong to the devil. Let him say kaddish for them."

Sometimes, though, Dave sees the rats in a more friendly vein, particularly the "Jewish" rats inside the shul, which, according to Dave, have their own minyan when the shul is empty of people: "Maybe I'll get Mrs. Miroff to make them a yarmulke and a talis. I'll get them a little prayer book. They're Jewish. One of them is named Abie. The other is Benny."

The trickster is a familiar figure in primitive religions, and he survives in civilized cultures in the form of the clown or comic. The primitive trickster's genius is his ability to incorporate disorder within the ordered world of everyday reality. Indeed, there is some of that in the comic, too. In a Lévi-Straussian sense, he represents nature's reentering culture "through the back door," so to speak: mocking the ordered universe structured by culture and suggesting, perhaps, various possibilities and permutations different from prevailing cultural norms. Dave's antics are a constant reminder that the Intervale Jewish Center is a world fabricated by culture that flies in the face of social, historical, and even biological reality. Surrounding it is a non-Jewish Bronx that is far more real than the Jewish Bronx of Intervale's congregants. Whatever contributed to Dave's peculiar sensibilities also made him particularly prone to crossing boundaries between young and old, Jew and non-Jew, male and female. A bachelor all his life, he is firmly rooted in an eternal adolescence, despite his increasingly advanced age. Unfettered by laws of *kashres* [ritual purity] or ethnic bias, he has long had intimate friends outside of the Jewish sphere. Moreover, subject to several breakdowns, he acts as if he were flitting back and forth between sanity and insanity. "Soon they're going to take me away from here. I'm going straight to Bellevue."

The merging of oppositions that characterizes Dave's thinking is both a weakness and a strength. It is a sign, perhaps, of mental instability, but it is also a source of power: by taunting congregants and neighbors about their anxieties over death and religious beliefs, he feigns, and perhaps convinces himself of, his own mastery of similar anxieties. By crossing the boundaries people set to define their own reality, he feigns mastery of different universes—both Jewish and Puerto Rican. By inhabiting a realm of disorder, he creates the illusion of being its master. Heading home from a Hatzilu outing, Dave looks out the window of the bus and watches as it approaches the Bronx just across the Whitestone Bridge: "Now the air smells good. I can smell the garbage. Where we were before, the air is too clean. It's no good for you."

As Robert Pelton argues in his study *The Trickster in West Africa*, "the trickster incarnates in every culture the oxymoronic imagination at play, literally 'fooling around' to discover new paradigms and even new logics."[8] To a certain degree, we can see Dave's behavior as the power of the powerless—namely, to debunk through ridicule. Ultimately, this is Dave's function for the Intervale congregation—to taunt the very forces they most fear and over which they have no control. There are no reprisals for Dave's irreverent behavior; he takes some of the awe out of death, God, and hostile, youthful neighbors.

In his study of humor, Freud maintains that all dirty jokes are either phallic or anal[9]—a point well taken in considering the themes of Dave's humor. Indeed, I am inclined to view the trickster as a walking dirty joke. The phallic side is life-affirming—the pleasure principle. It is a denial of death. The anal side signifies the opposite—death and decay. Although both elements are universal components of human consciousness, in the trickster they coexist in an unintegrated fashion. One side is the funny, ribald artist/poet; the other is a mean, foul-mouthed lout. Unfortunately for Dave, the latter side of him at times outweighs the former. Dave suffers from a good deal of inner rage; his humor sometimes shows a very mean face.

One cold, damp Saturday, Dave is busy cutting up vegetables and cake. His action seems even more frenetic than usual, and he is muttering loud enough for all of us to hear: "These fuckin' Jew bastards. You think I need this job? I don't need this job. The lousy few bucks a week. What do I need the aggravation for? Let them all go to hell! Anyone gives me any more trouble, I'll slit his throat."

Besides the vegetables—green pepper and cucumber—which Dave shreds and places on each plate, Mordechai has brought several large cans of gefilte fish in honor of Rosh Khodesh, the new lunar month. Dave cannot find a can opener. Mr. Abraham, swearing that he has brought at least half a dozen can openers over the years, goes out to his car to see if there is another one in the glove compartment, but he finds none. Dave puts the cans of fish into a plastic bag and carries them to the usually accommodating superintendent of an adjacent building. He returns a few minutes later with open cans of fish. Mr. Abraham, meanwhile, mutters a series of curses at Dave, who he knows has stolen the can opener, among many other things. (Only I, who have visited Dave's apartment, know the extent of Dave's pilferage of prayer books, kosher wine, and taleysim. The others can only guess.) Mrs. Miroff, who usually takes a good deal of care

REBBE AND GODFATHER

over the serving of the food, is not the least bit bothered by the missing can opener. She has long since gotten used to Dave's behavior: "He's a chiseler, a conniver," she confides.

Although Mrs. Miroff supplies Dave with a fairly extensive wardrobe of hand-me-down clothes, the relationship between the two is hardly one of peers. If it resembles anything, it is a mother–son relationship in which maternal instinct overrides disgust. It parallels Dave's relationship with Sacks, which, despite their closeness in age, is very much one of a tolerant father and an errant son.

Lately, considerable friction has entered the relationship between Dave and Mrs. Miroff. Despite his mutterings about not needing the job of caretaker, Dave jealously guards his position and resents Mrs. Miroff's meddling in the way he serves the food. Expressing his feelings as usual through his signs, Dave has painted the words "Stay out of this kitchen!" on the wall next to the burner where the coffee is brewed, and he threatens anyone who comes nearby with a huge bread knife, which he rather coyly refers to as his "penknife." Mrs. Miroff became a prime target after she accused Dave of putting less than the proper amount of coffee in the percolator in order to keep the rest for his own use. For weeks the coffee had been so weak that congregants began referring to it as tea. "*Afn ganef brent dos hitl*" goes the Yiddish saying ("On a thief's head, the hat burns," that is, he is hyperconscious of his guilt). Because he was indeed the culprit, Dave became irate at the reprimand. Sacks intervened, ordering Mrs. Miroff away from the kitchen, explaining, "You're better off losing an argument to a wise man than winning one with a fool." Later he advises Dave, "You shouldn't get so upset. You should consider her your mother, and as your mother she has the right to boss you around. She does the same thing to me. After all, she is an old woman."

Malachi Parkes joins the conversation: "She does the same thing to me. But I don't say anything because I consider her one of the daughters of Israel. She's right up there with the four mothers."

In fact, however, the real cause of tension between Mrs. Miroff and Dave was neither Dave's pilferage of the coffee nor her interfering in his work. The bone of contention was the presence during the summer of a young female photographer who had spent a good deal of time with Dave and whom Dave had become very fond of. Mrs. Miroff had quickly taken a dislike to the young woman. She resented the way she played up to the men, in particular the easy way she had with Dave, Mr. Sacks, and me. Mrs. Miroff had a rival. And Mrs. Miroff was suspicious. Why would a young woman want to spend time among old men? Sacks, she felt, should know better. "He's too old for young people, but he thinks he's too young to be with old people." He is an eligible bachelor, she reasoned, and a bachelor with money, to boot. Young women are attracted to money. Mrs. Miroff had very little influence over Sacks. Rather than listen to her, he is usually very quick to tell her off. So while the young photographer "wooed" Sacks, Mrs. Miroff had to sit by the side and seethe. And her fury was all the greater because of her affection for Sacks. If she could not complain about the photographer to Sacks, she certainly could to Dave, who, being less able to fend for himself, was more vulnerable and less likely to see through the wily ways of a young woman.

One of the more curious aspects of the conflict was that despite its rather long duration and sometimes vocal nature, it remained a purely private one. The conflict came out in the open only after the woman had photographed Mrs. Miroff placing a roll in her bag. Believing that the image might be misconstrued as an indication of indigence, Mrs. Miroff became irate. Her pride had been wounded and her privacy invaded. She approached Sacks and demanded action, but he refused to get involved: neither woman's presence was critical for the minyan, and the conflict in no way jeopardized the shul. Sacks's refusal to mediate only added further confirmation to Mrs. Miroff's concern that she was losing ground to a young upstart.

Finally Mrs. Miroff concluded that Dave had fallen hopelessly in love, and if things continued, Sacks might also be in danger. Mrs. Miroff took the offensive. She telephoned the photographer at home and told her never to come back to Intervale. She was causing dissension and making Mrs. Miroff feel like a stranger in her own shul. "Leave the old people alone," she told her. "Stop bothering us. We don't want you here."

When Mrs. Miroff told me what she had said, her face displayed a look of absolute triumph. She hadn't a drop of sympathy for the young woman, and regretted only having waited so long before taking action. The woman did not return to the Intervale Jewish Center. Dave tried to maintain contact. He called her repeatedly, though he was never able to get through to her, his calls being answered by her husband, who promised to relay the message. One Saturday he phoned repeatedly, then reported to me that neither she nor her husband was home: "A friend answered so I told her to take a message that this is Davíd Lentín, her Puerto Rican friend." Mrs. Miroff eyed Dave at the phone, shook her head, and commented, "Look at the old fool in love with a young tramp."

Mrs. Miroff isn't the only one upset by Dave's behavior. Unlike Mrs. Miroff, though, Mr. Abraham and Sacks have far more basic complaints against him than his amorous phone calls. Later that day, while taking some fruit from the refrigerator at Sacks's bakery, Mr. Abraham comments on the poor fare offered at the kiddush: "I don't know. Maybe you can explain something to me, some mystery that happened in shul today.

REBBE AND GODFATHER

This morning, when I took Mrs. Miroff to shul, I'll swear she had lettuce in the bundle. Did you see any lettuce in shul? I didn't see any. Maybe you could explain to me the mystery of the disappearing lettuce?"

"It's no mystery," Sacks responds. "It happens all the time. Just the other week I ordered fifteen taleysim for the shul. Where are they? Weissman, the man from Hatzilu, put them on a rack near the Ark. Today I come to shul, I ask Dave where the taleysim are. He says he doesn't know. 'Look, Dave,' I say to him. 'There are three keys to the shul. Flisser has an old key, it doesn't work no more. I have a key. You have a key. And Terry has a key.' " Terry is the black handyman hired to make repairs in the shul.

"Ah, go on!" Mr. Abraham interjects. "Terry hasn't worn a talis in years."

Taking my cue from Mr. Abraham, I try my own hand at a joke. "That means there can be only one culprit—you," I say to Sacks.

"Me?" Sacks responds. "I come to shul, I'm thankful that my talis is still there. And it's not Terry unless, like you wrote in your [*Natural History*] magazine article, he needs the taleysim for blankets to keep warm."

"In that case," Mr. Abraham suggests, "when you order new taleysim, you better order woolen ones. Or maybe down ones if we don't get the heating system fixed."

"So I tell Dave," Sacks continues, " 'Look. Let's not kid ourselves.' He doesn't answer me. He just walks away. Look, the guy is a kleptomaniac."

Despite the assessment, Sacks remains tolerant toward Dave. Whatever his failings, Dave is a member of the minyan and he contributes to the continued existence of the shul. Moreover, his contribution is of a special nature and goes beyond mere presence.

Dave's personal history parallels that of other congregants. His religiosity stems from the need to partake in the rites of commemoration. "When my mother died," he says, "I couldn't cope. I had a nervous breakdown. Anyway, one day I went into a synagogue and the rabbi explained to me that I feel guilty, but it's not my fault that she died and I'd feel better if I learned to say the kaddish. I told him I didn't know any Hebrew. But he said that's O.K. He'll show me with English letters. He said I should try it. I should give it two weeks. If I can't learn it after two weeks, then I should forget about it. So I tried, and after four days I was able to say the whole thing by heart."

In a community of elderly people, uncertain of their children's religiosity, they, too, need some assurance that the proper prayers will be recited when they die. On Saturdays, toward the end of the service when the kaddish is recited, the men shout for Dave to leave what he is doing in back of the shul and come to the front to recite the prayer. He does it, as he says, "from the heart." Like the wayward son determined to make amends for past wrongdoings, Dave's kaddish is the repayment of an obligation of a surviving child toward a deceased mother. And it has become the communal kaddish for the shul.

Watching Dave's tricksterlike, bawdy, angry, and poetic antics, I sometimes wonder how God responds to Dave's prayers. I ask Sacks what he thinks. "Quite well," is his reply. While not condoning all of Dave's behavior, Sacks staunchly believes in his role within the congregation. Nor is Dave the only case of God's receptiveness, in Sacks's view, to all of His creatures.

Ever since their first appearancce in the vacant lot beside the shul, the crowing roosters have become a part of Saturday services at Intervale. Now they are growing in numbers, and their voices have become a sort of choir, encouraged, perhaps, by the Saturday-morning chanting inside the shul. I comment frequently to Sacks about the outspokenness of the roosters, who seem to be vying for a place in the minyan: "Perhaps they have their own minyan."

It is the rebbe who responds. "Why not? God hears their *tefiles* [prayers] too. Even more so. Most of what we pray, we do mechanically. Frankly, most of us don't even know the meaning of the words we say. But what they say, they mean. So why shouldn't He listen to them? The same way even a whistle from Dave, God listens to. He means it. It's from his heart."[10]

·5·
"EVEN SOLOMON WOULD HAVE TROUBLE"

One Saturday, walking past the shops on Southern Boulevard on our way to the bakery from shul, I remark to Sacks that the Puerto Rican *botánica* selling religious statues, both pagan and folk-Catholic, has a sign outside that reads "Sale." "Imagine that," I comment. "A store like that having a sale."

"What's funny about that?" Sacks asks.

"You mean you don't find the idea of selling idols at a discount funny?"

"No. It's not so funny. After all, Avrom Ovinu's [Abraham our father's] father made idols, and he had a store to sell them. I imagine sometimes he sold them at a discount too."

A typical Sacksism. The man is an expert at locating the commonplace within the bizarre. He is an expert, too, in referring to the Bible to make sense out of life's peculiar twists of fate. Sacks is on familiar terms with the patriarchs of the Bible: he knows their human strengths and frailties, and he takes great pleasure in relating his observations to others.

The Sunday activities at Intervale can be divided into three parts. The first is prestation: congregants make donations to the shul and receive from Sacks in return a receipt and handshake. The second is the communal meal: Sacks arrives each Sunday morning either by squad car or taxi laden with half a dozen shopping bags stuffed with rolls, cream cheese, and cake. The third part is performance: through the review of the parshe, Sacks does for the whole congregation what he does on a regular basis for himself, namely merge the awesome world of the Bible with the familiar world of today. The performance begins as soon as Sacks announces toward the end of the brunch that it's time for a dvar Torah:

"There's a saying that if you sit down at a table without mentioning a couple of words of Torah, it's as if you ate *treyf* [nonkosher food]. So usually on Sundays I tell you the parshe of the week. So I'm going to spend ten minutes to tell you about the parshe for the simple reason—for two reasons. One, I haven't done it in a long time and I might forget how to do it. Number two, I think you're entitled not to eat treyf. Therefore without much further ado . . . Mr. Kaplan, go get two *khumoshim* [Bibles]!"

Kaplan retrieves the khumoshim, hands one to Sacks, and keeps one for himself. The two sit facing each other, with Sam in the middle and Mr. Abraham to Sacks's right. Kaplan follows the text closely as Sacks begins the review of the parshe. Sacks's presentations reveal the man not just as rabbi, teacher, and counselor but also as a master storyteller. Although he is particularly sensitive to the narrative techniques of the Bible ("Look at Genesis—in one line you have the whole history of the universe up to that point"), Sacks enhances and embellishes the material within the text through tone, rhythm, and dramatic effects. There is a wonderful interplay here between storyteller and story: the relevance of the Bible for Intervale's congregation does not come solely from the texts; to an equal degree, it is the result of Sacks's strength as a performer and his ability to digest the Bible and commentaries and recast them in an idiom that congregants readily understand. A selective examination of segments from a number of dvar Torahs reveals some of Sacks's performance techniques and sheds considerable light on the interplay between the teacher and the congregation on one level, and between Sacks and biblical heroes on another.

More than anything else, it is the Sunday brunch and dvar Torah that entice congregants to come to the shul. It makes pleasure and entertainment out of a didactic exercise that might elsewhere be rather esoteric. Sacks sees participation in the review as "an indirect route to God." If he makes it entertaining enough, a one-time visitor to the shul may become a regular and eventually, perhaps, a Saturday congregant. So Sacks places no restrictions on who may participate in the questions and translations. Any comment is treated with consideration. At the same time, the setting—a combination of food, convivial atmosphere, humor, storytelling, and reflections on everyday life problems—makes the review an event of

THE MIRACLE OF INTERVALE AVENUE

considerable meaning for those in attendance. And it does precisely what Sacks wants it to do: attract new members to the congregation, including this anthropologist.

The function of biblical text here shifts from myth to ritual in the sense that the lines are not just read, they are performed. Traditional Ashkenazic *lernen* [study] involves a rebbe or teacher reciting segments of the text in a singsong voice. Sacks does not do this, largely because his audience is not learned enough in Hebrew or religious texts to follow or be interested in such detailed explication of the Torah. Rather than read from the text, Sacks recites brief phrases in Hebrew, thereby creating the impression of translation, and continues with his own summation. He delights his audience with frequent integrations of analogies from everyday experience. The excitement in his voice mounts as the story reaches its climax. As it does, he moves from storyteller to preacher, bringing into high relief what he views as the moralizing intent of the biblical text. In doing so, the parshe is not just "learned"; it is experienced. As Barbara Myerhoff notes, "By merely absorbing us sufficiently, ritual, like art, lets us 'lose ourselves' and step out of our usual conscious, critical mentality."[1] In "losing" themselves, participants also give up their everyday time sense. According to Mircea Eliade, "Anyone who performs any rite transcends profane time and space; similarly, anyone who 'imitates' a mythological model or even ritually assists at the retelling of a myth (taking part in it), is taken out of profane 'becoming,' and returns to the 'Great Time.' "[2] Moreover, the regression to mythical time permits individuals to experience, albeit vicariously, the heroic exploits of mythical, larger-than-life figures.[3]

One result of experiencing biblical time together through the weekly review is the uniting of the individuals of the congregation into a group, performing as a group. Not even the Saturday service has a greater unifying effect. The Sunday dvar Torah is a performance in which Intervale presents itself to itself. God is the chief spectator on Saturday, while the women and the nonobservant stand on the sidelines. But on Sunday, even the spectators participate, caught by the storytelling in the leaps of fantasy that join separate worlds together over time and space and across the boundaries of separate individuality and experience. For the Intervale congregation, by participating in the review of the parshe, they are changing a biological act, namely, eating, into a collective cultural event. The group participates fully even in the process of translation, as individuals either supply words and definitions when Sacks hesitates or provide analogies as explications of the text.

SACKS: We'll continue with the Torah. Moses, being a good diplomat, satisfied Aaron and the Levi'im and told them they had no [special] day in

"EVEN SOLOMON WOULD HAVE TROUBLE"

the *mishkan* [Temple] in the *khanukas habayit*[4] because they are there all the time. And he tells them: "Your job is to work from age twenty-five to fifty. When you reach the age of fifty you become a senior citizen. You just tell the younger fellows what to do. You watch. They work.

DOROTHY: Be a supervisor.

SACKS: You'll be a supervisor as I was just told. In those days you worked from the day you were born, and I am not kidding you. Their infancy and childhood and all this was lost in the fact that you had to work for a living. You had to work to eat. And in those days, to have this novel idea that you work only from twenty-five years to fifty and at the end of twenty-five years of work you could retire, that certainly was novel. You didn't have to have no five-years marks on your sleeve like in the police department. When you got to the twenty-fifth year you were eligible for retirement.

JANETTE: Hash marks.

SACKS: Hash marks. But this is the most novel idea at the time. To us now who understand that you retire after a certain age, we can grasp the idea of retirement. But here they were retired and at the same time they were told they don't have to wait for the *malekh hamoves* [Angel of Death]. From fifty on, their job was to supervise as I was told here. Their job was to see that everything was done right. And relax. Sit back. Enjoy their old age. Like we do. There was a pillar of God's shekhine. A pillar . . .

KAPLAN: Fire.

SACKS: Fire at night only. *Umare'eysh laylo*. It was a pillar like a smoke, like a . . .

FLISSER: Cloud.

SACKS: Like a cloud. Beautiful! If I had such response all the time, half my job would be finished. Mr. Flisser . . .

FLISSER: I read the parshe yesterday, before you . . .

SACKS: That's beautiful. Really beautiful. You know, a professor is a person who has to teach. But [if] the people learn themselves, the professor gets the credit from teaching them anyway. But it's they who actually are the beneficiaries.

Later in the review Sacks mentions Moses' refusal to put out a fire raging in the desert because of his anger at the Israelites' complaining. Sacks then continues:

SACKS: You know, the Hebrews did not only go out themselves. There were a lot of people that went out that were not Hebrews. Or some mixed people that went out. And they were called *asafsof*. That means all the gathering. A crowd. Or whatever you want to call it.

THE MIRACLE OF INTERVALE AVENUE

KAPLAN: A mixed multitude.

SACKS: A mixed multitude. You see, that's beautiful. I thought at first that you were sleeping. But you aren't. (Sacks laughs.)

JEAN GELLER: Reformed Jews.

SACKS: No, no. Reformed Jews are Jews. Don't get me wrong. Reformed Jews are Jews. These were a mixed multitude who were not even Jewish.

KAPLAN: A rabble.

SACKS: A rabble. It was a crowd that always likes to go. In those days food wasn't so plentiful. As far as making a living goes, you didn't have a job. So when a crowd saw that something was happening, like there was going to be a big party there or this or that, they joined. There was nothing wrong with it. And when the Hebrews went out of Egypt, they went out *beyad romo*. It means with a strong hand. They went out. They were well fed. They were clothed and everything else. Naturally they were six hundred thousand all of a sudden going out for freedom. So they had a big rabble of crowds going with them joining the fun. And these people all of a sudden reminded themselves *zokharnu mi ya'akhileynu bosor*, "Who's going to give us meat?" They all of a sudden remembered *es hadag asher*,[5] the fish that they ate in *Mitsrayim* [Egypt] and the melons.

KAPLAN: The leeks.

SACKS: The leeks.

KAPLAN: Onions.

SACKS: And the onions.

KAPLAN: And the garlic.

SACKS: And the garlic. Onions and garlic, don't forget they remembered that, too.

JEAN GELLER: There was melons there?

SACKS: Oh, sure. The most delicious melons [grow] in Israel. They remembered that they ate all that in there.

KAPLAN: For nothing.

SACKS: For nothing. That is, that they worked twenty hours a day didn't count. But they didn't have to take money out of the pocket.

KAPLAN: *Umzist*.

SACKS: Umzist.

JEAN GELLER: Do you know how much a pound of garlic is?

SACKS: No.

JEAN GELLER: Two dollars.

SACKS: Two dollars a pound? They got it for nothing.

KAPLAN: Inflation after all those years.

"EVEN SOLOMON WOULD HAVE TROUBLE"

Digressions serve the purpose of "contemporizing," to use the sociologist Samuel Heilman's term, the biblical text.[6] Some come about in response to questions or associations from the congregation. Others take place through Sacks's insertion of factual, sometimes scientific information into his narrative, drawn for the most part from his readings of popular magazines—for example, in the following excerpt from *parshes Noyakh*.

SACKS: All right. Noah took two hundred and ten years to build the ark.

ABRAHAM: He was a slow worker.

SACKS: He wasn't a slow worker. He was definitely told by God to try to stretch the work as much as possible to get the people curious enough to come and ask what he's doing. And he answered to them and he told them, "Your ways are bad and God has intentions of bringing water and just wiping you all out." Of course they laughed at him. They didn't believe in him. And he kept on doing it for two hundred years, so they figured he was just an old nut. Let him work. At the age six hundred, Noah finished the ark. And when he finished that, God told him, 'Within seven days get everything. I'm going to bring the water on.' And he did. And you saw the animals coming two by two into the ark. These Noah did not have to solicit. God appointed these animals to themselves, and they came from all kinds of animals—the pure, the unpure—they came, insects or whatever. I wonder if the cockroaches came? No. If cockroaches came, they certainly survived. Noah! You shouldn't have taken them along! There's a good history of the life of a cockroach. It's so interesting that you have no idea. They're in moralistic standing sometimes better off than man. They come out at eleven o'clock for promenading or whatever it is. At twelve, and this is a proven fact by scientists who watch them, at twelve o'clock at night, midnight, all females have to go back to the post, twelve o'clock is curfew for female cockroaches. Males have a little more time to play around. Any female that's caught outside after twelve-o'clock curfew is actually eaten. It's eaten by the male cockroaches and they use it as . . .

KAPLAN: Dessert.

SACKS: Food.

LUCY: Such a story.

SACKS: I'm not telling a story. I'm telling you scientific facts. We go back to the khumesh. All right. [Everybody is laughing.] I'm glad you're enjoying this.

Although much of the activity centers on Sacks, members of the congregation find various ways to contribute to the event. The brunch that precedes the review, for example, is served by Mrs. Miroff and Dave, and before her bout with pneumonia, Lucy used to cut the rolls before they were served. During the parshe, too, members feel free to participate. Sam, Mr. Abraham, and Mr. Kaplan flank Sacks and follow the text both in the Hebrew and in English translation. They supply English words when Sacks is stuck, and they remind him where he is in the text when his frequent digressions lead him too far astray. For their part, others contribute too. Mr. Abraham, even when he is busy cleaning up the shul, still manages to slip in a quick one-liner. Janette, Jean, and several other women interrupt with questions or associations. Even Dave, who for the most part is locked in a world of his own, draws signs on paper plates that read "Sha! Der rebbe redt" (Quiet, the rabbi is talking), which he waves at noisy or otherwise troublesome congregants, and listens, particularly to the more off-color stories, which he retells to visitors and acquaintances, reminding them that "it's in the Bible." Although not everyone speaks during the review, it is the only event in which congregants participate that commands their near total attention. And in that sense it is truly a group project.

A particularly common way for the group to participate is through humor. Although Sacks has a storehouse of jokes that he draws on during the review of the parshe, it is Mr. Abraham who is generally the source of the best one-liners. (Sacks refers to himself as "Mr. Abraham's straight man.") At one review, Mr. Abraham had been busy walking in and out of the room doing odd jobs around the shul, including washing the hall floor, sweeping the main room, and fixing bathroom fixtures. (He acknowledges that one reason for attending is to have a chance to do some physical labor.) In the middle of a sentence, Sacks hollers, "Mr. Abraham! Come in here! This is getting dry. We need your humor in here. Sit down and you can go to sleep in the corner. Do interjections now and then to show that you're here because we're going on tape." Sacks continues with the parshe:

"Jacob was so enthused he picked up his legs, and with the help of God, naturally, as soon as he picked up his legs he was right in the place where he wanted to go. That was express. He didn't stop at the local."[7]

"The magic carpet's got nothing on Jacob," Mr. Abraham comments.

"That's just what I wanted," says Sacks. "That's what I've been missing in here!"

Responding to Sacks's explanation that the only time non-Jews are not permitted to eat Jewish food is on Passover, when the Paschal lamb may only be eaten by Jews, and in the case of a convert or servant only if he is circumcised, Mr. Abraham comments, "That's a hell of a price to pay for a meal."

Or take the following excerpt from a parshe on the laws regarding the Sabbath during the Exodus from Egypt:

"EVEN SOLOMON WOULD HAVE TROUBLE"

SACKS: If a man went to gather twigs in the desert for the fire on shabes, he was to be stoned.

ABRAHAM: If he was enough of a shmuck to look for twigs in the desert, he deserved it.

When Sacks uses humor, it is usually meant to serve as a reminder of the Bible's human face. Describing Rachel and Leah's argument over who would get to use the aphrodisiac to lure Jacob to bed, Sacks comments, "The women in those days certainly weren't bashful." Telling of Laban's willingness to let Jacob marry Rachel a week after he married Leah: "He married her with the condition that he had to work another seven years for her. And he did. But he got his money before. He got his pay before. And there was a good union man. He got his pay and he didn't walk off the job." Commenting on the difference in punishment that Pharaoh meted out to his wine steward and his baker, both of whom had served food containing a fly, Sacks, himself a baker, comments, "As usual the baker got hung."

Sacks's humor frequently refers to the fact that he and his congregation live in one of the world's most famous slums. Describing why Jacob came to Laban without any possessions, he narrates: "Esav sent his son to kill Jacob on the road. When he meets up with Jacob, Jacob tells him, 'Now, listen. Take all my possessions that I have. I'll become a poor man, and a poor man is just like a dead man.' He didn't know anything about the Intervale Jewish Center." Or take the following response to one woman's question concerning how we would recognize the Messiah when he comes: "If he comes to the South Bronx there'll be no problem. We'll just have to look for him inside a squad car."

Sometimes digressions from the text are prompted by a question from a congregant. One woman frequently asks rather moronic questions. "Do we have any pictures of Moses?" Or, "At that time, did they have any Reformed Jews?" Or "When Abraham circumcised himself, did they have any doctors and nurses in those days?" "Are the Egyptians *goyim*?" "What religion did people have in the Garden of Eden?" Sometimes these digressions are mindless distractions, but quite frequently they succeed in livening up the text if only by asserting its contemporaneity. In the case of the question about circumcision, Sacks responds by explaining that in religious households in Israel even today, the father circumcises his own son. "And if he has a lot of sons, I imagine he gets good at it." The anecdotal nature of his answer universalizes and concretizes an abstract or somewhat remote event. It makes what is distant seem much closer to home. Indeed, the humor often lies in the resultant anachronism, as in the following fragment from *parshe vayetse* relating Jacob's attempt to relieve the hostility between Joseph and his brothers:

THE MIRACLE OF INTERVALE AVENUE

SACKS: As I was saying in the car coming down here, it reminded me of the trials and tribulations of today. Joseph telling the dream to Jacob. And the father reprimanded him for the dream. But at the same time, it says . . . Mr. Abraham!

ABRAHAM: Yeah, I'm listening.

SACKS: Good. That it didn't say in the text, but I am glad you're listening. The ten brothers [of Joseph] went with the sheep to pasture them in other lands. In other words, you usually find in the Torah that when they wanted to go on a holiday or on a vacation or something or other, the shepherd, the *royeh*—what did they call them? The herdsmen, the shepherds, and in this case the ten brothers, they went to Shekhem. They went to this place like you would find in the wild west. You have those guys who take care of the herds, and they have a town in there where they [can] have a night on the town or something like that. In other words, they're going for a vacation. And Jacob's sons were the same way. They were getting a little too tired of having the sheep around their place, so they thought they'd take a vacation, and the place of a vacation was to go to Shekhem. There you could have a drink with the boys and this and that.

DOROTHY: [Like] you're going into town.

SACKS: [Like] you're going into town. You went to town. It's a diversion. It's a vacation from your work. And at the same time taking your work with you. They took the sheep with them because who were they going to leave it with there? Somebody had to take care of the sheep. So they took the sheep and they went to town. Now Jacob could have sent anybody to see how his boys are getting along. And the idea of sending just Joseph to find out how they're getting along, he had two alternatives. Two. One, if he sends a *sheliakh* [representative], if he sends one that was working for them, he would meet up with the boys and they would come there and they would tell them, "Hey, you! Mind your own business! Don't tell Pop . . ."

DOROTHY: Hush.

SACKS: Hush. And after all, don't be a squealer [they might have said]. In other words . . .

DOROTHY: Let's have a drink.

SACKS: Let's have a drink. You know, like this. And the other thing is if he sends Joseph, then they would have a little respect as Joseph being the actual sheliakh from the father. And they would act with a little bit more decorum. And they would respond a little better. And Jacob himself understood a little psychology. He says, "What is the sense of having twelve sons and have ten that are against one. And now they go away they don't even call Joseph to go and have a drink with them?" So he sends

Sacks reviews the rabbinical commentaries at home in preparation for the Sunday *dvar Torah*.

Sacks reviews the *parshe* of the week as Louis Kaplan follows the text.

Sunday brunch at Intervale usually draws a crowd of fifteen
or more congregants.

Rashim, previously a member of Rabbi Matthew's
congregation in Harlem, listens intently to the *dvar Torah*.

"EVEN SOLOMON WOULD HAVE TROUBLE"

Joseph to sort of bring all the brothers together, and when the brothers are together maybe they'll forget a little of the hate that one has for the other. So you see, all around it was working in a circle to try to get psychology, but God was in there at the beginning. He wanted to put down the framework for the play *Joseph and the Amazing Technicolor Dream Coat*. In other words, Joseph had to be sold in slavery and then the [play's] scenario could continue from here.

In *The History of the Yiddish Language*,[8] Max Weinreich argues that through panchronism, that is, by ignoring the separation between various time periods, the rabbis have been able to span generations to find precedent for rabbinic rulings. At Intervale, the spanning of the generations also bridges the gap between drama and comedy. A biblical analogy can lend itself as easily to good-natured jesting or play as it can to making the everyday seem heroic.

After completing the review of the parshe, Sacks discusses the trips Hatzilu is planning for the congregation. His weekly dvar Torahs are to some degree in competition with the organization's more lavish outings and repasts:

SACKS: But you don't want food for the soul, you want food for the stomach.

JANETTE: I live to eat and eat to live.

SACKS: As I told you beforehand, the Torah definitely says that you got to have a strong body to be able to sit down and actually learn the Torah. It doesn't want a weak person to sit down and learn. For the simple reason, every time he comes to a crucial point, he says, "Ohhh, *mayn boykh tut mir vey!* [My stomach hurts!]" Now, listen, as soon as there'll be trips, you'll be notified, we'll go out. Meanwhile you'll have to suffer here.

JANETTE: I don't suffer.

SACKS: You come in here and you have onion rolls, bagels, and cream cheese.

JANETTE: Why don't you bring me a little cottage cheese once in a while? I can't eat cream cheese. I could eat it, but it's too high for me in cholesterol.

SACKS: Will you listen to me? This lamentation is not yours by original. This lamentation was made by the people who ate *mun* [manna] in the desert when the Israelis went out. It's definitely written that the mun tasted exactly how they wished. If you would have eaten mun, you would have had cottage cheese. So these people complained. They wanted to have the *sir habosor*, they wanted to have the big pots of meat that they had in Egypt. You want cottage cheese. . . .

JANETTE: I have cottage cheese at home. I'll bring it in.

SACKS: Good, bring it in.

Sacks's playful use of a biblical analogy masked the preaching intent of the allusion. The Sunday brunch, which Sacks supplies, is a manna of sorts. Its sameness, week after week, places Sacks in the role of being like Moses, both the supplier of basic sustenance and also the one who determines the range of food available. Implicit in his reference to the biblical story is Sacks's awareness and sometimes resentment of the congregants' ingratitude for his efforts. Reviewing the parshe that describes the Israelites becoming disgruntled with the food, Sacks makes an explicit analogy between the complaints voiced over what he brings to Intervale and what Moses himself brought to the Israelites:

SACKS: Now in this little sojourn, he tells them that they only had the mun to eat. And the mun had the most beautiful taste. It tasted like anything that you would cook into honey. And whatever taste you want, that's the taste that the mun had. But naturally they were not satisfied with it. They wanted to have meat. And they wanted to have fish. And as the other people cried—crying is very contagious. The Hebrews, too, sat in front of their tents and they started to cry, too. They also started to cry. They also wanted to have that. God heard it and He said to Moses . . . first of all Moses says, "I can't stand this anymore!" He lost his patience. He says, "What am I? Am I their father? Did I bring them forth? Do I have to carry all this on my head?" he says. "And that I have to have everything?" God told him, He says, "No, you don't! Get yourself seventy elder people from Israel and you'll bring those seventy to in front of the mishkan, and I shall go down and I shall take some of your power and put it on those seventy, and they will become your ruling body. They'll rule with you and they'll carry over the burdens a little bit of the people." He says that he will do immediately. "But in the second you tell the people that I shall give them food, meat to eat not for a day, not for two days, not for seven days, not for ten days, not for twenty days, but for the whole month." And here is how this Torah is what happened here a half-hour ago. Moses said, "If you took all the *bakar* that they had, all the cattles, and you killed it, or you took all the fish that was in the sea and they brought it, *hayotse lahem?* Would it be enough for them?" If I brought all the bread in here, all the cake, all the stuff I have in the bakery that I left there, *hayotse lahem?* Would you have had enough today?

SAM: We'd still be short!

SACKS: You'd still be short. When I saw what was happening in here, I was saying to myself, this parshe of the week, it's so beautiful. . . . So he says, "*Hayotse lahem?* Would that be sufficient for them?"

The playful quality of this interchange, particularly where Sacks draws the analogy between his and Moses' plight, demonstrates the sense in which the review of the parshe is an activity that very much reflects Intervale as a community in dialogue with itself both as a congregation and as a greater collectivity, that is, as a people.[9]

Although anecdote and panchronistic humor cut through the awesomeness of holy text, it is not just Sacks's style that makes the parshe meaningful to the congregation. Sacks sees the biblical stories as a source of guidance for individuals' lives. He brings biblical figures down to earth and encourages congregants to see them as ordinary human beings, not too dissimilar to themselves. His central theme is the persistence of human frailties not only among the common folk of the Bible but even among the patriarchs and other ancient Jewish heroes:

SACKS: Jacob worked for the seven years and Laban says, "O.K., I'll keep my promise." And he made a big party. And naturally in the party they must have drunk something stronger than water. . . .

KAPLAN: Jacob got drunk.

SACKS: But at the end, in the evening, instead of taking Rokhel, Leah was the bride. In other words, the marriage ceremony was consummated with Leah.

ABRAHAM: It says here she was heavily veiled and in the dark. This fraud may be regarded as a retribution for the deception Jacob himself practiced on his father. His comeuppance.

SACKS: All right. The thing that we get from this, and I cannot emphasize this enough, the characters that are presented in the Bible are human beings. There's always brought up a fault, the human frailties, to stop successive generations from deitizing, from making those people as gods and worshiping them. We are not as other people are, we do not believe that the human being could take the place of a God. We believe that there is one God and we have ancestors who were very righteous, very religious, but at the same time there was times in their lives where they succumbed to the frailty of being human. And this was one of the times. Now, Jacob deceived his father and he wore a mask. He wore the goat's [skin] on his hands, and as he tried to get the blessing that was due to his older brother, he in turn was deceived by his wives. They put a big veil on her, and he did not know his deception till the morning he got up. When he got up in the morning he found out he had the wrong wife. He did not have the wife that he bargained for.

JEAN GELLER: Did he like her?

SACKS: He never did.

Sacks's admiration for the wisdom of the Bible in blending human frailties with saintliness goes beyond the reminder not to deify human beings. He also recognizes the ease with which ordinary people can identify with their biblical forebears and see their own plight in the dilemmas faced by them. "Religious leaders make a mistake in making biblical figures so godlike. They make them more distant from ordinary people. What I do is I present them in such a way that people will identify things in their lives with the Bible." Biblical heroes set examples for us to follow. Moreover, a recognition of their saintliness despite their frailty softens the blow we feel when we cannot measure up to our highest standards. The disappointment parents feel in their children's not meeting certain expectations provides one example:

SACKS: Gershon was Moses' first son. [Named,] he said, "Because I was a *ger* [stranger]." And the other one was Eliezar. Moses had two sons. And here they're mentioned, and once before they were mentioned in the Bible. And no more.

LENA ZALBEN: What were their names?

SACKS: Gershon and Eliezar.

LENA ZALBEN: Oh, that's a relative of mine.

SACKS: These are the two sons of Moses. The reason why Moses' sons were not mentioned, although the father actually wanted his sons to be his successors, but they were not [mentioned] because they show us in the khumesh that we cannot depend upon a certain hierarchy or whatever it is, a monarchy or a dynasty. Moses was rewarded for what he did, and his children would have been rewarded in their own right if they were fit for it. Apparently they were not. And therefore [the Bible] just mentions they were his children. And that is all.

The story also points to other concerns parents have, concerns that Sacks alludes to in the next statement:

SACKS: And Korakh, who went against Moses, he was swallowed in the ground. But his children, Korakh's children, did not agree with the father when he went against Moses. And they in turn were not punished for their father's deeds. They are mentioned in the Torah. They were given the land that was given to them.

KAPLAN: Didn't he have important descendants?

SACKS: Who?

KAPLAN: Korakh's children.

SACKS: Korakh's children later on in history, they had important descendants. From them came the Levi'im. And their descendants were of some consequence.

The story of Noah contains both the underside of Noah's righteousness and the ambiguity of relationships between the generations. Although Noah was a righteous man, Sacks reports the following as the biblical portrayal of him:

SACKS: The story is this. They were in the boat for forty days, and after forty days God remembered Noah and God told to Noah, "The rain stopped, the water started to recede." And as the water receded the ark was floating, and it happened to land on Mount Ararat. At the edge of a mountain the boat landed. The boat landed some five or six thousand years ago. Last year there was still an expedition thinking they could find that boat. So you see our Torah is not extinct. One of these days someone will come up with a piece of boat or wood and they'll prove that it was Noah's ark and we'll have it. First, when the ark landed permanently on the mountaintop, he opened up the window that he had, Noah, and he tried to send out the raven. Now the raven went, flew back, went in, flew back again. And Rashi, I don't know, he gets different explanations. He says the raven was afraid that Noah was trying to make time with his wife. And therefore he did not [go out for long]. . . . That's exactly what he says, so don't look at me like that.

ABRAHAM: Who you talking about? Mrs. Raven?

SACKS: Mrs. Raven. And therefore he refused to leave her alone and he flew back to the ark. Mr. Abraham, never ask any questions on fact.

ABRAHAM: No. You have to ask a raven *maven* [expert].

Sacks continues with the story. Noah sends out a dove this time.

SACKS: He [the dove] did not return and therefore he has proof that the water had receded and he had found a resting place. He waited another week or thirty days, I don't know, *shloshim yom*. He waited a period of time, and then he opened up the door of the ark and he and his sons and their wives and all the animals left there with the blessing of God that God told them to occupy this fresh land and *pru urvu milu es ho-orets,* which means . . .

KAPLAN: Be fruitful and multiply.

SACKS: Multiply and fill the land. And now we get to the character of Noah. We get a little introspect of how much of a *tsaddik*, a righteous person, he was. He was a farmer originally and he was given permission to grow, and the first thing he grew was grapes, and the second thing he did, he had wine, and the third thing he did, he got drunk. [Everybody laughs.] So you see, he was righteous according to his *dor*, according to his generation. At least he grew the grapes.

DOROTHY: He can't help it if he got drunk.

SACKS: If he got drunk. The story here is that his grandchild, Canaan, who was the son of Ham, saw how Noah was rolling around. Naturally the only robe that they wore was just a cloth. He disrobed himself, and his nakedness was prevalent. I suppose he had some excrement coming out, like a drunken man, which you see in the streets here, whether in Park-chester, Eastchester, or wherever. I don't know if he smelled as bad.

KAPLAN: In Hunts Point.

SACKS: Hunts Point you don't see so many drunks. You want to see real

drunks, you got to go down to Parkchester. There you see the real
drunks. And they're so drunk, they stink a mile before you get off from
the station on Parkchester. Don't go out of the Bronx. You can find
everything good and bad right here in the Bronx. So his grandchild made
a mockery of the situation of his grandfather. And he said shame on him
and was laughing at him.

DOROTHY: Shame on the grandchild!

SACKS: Shame on the grandchild, too. The other two sons, Shem and
Yofes, took a cloth and put it on their shoulders and walked backwards not
to see the nakedness and the shame of the father, Noah. And they
covered him. They covered him with the blanket, at the same time not
exposing his derogatory appearance even to their own eyes. They didn't
want to see it. They covered him. And Noah slept it off. When he was told
of the situation that happened, he went out and he cursed Canaan. He
cursed his grandson and said, "Because you shamed your grandfather,
therefore you will be in later years the servant to the descendants of Shem
and Yofes." And these were the ancestors of Abraham. Shem was the
ancestor of Abraham, Isaac, Jacob, and Israel. And in the end, Erets
Canaan was taken from them and given to the twelve tribes of the Israelis.
So we see how everything is tied in and God doesn't leave any loose ends
lying around.

Biblical analogy serves a dual role. It provides a didactic story and
presents a life plan for the congregation. A moral dilemma is easier to face
when placed in the context of a biblical event whose hero faced the same
problem and eventually overcame it. For example, Sacks's role as Moses,
the leader of a cantankerous crew of people, is literally infused with
meaning when he reflects upon the many trials and tribulations of his
biblical namesake. A less imaginative man would cringe at the behavior of
some members of Intervale's congregation. Sacks sees the congregation as
similar to the rabble that Moses led out of Egypt. In this sense, the
didactic quality of the story has an affirmative aspect: it legitimizes the
current plight of congregants by framing them within the context of biblical events.

Resorting to mythical and/or ritual frames of reference has considerable
impact, too, on the sense of time of members of the congregation. Since
they experience linear time, for the most part, as an adversary, the cycli-
cal time of myth and ritual offers them a more benevolent face. As Barbara Myerhoff notes,

Ritual alters our ordinary sense of time, repudiating meaningless
change and discontinuity by emphasizing regularity, precedent, and
order.

"EVEN SOLOMON WOULD HAVE TROUBLE"

In ritual, all forms of change are interpreted by being linked with the past and incorporated in a larger framework, where inevitable varia- tions are equated with grander, tidier totalities.[10]

Sacks applies the same affirmative logic to the plight of individual con- gregants. After the death of her older sister, Mrs. Miroff was uncertain whether or not to sit shiva. The sister had been a very selfish woman, and Mrs. Miroff had suffered throughout her life on her account. At first, Sacks was uncertain what to advise. Then, after reading over the parshe of the week, he reflected that in describing Sarah's death, the Bible uses a small Hebrew letter *kof* for the word *likvoso* [Gen. 23:2] when Abraham mourned. The explanation given is that Sarah had lived a full life to an advanced age, so Abraham's grief could not be excessive. Mrs. Miroff's sister was nearly a hundred years old and she, too, had lived a full life, so Sacks determined that it would not be appropriate for Mrs. Miroff to mourn too conspicuously for her sister. Besides which, Mrs. Miroff did not particularly care for her sister. Although from the standpoint of *hala- khah* (religious law), as a sister Mrs. Miroff was obligated to mourn, Sacks's decision was typical of his use of the Bible to rationalize pragmatic decisions that bend Orthodox practice.

It is a particularly poignant reflection on the unique quality of the Intervale community that the social worker assigned by JASA [Jewish Allied Services for the Aged] to handle congregants' social welfare needs, emerged from the encounter with the Jewish father he never thought he had.[11] Sacks is describing the story of Jacob's dream in which angels are going up and down the ladder. He explains that the reason for the ladder (angels obviously don't need a ladder) is so that people shouldn't get too upset that angels are climbing without one:

SACKS: There was God sitting on top of the ladder. *Vehiney adoshem nitsov olov,* and He told him, "I am the God of Abraham your father, and the God of Yitshak, the God of Isaac." Now here Jacob is told that God is the God of his father Abraham. Abraham was his grandfather. But in those days a grandfather was considered a father of the grandchildren, too. And it was not only the immediate father that was given the title of father, but a grandfather. Any elder or even a great-grandfather who happened to live was considered a father of all successive generations. He was the father. On that precept that the grandfather was considered the father, I gave to the social worker from JASA his name. He had no Jewish name. He wasn't brought up as a Jew. He was brought up by Christian parents who are descended from Jews. Hitler reminded him that he had Jewish blood in him. He came in here as a refugee. But he married Jewish. And all the kids are Jewish. Everything is Jewish. But when he

THE MIRACLE OF INTERVALE AVENUE

was called up to the Torah—he was never called up to any Torah except here when I called him up—he didn't know his [Jewish] name. He had no [Jewish] father. But he knew his grandfather who was Jewish and his grandfather's name, Elyohu ben . . . and that is his official call-up name. Until a hundred and twenty, that will be his Jewish name.

If the example demonstrates anything, it is the remarkable ability Sacks has to bend religion to meet the existential needs of individual congregants. Sacks's reasoning aside, without a Jewish mother, the man would still have to convert to Judaism to qualify as a Jew by Orthodox law. The biblical allusion casts an aura of respectability, perhaps even psychic harmony, over actions that are in keeping with personal needs whether or not they fully mesh with Orthodox law. Little wonder that congregants, very few of whom are truly observant Jews, find Sacks's narratives so meaningful. The narratives change the focus of the biblical story by stripping bare the human elements and reestablishing a dialogue between man and God. Describing Moses' seeking God's advice, Sacks relates:

"Moses immediately, when he's presented with a problem that he thinks is beyond his capacity to decide, he asks God for advice because he and God were buddies. They used to talk *pe al pe* [face to face]."

"*Pe al pe*," Mr. Kaplan reiterates.

"They used to speak like I speak to Mr. Kaplan. And he spoke that way to God. So he said, 'Goddie, or God, these people are asking me whether they should send spies to the new land that we're about to occupy.' And God answers him, 'Sure! *Shlakh-lekho anoshim*. Go ahead! Send people.'"

In his study *The Uses of Enchantment*, Bruno Bettelheim argues that despite their similarities, significant differences exist between myth and fairy tale. Myths convey a sense of being about absolutely unique, awe-inspiring events that do not happen to ordinary mortals; fairy tales, whose events are indeed impossible, generally occur to ordinary people.[12] Moreover, myth and fairy tale speak to very different parts of the self: "Myth projects an ideal personality acting on the basis of superego demands, while fairytales depict an ego integration which allows for appropriate satisfaction of id desires. The difference accounts for the contrast between the pervasive pessimism of myth and the essential optimism of fairytales."[13] Sacks's narratives suggest the quality, almost, of a blend of myth and fairy tale. They depict awe-inspiring events happening to ordinary people while at the same time portraying mythic heroes as something less than perfect. The narratives are neither totally pessimistic nor optimistic. They rest heavily upon the belief that good and evil coexist. Yet, like fairy tales, his explications of biblical stories are a subtle dissuasion from despair. Perhaps the most appropriate framework for understanding Sacks's narratives can be found in the psychoanalyst Erik Erikson's analysis of the state of mind of old age, "governed by the struggle for Integrity versus a sense of Despair and Disgust, and that out of this conflict a certain Wisdom may emerge under certain favorable personal and cultural conditions. . . ."[14]

If the fairy tale introduces children to the idea of death, particularly the death of parents, biblical narrative affirms the benevolence of death— both as a heroic triumph and as a peaceful conclusion to a good life (as in Abraham's mourning for Sarah). In this sense, in particular, the biblical narrative flies in the face of the tendency of contemporary culture to deny death altogether. This, too, is a source of strength. As Walter Benjamin notes, "Death is the sanction of everything that the storyteller can tell. He has borrowed his authority from death. In other words, it is natural history to which his stories refer back."[15] Sacks's narratives incorporate betrayal, human frailties, and ultimately death, and make each element part of a much larger bundle of common human experience. The task of his narrative is not to vanquish these experiences but to tame them and rob them of the threat of despair.[16]

Indeed, it is the peculiar wisdom of the storyteller that shapes the character of the Intervale Jewish Center and distinguishes it from being what it might otherwise be—a conglomeration of feisty, eccentric individuals. The "Miracle of Intervale Avenue" is, after all, a story that Sacks has spun, which, like all storytelling, succeeds in making the commonplace heroic and the heroic closer to ordinary mortals.

In his essay "The Storyteller," Walter Benjamin contrasts the historian and the chronicler. The former is the writer of history, the latter is its teller:

> By basing their historical tales in a divine plan of salvation—an inscrutable one—they [the chroniclers] have from the very start lifted the burden of explanations from their own shoulders. Its place is taken by interpretation, which is not concerned with an accurate concatenation of definite events, but with the way these are embedded in the great inscrutable course of the world.
>
> Whether this course is eschatologically determined or is a natural one makes no difference. In the storyteller the chronicler is preserved in changed form, secularized, as it were.[17]

As its chronicler, Sacks records the history of the Intervale Jewish Center as the history of a covenant between God and man in which both have invested their separate immortalities in the preservation of the minyan. By having their minyan, congregants are assured that God has not forsaken them in old age, and He, too, within the devastated landscape of the South Bronx, has not been forsaken. Indeed, the very setting of the Intervale Jewish Center lends to the story a heroic quality not unlike that of the world that Noah inhabited after the Flood, or that the Israelites traversed on their journey to their Promised Land.

On a cold Sunday morning in February, Sacks precedes the dvar Torah by explaining to the congregation that Horowitz has moved to a "home" for the aged. During the ensuing discussion, someone comments that "the shul is known as the miracle shul."

SACKS: By the way, let me explain to you how much of a miracle this is. Horowitz has been a steady member here for almost forty years, more than forty. I've been here over twenty and Horowitz has been over forty. Now Horowitz has reached the stage where he is just on the borderline between being mobile and immobile. And since he is a loner, he is alone. On the advice of myself and his family, we told him this is the best time for him to go into a home because the home will not accept him when he's immobile, when he can't do anything. So now's the time. He left and he's in a home now and he enjoys himself. He says it's like a palace.

Someone asks where the home is.

SACKS: I don't know where it is, but wherever it is, he's enjoying himself. He has a good time. But the thing that I want to bring out about the miracle minyan is, he was always counted in here. Henekh be-reb Khayim was counted in as the ninth or the tenth person. Two weeks before he had decided and we all were deciding it, all of a sudden [came] a person, a young fellow that we have seen intermittently but not steady, Rashim ben-Ruel ha-Kohen, a colored fellow, but he is Jewish and religious and he has made this point now that he comes every Saturday. So two weeks before Horowitz left we had the substitute right in here. And we had the replacement, as the gentleman can verify the statement that not only did we have a minyan yesterday, we had twelve or thirteen men. We had four or five women, I think we had five women. So the miracle of the minyan is not this. The miracle is that you people come here and that you people keep this place open. And with the help of you people keeping the place open, God will see the person comes in to have a minyan.

FANNY: I come here every Saturday.

SACKS: Right. So this is the thing. I don't believe in miracles. I believe in the work of God. As we're talking now about miracles, the parshe that we read yesterday is called—yesterday was *shabes shira*. It explains how the Jewish people, when they ran out of Egypt, had to cross the Reed Sea, the Red Sea, the *yam suf*. Imagine this, six hundred thousand people standing on the edge of the sea, with the water, right in back of them *kol rehev mitsrayim*,[18] all the cavalry of the best of Pharaoh, are chasing after them. Well, listen to this. And He tells them, He says, 'Why are they crying to me? Take up your stick! Hit the water.' That they did not show in the movie [*The Ten Commandments*]. The water parts. And *ruakh kodim,* an east wind, comes and actually dries the bottom of the sea, dries it. And the Jewish people can walk. Now there is one thing in there that has not been emphasized. Before the water parted—this is if you can read in the paper in the book—He tells them, "Enter the water!" And nothing could have been accomplished if some of those Israelis actually did not enter the sea. When they entered the sea first, the water parted.

KAPLAN: They had faith.

SACKS: They had faith. The amuno was great enough to actually accomplish that, and what you call this miracle, it's not a miracle. It's the amuno, the belief in God that creates the opportunity for a thing to come about. The same amuno as you have when you start out in the morning. You don't know that Friday they broke in here. Saturday the boiler was flooded, or Thursday they broke in. When you came in Saturday morning, the place was beautiful, right? It was so warm that the people came in here and they said, "Oh, the radiators are warm." You see, that's the amuno. Amuno is a faith that creates the miracle before it happens.

Sacks finishes the narrative with a capsule preview of next week's parshe. Even as he speaks, individual congregants pick themselves up and, weighed down with bundles, gradually make their way out of the shul. Mrs. Miroff waits patiently for Mr. Abraham, who drives her to and from shul every Saturday and Sunday. One Sunday, after the parshe, Mr. Abraham tells Mrs. Miroff that there's not enough room in the car for both her and Nelly, her black companion. Mrs. Miroff offers to share a cab with Sacks, but, preferring to walk and suspecting some amorous intent, Sacks advises her to go with Mr. Abraham.

"I can't. He's got no room in the car."

"What do you mean, he's got no room in the car?"

"That's what he told me."

"Mr. Abraham," Sacks calls out. "You'll take Mrs. Miroff home?"

"I can't fit them both in. I've got too much junk in there already because I'm clearing out my property over on Charlotte Street."

"All right. Let me see what's doing there." Sacks gets up and heads outside. Mr. Abraham, Mrs. Miroff, and Nelly follow. He returns a few minutes later alone.

"You got it straightened out?" I ask.

"Of course I got it straightened out. If there's room for one in there, there's room for two. Mrs. Miroff can always sit on Nelly's lap. So I got them both in. Let me tell you something. The decisions I have to make here, even Solomon would have trouble with."

· 6 ·

"MAYBE IT'S BRODSKY"

Death sets its own priorities. Haggard-looking octogenarians survive while younger people succumb. Even the seemingly fragile minyan carries on, almost in defiance of death. Congregants appear week after week, and I, for one, believe they will continue to do so forever. There are periods when death seems vanquished, as if it, too, were old and tired. Other times, death strikes unexpectedly: within a short period several long-standing congregants pass away.

During the third year of my study, five women died. One I did not know at all. Another, Janette, I knew only slightly. She was an intelligent woman who always sat opposite Sacks during the brunch and dvar Torah. In winter she wore an old fur coat and matching hat, which, together with her ruby-red lipstick and blue-green eye shadow, made her seem glamorous. Janette entered the hospital to have a tumor removed. Though seemingly strong, almost youthful, her body did not withstand the shock of the surgery: she died shortly after the operation. Death is no stranger at Intervale, but still, Janette's death was disturbing. It was treated both as a topic of conversation and as a lesson: "She should never have had the surgery. They should have left well enough alone."

Choice, however, rarely is a factor in the deaths of members of the congregation. Pauline Goldberg, an argumentative and sharp-witted

woman in her early seventies, died suddenly of a stroke. Not long before
her death, she had sat next to Sacks, bewailing the strains in her relationship with her children, both of whom were pleading with her to leave the
area. "Who's going to sit shiva for me when I die, Mr. Sacks? My
daughter won't. My son won't. Will you?"

Sacks turned the question into a joke. "I'll tell you what, Mrs. Goldberg. I'll make you a deal. I'll promise to sit shiva for you if you promise to
sit shiva for me." Sacks has fulfilled his part of the bargain: he recites the
memorial prayer each year on the anniversary of her death.

Lena Michaels had come to Intervale from Rabbi Matthew's congregation in Harlem. She was a dignified woman. Her wide-rimmed hat, long
dress, white gloves, and dark skin made her look more like a proper
Sunday churchgoer than an Intervale congregant. Offended by the inevitable fights over food, Lena Michaels generally avoided the Sunday
brunches and outings, preferring instead the more dignified Saturday
service.

Lena Zalben was the fifth woman who died that year. Although she
would commiserate with Lena Michaels on "the carrying-on of those
shnorrers," she was a regular at the Sunday events. At times Lena Zalben
saw the Intervale Jewish Center as a source of conflict rather than as a
place of refuge. Lonely and needing a sympathetic ear, she would walk
the half-dozen blocks to visit Mrs. Miroff in her sewing shop.

Mrs. Miroff maintains a hole-in-the-wall tailor shop on Faile Street, in a
building adjacent to her apartment. A homemade metal grate covers the
window and two large locks secure the door. But since the shop is adjacent to a numbers parlor, the location provides heavy street traffic—
adequate security against vandalism. At night, too, the store is often
guarded by burly street people who use the surrounding walls of the
entranceway for shelter, sleeping two or three bundled together.

The inside of the shop is like a showroom of an old thrift shop. It is
dimly lit, the two fluorescent fixtures trying hard to illuminate the room.
The walls are covered with fading beige wallpaper. A sign that reads "No
Smokeing" (the orthography is obviously Dave's) hangs on the wall. End-
less items of unclaimed clothes overwhelm the racks from which they
hang. Mrs. Miroff sits next to an ancient Singer sewing machine. It is her
tie to life. "A human being is like this machine," she comments, switching
the toggle switch to the on position, then, after a few seconds, switching it
off again. She invites her guest to do as she does—tilt her head sideways
to bring her ear close to the machine and listen to the still-whirring sound
as the motor gradually loses momentum. "It takes only a little bit to get
going. But once it starts, it takes a long time to stop." Mrs. Miroff is
seldom alone in her shop. Neighborhood people stop by to have hems

lowered or raised and sometimes to have a dress remade or a suit altered. Her clients are black and Puerto Rican. Jews are accommodated free. Dave receives her hand-me-downs—the clothes that are never claimed; Sacks and Mr. Abraham come to her for mending a zipper or a button-hole; her daughter Florence comes to have evening gowns made. Even Lena Zalben would have her clothes altered by Mrs. Miroff.

Besides Lena, other nonclients frequent the shop, including Nelly, her slightly retarded companion. The relationship between the two is more practical than affectionate. Nelly needs supervision, and Mrs. Miroff does not see well enough to leave the area unescorted. Although neighbors refer to Nelly as Mrs. Miroff's "black daughter," Mrs. Miroff sees Nelly more like a pet than a relative: "You cannot reason with her. If you tell her something she'll do the opposite."

"Would she help if someone tried to harm you?" I ask.

"No. She would just run away."

The other regulars at the shop are Mrs. Hutchison, an elderly black woman who drops by whenever she visits the numbers parlor, and various black men, mostly in their thirties. Sometimes they take chairs from inside the shop and sit outside just in front of the window; other times, particularly on cold winter days, they huddle inside the shop. In either case they form a formidable-looking human wall. Mrs. Miroff refers to them as "mine bums." They occupy a flat in an abandoned building at the corner of Faile Street and Hunts Point Avenue. According to Mrs. Miroff, the bums live communally: one "owns" the apartment; a second aquires food by scavenging from the Hunts Point market, while a third is the "cook."

Although Mrs. Miroff has her "specials," bums who use the shop as a regular place of refuge, on some days whole groups come in. Mrs. Miroff is familiar with them all. One freezing December day I encounter Buck, Spike, Annie, and Honey inside the shop. Honey is the only one I recognize. Mrs. Miroff doesn't care for her: she is too loose with the men. Indeed, Mrs. Miroff's prudishness is one reason she frequently chides the bums. One of her favorites and consequently a frequent target for her chastisement is Lawrence. Lawrence is a hulky man with enormous hands, which, Mrs. Miroff assures me (I suspect with a little exaggeration), have killed more than one man. Although she will not leave visitors alone with him in her shop out of fear for their safety, Mrs. Miroff hasn't the slightest fear of him. Once, when he began to kiss a girl outside the shop and call her "Momma," Mrs. Miroff gave him an earful:

"Why do you call her "Momma"? Your momma's not like that. This girl is a tramp."

Lawrence apologized: "You're right, Mrs. Miroff. [He pronounces her name Mire-off.] My momma's not like that."

Mrs. Miroff generally warns the men not to bring their girlfriends into the shop: "This is for business, not for fooling around." She ignores Honey. While she is busy at her machine stitching the torn pockets of a coat, Honey and her friends are talking and passing around a bottle of Thunderbird. The men drink straight from the bottle. Honey plays the lady. She pours the cheap liquor into a plastic cup "out of respect for Mom."

Annie is thirty years old and white. Her skin is pallid, her hair un-kempt, and her front teeth are missing. She comes from San Diego. In 1971 she got married, had a baby, and adopted her husband's two chil-dren. But he beat her. She left him when he began to beat the child. She came to New York, was unemployed, and found that she could "make money by jerking men off." Later she became involved in the cocaine trade. She moved to Hunts Point after getting in trouble with a dealer.

Honey is black and much younger-looking than Annie. Mrs. Miroff considers her pretty—a rare compliment from someone who jealously guards her feminine vanity. Honey's common-law husband is in Danne-more penitentiary for selling heroin to federal agents. She doesn't know how long he'll be there, but adds, "I couldn't care less either. Besides, I've a boyfriend who takes care of me. He gives me clothes and food." Honey has lived in Hunts Point since the mid-1970s. She spent some time at Spofford, a juvenile correctional facility just around the corner from Mrs. Miroff's shop. She is a mother and had her first child at age fourteen. After her husband was arrested, she intended to move in with her mother, but the mother and her mother's boyfriend both "shot smack," and Honey couldn't stand to watch them shoot up. Her sister lived on Hunts Point Avenue, and she moved in with her for a while until they were evicted for having loud parties. They moved to a private house on Cassa Street but were evicted when the building was slated for renova-tion. They then moved to the same abandoned building on Faile Street where the bums live. She and her sister occupied an apartment on the third floor until a fire forced them out. The fire was started when someone tried to get even with Lawrence, who refused to share a chicken dinner. "Now we're just out on the street."

Buck grew up in the area, and he has known Mrs. Miroff from his early childhood. He belonged to various gangs and eventually spent some time in prison. He no longer lives in Hunts Point—"I'm just here to visit Spike." Mrs. Miroff likes Spike, and it's apparently on account of him that the rest of the group is tolerated inside the shop. Spike "freelances" at the market. He uses drugs, and he steals only when he needs a fix. He likes Hunts Point because it's possible "to make money here without having to rip people off." Spike used to belong to a local gang called the Rogues of

THE MIRACLE OF INTERVALE AVENUE

Fort Apache. In the old days they would fish in the nearby swamps, and Mrs. Miroff once showed them how to prepare a fish stew over a fire in the nearby park. As Spike tells me these stories, his uncle walks into the shop to borrow seventy-five cents from Mrs. Miroff. He then steps outside to smoke a cigarette, "out of respect for Mom. I know she don't like the smell of smoke."

Most of the bums "freelance." They gather outside the entrance of the market and wait for a friendly truck driver who hires them to help unload. They can make anywhere from thirty to sixty dollars a night. Since they work sporadically and they squander their earnings on alcohol or gambling, they are constantly short of cash and regularly ask Mrs. Miroff for a dollar or two to buy a bottle of wine. Sometimes they reciprocate by giving her fruit or vegetables that they "acquire" at the market. Some of her regulars even come to her before going to the market and ask her what she needs. Watermelons, a staple of the Intervale Jewish Center's Saturday kiddush, need to be ordered almost a week in advance. "Watermelons they get only on Sundays," Mrs. Miroff explains. "There are less guards around."

Andrew, the gentlest of the bums, is a small man in his mid-thirties whose head is always covered in a blue knit cap. His jet-black face is covered by white blotches—an effect, apparently, of poor nutrition and chronic alcoholism. Andrew is very proud of having recently become a grandfather, although, to the best of my knowledge, he has very little contact with his family. When I first began to visit Mrs. Miroff's shop, Andrew would occupy some of his time cleaning the doorway. Part of the day he would roam through the neighborhood with a grocery cart lined with a thick black plastic garbage bag, collecting old beer and soft-drink cans. When his cart was filled, he would head to one of the many junk shops a few blocks away. On a good day he can make as much as twelve dollars for the scavenged metal. Recently, though, Andrew seems less able to pick himself up. He is usually slumped on a chair, drunk, either inside or outside the shop.

Mrs. Miroff is very proud of her relationship with the bums, particularly for the remarkable degree of control she has over them. She regularly points out the various kindnesses they do for her, bringing her fruit from the market and other gifts, as a way of reciprocating for good turns she has done them. Nor are her good turns always as basic as sustenance and shelter. Ernie, for example, stores his watch with her so no one will steal it when he is drunk. And Lawrence stores his Bible with her.

To some degree, Mrs. Miroff's relationship with the bums resembles her relationship with Nelly: it's quite practical. The bums use the shop as a place to seek shelter in winter or to cool off in summer, and Mrs. Miroff has taken to feeding them lunches of hard-boiled eggs on a roll with coffee. In exchange they offer her both protection and company. An outgoing person who needs to be the center of attention, she cherishes the access the shop gives her to the hustle and bustle of the street.

One Sunday, reflecting on her feelings of loneliness after more than twenty years a widow, she tried to explain her relationship with the bums: "They don't see me like an old lady. They think I'm one of them. Yesterday was my husband's yortsayt. So Lawrence says to me, 'Why don't you ever get married again?' I said, 'I didn't get the right man and I don't think it's the place to get married.' So he came over to me. He fixed my hair like he wanted to tell me he would want me. The young boys tell me they want me. But he didn't have the nerve for to do it openly. So he was looking to fix my hair. And I was sitting that time by myself. [So I thought I] better go away from the store quick because he was alone and I was alone. And I was afraid he'd say something and I'd say something. And I said, 'Get out, bums!' That's what I hollered. 'Get out!' You see, when I say bums, there's [usually] a lot of bums there. But [this time] it was only me and him. So that means [I am saying that] he is a bum. And I don't want to tease him. So I closed the store. And when I closed the store I was running upstairs. Then Charlie, the very black one, wants to tell me, 'So, why don't you marry me?' 'Charlie,' I answer, 'you're not the marrying type. I should marry you? At my age?' You see, they all want me in a way of something. 'Oh, you're the best woman on the block,' they tell me. They never met another woman like me. And that's it. This is life. It's the twentieth yortsayt. It's twenty years. I felt so bad yesterday."

No other congregant has quite such intimate contact with the street people as does Mrs. Miroff. Indeed, some congregants are even careful not to get too friendly with neighbors. Flisser, for example, maintains, "Sure, we're friendly. If there's a package from the mailman, we'll help each other out in that way. But not to let them into the apartment. I don't want them to look around. What they don't know can't harm."

Even Sacks, who rarely feels threatened by street people and is himself pretty much a walking landmark in Hunts Point, is impressed by Mrs. Miroff's way with the bums. Since the two are neighbors, they often discuss the various goings-on on their block. One day Sacks says to her admiringly, "You know, Mrs. Miroff, the kind of people you let into the shop, I wouldn't trust even if they were all the way on the other side of the street from me."

Delighted by Sacks's comment, Mrs. Miroff responds by describing a recent incident illustrating her command of these people: "This week I had some trouble. One of them they call 'Boilerman' gave me a push after I told him to keep the door closed. He kept coming into the store to give things to Andrew, and the store was getting cold. Anyway, when he hit me, a woman runs on the street and yells, 'He hit Momma!' The neighbors got alarmed and told the police, who were not far away. The police told me I should press charges."

"Don't press charges," Sacks advises. "Leave it the way it is. The way you operate is simply beautiful to watch. If the cops start to intervene, it will only jeopardize your position. So you're better off not pressing charges. I don't know how you do it, but sometimes I see the bums involved in the biggest fights, they could be throwing bottles at each other and killing each other right outside the shop. When you walk outside, even in the biggest fight, everything just melts away. You say, 'Stop!' Even a bullet would stop in midair."

Sacks, too, recognizes the romantic quality to her relationship with the street people. Once, when, using Mrs. Miroff's term, I referred to them as bums, Sacks countered: "Let me explain something to you. They're not bums. They are, what should I call it, they're her knights in shining armor and she is the damsel in distress. So they have a bottle on them instead of a sword. Or they sweat instead of wearing armor. To her, they are knights in armor. The image is perfect. The knights rescue her from being alone."

Fiercely independent, and more inclined to give than to take, Mrs. Miroff tends not to have close peer relationships, particularly not with women. She is too proud to sit idly by and wait for someone else to serve, too self-possessed to let others take center stage. Her closest friend at Intervale was Lena Zalben, but the relationship was not entirely reciprocal. Lena liked Mrs. Miroff, but Mrs. Miroff often thought of her as a nuisance, particularly because Lena liked to spend time inside Mrs. Miroff's shop, occupying the seat of a potential client and filling the air with idle chatter. Like Mrs. Miroff, Lena was born in Russia and learned to be a seamstress as a young girl. In 1916, when she was fourteen years old, she left Russia and came to the United States. While Mrs. Miroff eventually set up her own business, Lena worked for thirty-one years as an employee in the garment industry, eventually rising to the position of forelady. Then one day she tripped and fell just outside the shop. She banged her head on the concrete, broke a shoulder and her nose, and could no longer return to work. She stopped sewing altogether. If she had clothing that needed mending, she would ask Mrs. Miroff to do it. Mrs. Miroff resented the pathetic sense of helplessness that lay behind the request. Lena was everything that Mrs. Miroff was not: resigned to her fate. She used to describe visits she would make to a friend's neighborhood in Brooklyn for the High Holy Days: "When I came there shabes, I used to think that I'm in Israel. There's so many shuls there."

"How come you never considered moving there?" I asked.

"Ah, I don't know. Because it's easy for me where I am. I was brought up here. I like everybody here. And you know the park, the little park there on the corner. I sit there. It was a pleasant place to sit. Now all the drunks are there."

"Doesn't that make you want to leave?" I ask.

"No. So I won't sit there. That's all. I'm so many years here that I think I was born here. Forty-three years I've been living here."

During the summer, congregants arriving before services usually move a few chairs outside the synagogue and position themselves facing the sun. One Saturday, Sam and Lucy arrive early. Lucy looks tanned and apparently has spent part of the week basking in the sun outside her building. She is in good humor, but when Lena Zalben arrives a few minutes later, Lucy ignores her. Instead she engages me in conversation: "How's business, Jack?" Somewhat surprised by the question, I explain as best I can the peculiar nature of my "business." Lucy drops the topic and concentrates on absorbing the warm rays of the sun, looking rather content, as if the sun were making the limbs of her body more supple, herself more youthful. Mr. Abraham arrives with Mrs. Miroff, and Lena tries to engage her in conversation:

LENA: Tomorrow I'm not going to be here.

MRS. MIROFF: Who says I'm not going to be here? I'll be here.

LENA: No! Me. Me. *I'm* not going to be here. What's the matter, you don't hear what I say? I know you'll be here. Tomorrow I'm going to Co-op City. My nephew, the one that lives in Long Branch, he's picking me up and we're going to Co-op City for a family reunion. He's so good to me. Last week he picked me up at my home and drove me to New Jersey to see my sister's grave. They had people there praying like this. [Lena imitates Orthodox Jews holding prayer books and "shokling" or swaying as they pray.] Then he took me to a nice fish restaurant. I'm telling you, I never had such good fish. I told him he didn't have to drive me home. But he drove me right to my house. Imagine that, all the way from Long Branch. It's far. It's maybe fifty miles.

Mrs. Miroff has been growing increasingly impatient with Lena's story. Finally she throws her arms up in disgust and walks away.

"What's the matter? Did I say something wrong?" asks Lena.

Mrs. Miroff begins to shout hoarsely: "You tell me how far Long Branch is from the city. What? You think I don't know. Any intelligent person [who] lives for a while knows how far Long Branch is from the city!"

Lena apologizes: "I'm sorry. I was telling you about my nephew. He's so good to me. But then why shouldn't he be? I lived with my sister. He'd go to her and say, 'Ma, I saw a suit I like.' And she'd say, 'What's the matter with you? You know we don't got extra money for something like that.' And I would give him the money. My sister didn't let me do a thing around the house. Everything she did for me. 'You work,' she'd tell me. 'I sit home all day. So why should you do anything when you come home?' Then one day I came home and I found her there. Dead. Imagine that. You live through things like that and you don't get a nervous breakdown or something. And I'm still around."

As soon as Lena reaches the topic of her sister's death, Mrs. Miroff excuses herself again and walks toward the shul. The problem is less that she has heard the story before than her intolerance for Lena's obsession with dead family members. But she is upset, too, about Lena's underestimation of her own self-worth, particularly in regard to her relative's generosity. Lena had long ago sacrificed her independence to help her widowed sister raise an only son. In Mrs. Miroff's view, Lena had sacrificed too much. Regarding her own children, Mrs. Miroff likes to stress her own beneficence. When her children take her to visit with them, she usually cooks the food and brings it with her. She does so because "they all like the way I cook. Even my son-in-law. He's part of the family, too." Other congregants cook to avoid eating treyf food. One woman described how her son, worried about her health, insisted that she eat bread on Passover: "Ma, do it for me." Now she balks at the offer to spend the holy days outside the neighborhood: "*Yontov* [holy day] I got to be in shul. I got to be with the old people."

Though devoted to her children, Mrs. Miroff now believes in setting limits on what she will sacrifice for them. Her own need for an independent existence must take priority. Several years ago, suffering from an illness that was sapping her strength, she consented to leave her familiar surroundings temporarily and move in with her son. When she returned, she raved about the first-class treatment she received. "My son and daughter-in-law took very good care of me. They treated me like I was a baby. They even fed me."

"You must have liked that," I commented.

"No," she replied.

"Why not?"

"Why not? Because I'm not a baby. I'm too old to get born."

Response to family obligations was not the only difference between Lena and Mrs. Miroff. Mrs. Miroff is regal, outspoken, and, when need be, hard as nails. Lena was soft-spoken, easily swayed, and very much a follower. Mrs. Miroff virtually rules Faile Street. Lena, who lived some six blocks from Mrs. Miroff, was grateful just to be in a renovated one-bedroom apartment at the intersection of Hunts Point Avenue and Southern Boulevard.

"MAYBE IT'S BRODSKY"

I visited Lena several times at home, the last time shortly before her death. As we head toward the elevator she greets various people and they watch her as she walks, slowly placing one foot in front of the other. A few minutes later, we approach the elevator, and several teen-age girls hold the door open for her. Chattering in Spanish, they seem patient and unperturbed by the slowness of her gait. Once inside, Lena talks to each of them. "Why don't you go outside and play? It's so beautiful outside. Go, children. You should have a good time." They respond in the same amicable way. The elevator stops on Lena's floor. The door opens. Lena doesn't move until the children remind her that this is her floor. At first she's lost, uncertain which way to go. I remember from previous visits and lead the way. Outside her apartment she begins to search her purse for the keys. She becomes worried that she may have lost them once again. After a suspenseful moment or two, she finds them and tries each key in the two locks, uncertain which key goes where. She becomes frustrated and asks me to try. I open the door and we enter the apartment. It is clean. Except for the large number of photographs on the sofa, the living room is relatively uncluttered. I stay to photograph her for a while, then I move on, though I promise to return.

The following Saturday after shul, Mrs. Miroff agrees to walk part of the way home with me and Lena. She intends to take a bus as soon as we reach Lena's apartment building. But when we reach Lena's home, Mrs. Miroff looks tired. I encourage her to come upstairs. She hesitates, but feeling the strain of the walk, she agrees to come up, as long as I promise to keep the stay a short one. Inside the apartment, Lena begins to point to the photographs of dead relatives that occupy the surfaces of all of her funiture. Mrs. Miroff becomes agitated, and I, watching her, realize why she hesitated to come up. Listening to Lena's tour, Mrs. Miroff tries to marshal my support.

"You got to leave the dead people alone, right, Jack?"

"Yes," I agree. "But someone has to remember them, too."

"Remember, yes. But not through pictures."

"You can't tell someone how to live," I advise.

Lena continues to point out the various faces in the photographs: ". . . and my sister, my older sister. Her husband was a big builder and he died young, too. And she died. And my sister. We were nine children and I'm the only one. I'll give you a little orange juice? Coffee? You want a little?"

"No," I reply.

"Sure?"

"I'm sure."

THE MIRACLE OF INTERVALE AVENUE

"Did I ever tell you about my sister's son? My nephew. He calls me every Monday night. They had an unveiling for his father-in-law. So his wife made such a fine dinner. From the cemetery she went."

Mrs. Miroff tries to cut in. She talks about the children who come to see her after graduating from the school around the corner from her shop. But Lena has no intention of letting her change the subject. She resumes the tour of the photographs.

"That's my brother that died last year. He was such a beautiful person, too. He had children, all college graduates. He had cancer at the top of his thigh. He died young, too."

"How old was he?" Mrs. Miroff asks.

"He was young."

"Fifty?"

"No. He had got two sons already. He must have been over fifty. Because this is the son in college, and the daughter is a high school teacher, too. So why should I hide it? I have nothing else. I figure I look at them and I'll just go to sleep. That's all."

"Lena," Mrs. Miroff interrupts, "you're supposed to live, too. This is not a life!"

"It's too late. Listen. What am I going to do?"

"This is to look to death. Look to life. It's beautiful. Put flowers. Put here a beautiful object. Put flowers!"

"Put flowers? I got flowers."

"Lena, you got to live!"

"I haven't got a life. All the best years of my life are gone. You know, when I go to sleep I always talk to them [the photographs], and I say I don't care if I die. You know, I bought a grave next to my brother, my mother—my sister, I mean. And when I go to the cemetery with my nephew in Long Branch, he says everything himself. Over there, there's no *zoger* [prayer reciter], you know. So I look at him and I cry. It hurts me. Because his father died young, his mother died so young. So I said, 'Bernele, would you say kaddish for me, too?' He says, 'Aunt Lena, please! I don't want you to talk like that. Please don't talk like that.' "

"He's right!"

"If you'd see the way he cried. So we bought a plot when my sister died. [Now] they wouldn't give that plot for five thousand dollars because it's a small town and they need it for their own people. But being [that] her father-in-law was the first Jew there—Feinberg—when the father-in-law died, they closed the stores. Everyone was going to the funeral. Police and everybody. So I paid a thousand dollars. I paid it out, you know, by the month. And then he put one pink stone—it cost eleven hundred. So on her stone and the whole thing next to her is my name. So you see, I didn't bother nobody when I was alive. They will only have to put me in the thing where I'm going. Did I do a foolish thing that I did? No. Why? You don't die when you have a grave. You can live for twenty more years, right?"

"As long as the country exists, you got a grave," Mrs. Miroff offers.

"You ought to see how beautiful. A pink stone. We paid eleven hundred dollars for it. On her side the whole story . . . You know, when her husband died, he died so young. At the time they [men] weren't allowed to [lie next to women]. He lay with the family, one aisle further. She died so many years after."

"Lena," Mrs. Miroff interrupts, "if you want to work, why don't you make me coffee?"

"What? Of course, my God! You want a juice? Or you want an orange?"

"I don't want orange juice. I want coffee."

"Come here. Come here, *mamele*. See what you want in the refrigerator."

"Coffee."

"Come here!"

"Coffee. Coffee. Not guilty!" Mrs. Miroff, the mother-in-law of a lawyer, imitates a defendant on trial.

"I got coffee. I got everything."

"Make coffee!"

"I'll make coffee. I got coffee. I got everything. I'm so glad you said that. Look at the fridge. Mamele, I'm sorry I got no more orange juice. I got grapefruit."

"I don't want orange juice!" By this time Mrs. Miroff, even with her hoarse, whispery voice, is screaming.

"What do you want?"

"Coffee!"

"Only coffee? Oh, good."

Lena takes a jar from the refrigerator containing a pint of already brewed coffee and heats it in a saucepan. As she pours it into a cup, she asks for the umpteenth time whether I would like some also. I decline, a little suspicious of the contents. Not long after this visit I was warned by one of Lena's friends not to eat anything in her home because "she mixes things up. You never know what she's serving you."

By that time, though, Lena was terribly senile. She sometimes failed to recognize me and she often seemed completely confused. One Saturday I found her walking to shul, seemingly unaware of where she was headed. I watched for a moment, then pointed her in the right direction and walked with her, although she scarcely recognized me. A few months later, on the third day of Hanukkah, Anne Copeland, an occasional visitor to the

THE MIRACLE OF INTERVALE AVENUE

Intervale Jewish Center who lived in the same building as Lena, arrived in shul for the Sunday brunch and announced that Lena had died.

The news came as a shock because, aside from senility, Lena seemed to be in good physical condition: death proved unpredictable once again. The news hit Mrs. Miroff particularly hard. She questioned Anne Copeland intensely: When? How? Most of all she wanted to know whether Lena was still alive on Saturday, the day after the two had last spoken on the phone. Lena had called Mrs. Miroff and explained that she wasn't feeling very well. But Mrs. Miroff had had difficulty hearing because Lena refused to lower the volume of a radio near the phone. Mrs. Miroff refused to continue the conversation, insisting that Lena call back when she was prepared to speak without a radio in the background. Lena never called back, and Mrs. Miroff now felt terribly guilty. Perhaps Lena had been calling out to her in desperation, and if she had shown a little more patience, Mrs. Miroff might have saved Lena's life. Or perhaps, and this concerned Mrs. Miroff the most, all Lena wanted was to reach out to her in the last moments of her life so as not to die alone. In that case Mrs. Miroff felt that she could never atone for having failed her.

It was the third day of Hanukkah, the holiday celebrating an ancient victory against insurmountable odds. The Temple in Jerusalem had been restored and its defilers ejected from the land. But today, on the anniversary of an ancient miracle, the Intervale Jewish Center was nearly empty. A heavy blanket of snow covered the streets outside, and most members of the congregation, fearing for their safety on the slippery sidewalks, stayed home. A terrible sense of loneliness surrounded us all. There would be no miracle at Intervale on this Hanukkah. Lena was dead; the ranks of the congregation continued to thin.

As Sacks begins the review of the parshe, the phone rings. Dave picks up the receiver: "Davíd Lentín, the Puerto Rican. You got a church. This is not a synagogue."

"Come on, there. Cut it out!" Sacks barks at him.

"It's Fran Rossner calling about Lena," Dave announces, suddenly serious. Fran is a regular Sunday visitor who was friendly with Lena. Sacks gets up and takes the receiver. "Listen, Fran, is she dead? Who was notified? The family was there? So who got the bank books? The niece did? O.K. So listen. *Borukh dayan emes* [Blessed is the true Judge]. I know how she lived. I know how she died. She lived like a human being, like all human beings. She breathed air, and she breathed oxygen."

"And she drank water," Dorothy offers.

"And she drank. She had food. And she wasn't a young woman," Sacks continues. "How old was she?"

"Seventy-two," Mrs. Miroff comments.

"MAYBE IT'S BRODSKY"

"She wasn't *your* age," Sacks says to Fran. "She was about ten years younger . . . [I mean] older than you. O.K. Fran, Did they tell you anything about where the funeral will be? You don't know. All right. Can you call back when you find out the niece's phone number? Good. I'll speak to you later."

Sacks puts down the receiver and explains that Fran Rossner had called and that Lena's bank books had been located. "She had a lot of money in the bank books. So we'll take the bank books and we'll bury her with them."

"She has a plot," someone offers.

"She bought it next to her sister," Dorothy adds.

"In New Jersey," Mrs. Miroff joins in.

"She paid for it. A thousand dollars," Dorothy adds.

"She ain't got no *kinder* [children]?" asks Mordechai.

"She was never married," Dorothy responds.

"She was never married," Sacks confirms.

"They said she was seventy-two," one woman comments.

"Who?" asks Sacks.

"Mrs. Miroff," the woman replies.

"She told me," Mrs. Miroff confirms.

"You don't have to tell the truth," Dorothy comments.

"I don't think so. I think she was much older," Sacks insists, trying to allay fears of congregants that their own time, too, might be up.

"Yeah, she looked older," Anne agrees.

"A few years here or there . . . ," Mrs. Miroff replies, still insisting on the figure she announced earlier.

"Mrs. Miroff, a couple of years here, a couple of years there." For once he is about to agree with Mrs. Miroff. He stops himself and resumes the review of the parshe. Suddenly the phone rings again. Dave answers and scribbles down the telephone number of Lena's niece in Co-op City. Sacks asks whether anyone is willing to make the phone call. No one volunteers.

"What are you going to say to her?" Kaplan asks.

"You call her up and . . ."

"Ask about the funeral," Dorothy suggests.

"No!" Sacks responds emphatically. "Don't mention funerals!"

"No?" Dorothy asks, surprised.

"You just tell her we're having the Hanukkah party here. That Lena usually comes and she's not here. Then we'll let her carry the ball further," Sacks argues.

"We'll find out what's what," Dorothy agrees.

"She was talking to me once . . . ," Mrs. Miroff begins to reminisce.

"Don't. . . . What she was talking to you, forget," Sacks interrupts.

THE MIRACLE OF INTERVALE AVENUE

"Not Lena was talking to me. The niece."

"The niece, all right. Who wants to call? Should I call?" Sacks asks.

"Yeah, you call," everyone agrees.

"You're the diplomat," Dorothy adds.

"Yeah, you do it," Anne agrees.

"She'll deny everything." Mr. Abraham tries to lighten the mood.

"*Koved*, some respect please," Sam insists, suddenly alert. Then he muses, "How do you like that? Overnight."

Sacks calls the niece. She is already aware of Lena's death. She asks for the address of the Intervale Jewish Center. "I imagine you'll be sitting shiva or whatever? No? And she has no sisters or brothers left. All right. We'll say a prayer for her here. The kaddish as far as I know is only on a Saturday." Sacks asks for the niece's address. He intends as always to send a condolence card. He then advises her not to bring Lena's old clothes to the shul since people will see them and it will make them feel sad. If there are any religious articles such as prayer books, those she might bring to Intervale. Sacks puts down the receiver and announces: "Unfortunately, I'm sorry to say she did pass away nine o'clock last night."

"She died last night?" Mrs. Miroff asks, sounding somewhat relieved.

"She died last night at nine o'clock. Anyone who wants to send a card . . . she has no one to say kaddish after her because she had no . . ."

"She has a nephew. She raised him up," Mrs. Miroff interrupts.

"She has a nephew," Sacks agrees. "All right. She has a nephew. The only thing is, when Dave says kaddish or we daven, we'll think of her, too."

If death sometimes hides a kind face, it revealed itself in Lena's death. She had long outlived her use for life, in large measure because life had outlived its use for her. No longer able to work, the sister whom she had supported now long dead, and the sister's son grown up, Lena talked as if her life no longer had much value. Preparing for death seemed her final task. Acquiring a grave and a tombstone gave her a sense that she would leave this world the same way she had lived in it: a burden to no one.

Lena's obsession with death created a barrier between her and Mrs. Miroff. Lena had embraced death almost as a friend. Mrs. Miroff considers death a gruesome enemy, to be met head on and forced to keep its distance. Indeed, Mrs. Miroff's vitality is generated from her struggle with death: her fascination with the bums is very much a part of that struggle. Like death, they are wild, destructive, even life-threatening. Controlling the bums is like taming death: a triumph of iron will over malleable matter.

Lena had resigned herself to a passive end of life. Mrs. Miroff has done the opposite. Mourning her husband, she had "adopted" Nelly, the retarded black girl. Dreading dependency, she has become even more fiercely independent as she has grown older, taking into her orbit an ever-widening circle of needy street people. And, while both women took pride in their femininity, Lena's pride was limited to her past: "You should have seen me. All the men used to turn their heads." Mrs. Miroff still considers herself desirable and attractive: "All the bums want me by way of something. They all want I should marry them."

Yet the two women were friends. It was as if Lena saw her vitality within Mrs. Miroff and admired her for it, while Mrs. Miroff saw her vulnerability and helplessness in Lena. In their extreme responses to old age and death, they seem to represent the dual components of how all people respond to life: a combination, often poorly integrated, of fatalism and defiance. As passive as Lena seemed to be, she still clung to a bit of independence in maintaining her own apartment, unaided by charity. As defiant as Mrs. Miroff seems, she, too, recognizes that ultimately there is a limit to life and is grateful for each moment of time she remains on earth: "I'm happy just to be alive," she says.

Like old people everywhere, the members of the Intervale congregation are engaged in a constant struggle to come to terms with death. They are forever occupied with performing the rites of commemoration for departed loved ones, and they prepare also for their own death: both learning to accept it and finding various means of defying it. Little wonder that the religious life of the Intervale Jewish Center revolves around the rites of commemoration. Even the synagogue has an element of commemoration to it—partly in its physical structure and partly as a social institution. Most synagogues have commemorative plaques listing the names of the dead. Intervale's commemorative plaques were lost during a break-in several years ago, along with the brass plumbing and an enormous brass menorah. The pipes and menorah were replaced, but the memorial plaque and the names it contained are lost forever, reflecting, in a sense, the peculiar feature of the Intervale Jewish Center as a synagogue most of whose members were drawn to it quite recently and only after their own synagogues were closed. The relationship between the shul and its congregants is one of shared survivorhood: it is a relationship forged by common need and shared experience. The Intervale Jewish Center has witnessed the demise of almost all of its congregants; the current congregation has witnessed the demise of the other synagogues in the area.

There remains, nonetheless, an echo of the former congregation—almost a ghostly presence. The long oak pews have nailed to their backs tiny brass plates inscribed with the names of the former congregants. And from the fluorescent fixtures hang the names in Yiddish of the congregants who paid for their purchase. These have acquired the aura of the

THE MIRACLE OF INTERVALE AVENUE

sacred. When a group of young volunteers offered to clean the synagogue and remove the spare benches, Sacks balked at the suggestion:

"As long as I remain here, the character of this place will remain the same. You know, the khumesh tells us that when Moses descended Mount Sinai and saw the golden calf, he threw the tablets at the calf and they broke. God commanded him to make new ones and place them and the fragments from the old ones into the aren koydesh [Ark]. The people who used to pray here, who were members of the congregation, have their names on the benches. They paid for them and the benches belong to them. It's not our right to throw them out."

Recently the owner of a private hospital in the area became interested in the shul. He commissioned a sign painter to make a brand-new sign reading "Intervale Jewish Center." The pathetic, broken old one was removed and thrown into the rubble-strewn lot adjacent to the shul. Mrs. Miroff, seeing it lying there, cast a disparaging glance at the new sign. "That's not for us. This one is for us. We're old people, we need old things." She insisted that the sign be saved. Sacks, Dave, and I dragged the heavy metal sign from the yard into the shul, where it now sits, propped up along the side wall, preserved.

Both the sense of loss and the need to preserve are present even in the synagogue ritual unrelated to the rites of commemoration. During a sermon in the Rosh Hashanah service, Sacks remarked that while singing one prayer he could hear the voices of all those congregants who were no longer there. Even his old friend Brodsky's voice was present, as usual, loud and off-key. Of course, Sacks's observation may have had an ulterior motive: if the ghosts were present, he had a minyan. But there were other occasions when congregants expressed a sense of presence rather than loss—certainly in the form of distinct and fond memories.

In mid-January, Lucy observes her father's yortsayt. For yortsayt, individual congregants approach the bima during the reading of the Torah and either hand Sacks a slip of paper containing the Hebrew name of the dead person or, in the case of a spouse or close relative, communicate the information orally. Sacks takes the Torah, rests it firmly on his shoulder, and recites the *El Mole Rakhamim* prayer, inserting the name of the relative for whom the prayer is recited. The responsibility is a communal one in the sense that individuals often know the appropriate date of one another's yortsayt, or they can be asked to see that the prayer is recited even if they themselves are not present. The Saturday of her father's yortsayt, Lucy is ill and unable to attend services; she gives the slip of paper with her father's and her father's father's Hebrew names to Sam, her husband. Sam, though, does not stay for the whole service; he leaves around noon, too early for the memorial prayer. So he hands the slip of paper to Mr. Horowitz, who, when the time comes, hands it to Mr. Sacks, who hands it back to Mr. Horowitz, who will later return it to Sam or Lucy, as if it were a receipt to indicate that the prayer has been recited.

When Horowitz sits down with the slip of paper containing Lucy's father's name, Mrs. Miroff remains at the bima, indicating to Sacks that she wants the prayer recited for her husband, Benny. As she does every year for his yortsayt, Mrs. Miroff has prepared for the congregation a small feast of chick peas, fruit salad, and gefilte fish.

Yortsayt is a special time for Mrs. Miroff: a public event in shul to be shared with the group; a private moment at home to recall her husband by rummaging through the spare bedroom of her apartment in search of old photographs. One Saturday I visited her on the day of yortsayt. It was the first time she would allow me upstairs into her apartment. "To be alone for so many years after he died—I cried in shul thinking about it," she said. "He was such a strong man. One day he sees double and my son told him to go to the hospital. He had cancer. It spread, and in a year he was dead. Every day I would go to the hospital. He wouldn't let me out of his sight. One day I got stuck in the elevator. He thought I had gone away and he kept screaming, 'Elsie, Elsie!' Mrs. Miroff let herself cry for a moment only. She put the photograph down, then walked into the kitchen where she busied herself heating up some brewed coffee in an ancient cast-iron percolator.

During the service, Dave is busy slicing cake for the kiddush. He stops when he is called to lift the Torah at the end of the reading so that it can be tied and put away; and again near the end of the service, he is called to the front of the room to recite the kaddish. Because he is either preoccupied elsewhere or just being coy, Dave sometimes needs a little coaxing. Eventually he drops the knife he is using to slice the cake and heads toward the front. On his way he jokingly coaxes one of the other men to go up instead of him: "You go. I'm not really here anymore. My body is here, but my spirit is upstairs. Someone's got to say kaddish for me. Maybe I need a couple of egg crates for a coffin. I'll just dig a hole in the ground— here outside in the yard—and bury myself. I can even say kaddish for myself. I'll put a plug in the box, attach a wire, and I'll make a recording. This way there'll be someone to say kaddish for me, so it'll speed things up when I go upstairs."

For whatever reason, the memorial prayers seem to have left their mark on each member of the congregation. During the kiddush, Sacks too has death on his mind:

"This week I read an article in a magazine about a man who is presumed dead. They place him in a body bag, but they forget to close the zipper entirely. Someone later tries to close the zipper but somehow has some trouble doing it, and as he tries to close it, he discovers that the man is still alive. You know, there was a novel written about the man Jesus brought back to life. I can't remember the name of the novel now. But imagine the things you would know if you were brought back to life."

"There's a joke about that," Mr. Abraham comments.

"Yeah," Sacks acknowledges, "I just told it to you. My son Arthur heard it on television. Harry and Sam are busy talking about baseball when Harry says to Sam, 'Do you think they play baseball up in heaven?' 'I don't know,' Sam answers. 'What do you think?' 'I'll tell you what,' Harry answers. 'Let's make a deal that if one of us should die before the other, the one who dies will come back and give some kind of sign to the other whether there is baseball or not in heaven.' A few days later, Harry drops dead. And that night Sam is sleeping when all of a sudden something enters his room, and when he opens his eyes he recognizes his good friend Harry who passed away. 'Sam,' he says, 'I've come back to keep my promise. I've got good news for you and I've got bad news. The good news is yes, there's baseball up in heaven. The bad news is you're pitching next Saturday.'

"Actually," Sacks adds, resuming the previous discussion about the man that Jesus brought back to life, "I only want to die once. The truth is, I'm not afraid of death. Just of dying. I would like to die while I'm working. If that's the case, I don't mind working all day. You know, the Bible tells us that King David wanted to know when he would die. God told him he would never die while reading the Torah. So all day long he studied the Torah. Then one day he heard something. He went to the window [to see what it was], and he died."

"I don't plan to stop working," Dave adds his voice to the discussion. "When I die, I'm going to *shmeer* [paint] up there. If I can't paint up there, I'm not going. You can refuse to go, you know!"

"What kind of conversation is this?" Lucy asks, irate. "Why all this talk about death?"

Perhaps the theme of the conversation was set by a rather strange incident earlier in the services: a man dropped by, placed a bottle of whiskey and a cake on the table, saying they were in honor of a yortsayt, then left as quickly as he had come. Had the man stayed, he would have been the tenth man; he would have made the minyan. Since, in a pinch, Sacks considers God the tenth man, that made the visitor almost fit the bill as His earthly representative. His errand suggested both the centrality of death as a bond among the congregants and its influence toward renewing the minyan. But by his refusal to stay and participate, the visitor also symbolized the absence of a second generation to guarantee both the future of the congregation and the recitation of the prayers of

Mrs. Miroff owns a
seamstress shop
where friends and
neighbors congregate.

Sam Davis shared this apartment with his wife until she
entered a nursing home.

Mrs. Miroff attributes her longevity to work; she often says, "When my machine goes, I go."

Mrs. Miroff, here with her granddaughter, is visited daily by her daughter who works in the area.

commemoration. In the precarious balance between death and life at the Intervale Jewish Center, the incident seemed to serve as a warning that ultimately death would gain the upper hand.

The anthropologist Ernest Becker argued that all cultural systems are denials of death.[1] By establishing a symbolic universe as a counterforce to the material world, cultural systems negate not only the physical reality of death but its psychological reality, too. Of course, those closest to experiencing death are the most responsive to the cultural and psychological defenses against it. Elderly people in particular inhabit a panchronistic universe in which past and present merge so completely that departed loved ones remain very much alive long after their physical extinction. Although Sacks has a rational explanation for the phenomenon, he, too, maintains a degree of contact with his deceased wife:

"Although I do not believe in reincarnation, the dead do return sometimes in the form of a dream. They don't actually return; it's all part of the dream. Like when I was having a problem with the people I work with in the bakery. At night I dreamt I was having a conversation with my wife and she was advising me exactly as she used to do when she was alive. I realized when I awoke that subconsciously I was advising myself how to deal with the problem."

Other congregants have experienced even more intense feelings of the continued presence of spouses. A year after her husband's death, Fanny still talks to him: "Sometimes I lose things. Like my keys. The other day I couldn't find them. So he talked to me. He told me to go look underneath the pillow on the couch. So I went there, and sure enough I found them."

"I don't see so good," commented Rose Cutler just before her ninety-fourth birthday. "Last night I look in my apartment and I see my husband like he's still alive. Then I blink and I don't see him no more. Imagine that. He's dead already twenty years."

Communication with the dead is motivated by our inability to acknowledge extinction. The unconscious, according to Freud, "does not know death."[2] Having constructed a symbolic universe through language and culture, we are locked within it whether it meshes with or negates reality. Indeed, our beliefs cause us to experience reality as a rude and only partial awakening. Perhaps this is why death jokes are so poignant, particularly for elderly people. They use the incongruity between belief and reality to mock our denial of death. The following joke stemmed from a conversation between Sacks and Mr. Abraham concerning one congregant's physical condition, which had been deteriorating for months. I begin the conversation by mentioning that the man looks a little better today.

"My father, *alevashulem* [may he rest in peace], used to say, 'I'd rather have people say how bad I look and still be alive, than say how good I look and be dead.' "

"You know what they say," Sacks responds. "Before *me toyt, me lebt* [before you die, you live]."

"My uncle, alevashulem," Mr. Abraham continues, "used to tell this story about Joe in the hospital and every day someone asks, 'How is Joe?' 'Oh, he's improving. He's improving.' One day someone asks, 'How is Joe?' 'He died yesterday.' 'What did he die of?' 'He died from improvements.' "

"Why is it," Sacks asks, "that only your dead relatives seem to have anything to say?"

Why, indeed? Perhaps because a peer relation to death is the source of their authority. Borrowing from that same source of power, congregants are quick to remind much younger acquaintances of their own special status deriving from proximity to death. They typically respond to statements about future plans with the phrase "If I live that long." When an acquaintance tried to persuade Mr. Abraham to buy a savings bond, he asked the man when the bond would mature. The man replied, "In twenty years." "In that case," Mr. Abraham responded, "let me first check with the man upstairs to see if I'll be around to collect." On another occasion the manager of the legal firm he works for asked that he give enough notice before he retires so they can break in a new man. "Sure, I'll do it. Just so long as the man upstairs doesn't retire me first."

The fact that elderly people continually sense the nearness of death gives them a distinct worldview, quite different from that of younger people. Not only does firsthand awareness of death give them a personal sense of power from facing what others evade, but it also contributes to a complex and ambivalent relationship between the dead and their survivors. That ambivalence is a central theme in many death jokes, including this one told to me by Sacks:

"This guy was on his death bed and his wife was there, his son was there, his daughter was there, and everyone is telling him, 'Don't worry about it. You'll be all right. You'll get up.' And all of a sudden he says, 'Moishe, you're here?' 'Yeah.' 'Khaye-Sore, are you here?' 'Yeah.' 'Malke, you here?' 'Yeah.' 'So if everybody's here, then who is minding the store?' "

Sacks's joke, in his typically optimistic way, places the dying man in a superior vantage point from which he can playfully tease the living. Mr. Abraham has a similar joke, though far more cynical:

"A man is on his deathbed, and the family is gathered around to discuss the funeral arrangements. As they're talking, they keep finding ways to save money. This one says not to bother with a fancy coffin, a pine box is good enough. The other son says not to bother with a limousine, they'll just use their own cars. All of a sudden, the dying man sits up and says, '*Boyes*, help me out of bed. I'll save you the expense. I'll walk to the cemetery.' "

At Intervale a good deal of the ambivalence in the relationship between the dying and survivors revolves around the question of religious observance and the desire for a kaddish (someone to recite the mourner's prayer). Intervale, like the Bronx in general, never was a bastion of Jewish orthodoxy. Most congregants have turned to religion late in life as a way of assuming their place among the generations and achieving what Barbara Myerhoff refers to as a sense of continuity[3] despite the many discontinuities of their childhood and adult lives. Their children are even less observant than they themselves have been, so they have good reason to doubt whether the proper prayers will be recited when they die.

A year after I arrived at the Intervale Jewish Center, I began to join Sacks and Mr. Abraham at the bakery on Saturday afternoons. I participated in conversations and later I shared Sacks's concern for Mr. Abraham when he was diagnosed as having an illness similar to the one that killed his brother several years earlier. His impending operation and the threat the illness posed to his life were particularly close to the surface in all of our minds. As usual, one Saturday afternoon, I walked with Sacks to the bakery after kiddush. Mr. Abraham had driven Mrs. Miroff home and then gone off to his run-down three-story property near Charlotte Street to make some repairs and try to collect some rent. He would join us later.

Sacks puts his plastic shopping bag down on the table. He takes off his hat and replaces it with a yarmulke. He walks past the tables and chairs and heads to his private domain—the oven and workbench area in the rear. Sacks fishes through a refrigerator and pulls out some oranges and a salami wrapped in brown paper. From another refrigerator in front of the bakery I take out cans of club soda and cola. Then I hunt through a freezer for rolls, which I place inside the oven to thaw. As I set paper plates on the table, Sacks prepares a separate lunch for his new cat, Pinkie. While we work, I ask Sacks whether he's concerned about Mr. Abraham; he gives a curt "Of course!" then resumes working in silence. The silence is thick and there is little I can do to penetrate it. It is broken only by the arrival of Mr. Abraham.

Sacks begins to talk about the Isaac Bashevis Singer book he is currently reading, *The Family Moskat*. He is apparently struck by a sequence in the plot that is terribly ironic:

"One character in the book is a fierce Hasid who avoids any contact with members of the opposite sex. His family insists that he get married, and of course he ends up with three daughters. So he has no one to say kaddish for him."

"You know," Mr. Abraham responds, "that reminds me of a next-door neighbor I used to have when I was living on the Concourse. This guy was an officer in the Israeli army. He was a very nice guy. Anyway, when he came here, he worked for someone who gave him a real rough time. One day I see him and I ask him how things are going with his boss. So he says to me, 'The boss is a great guy. He's just the kind of guy I'd love to say kaddish for.' "

We all laugh, and then become silent while we resume eating our sandwiches. Mr. Abraham is the first to break the silence:

"When my brother died, I didn't know who was going to say kaddish for him. One son lives in Nova Scotia, and where he lives, they can't get a minyan, so he couldn't say kaddish. The other son isn't religious, so I wouldn't trust him even if he was near a minyan. So for eleven months I made the six forty-five A.M. minyan and I said kaddish. My wife kept telling me, 'You don't have to do it. He has children and they're supposed to say it.' Anyway, I figure when it's my turn to go, I'll find myself one of those 'beards,' as a friend of mine calls the hasidic yeshiva students, and I'll pay him two hundred dollars to say kaddish for me."

Sacks puts down his sandwich. "Mr. Abraham, let me tell you something. You don't have to pay any yeshiva bokher to say kaddish for you. What you did for your brother was really for yourself."

Mr. Abraham seems pleased by Sacks's reassurance. "Thanks a lot," he says. "You just saved me two hundred bucks."

The idea of striking a bargain with death, of negotiating for time, comes up in Elisabeth Kübler-Ross's study of dying patients.[4] At Intervale, because of the implicit recognition of how disreputable each party to the agreement is (who will voluntarily submit to death, agreement or no agreement?),[5] I am tempted to use the term "cheating" rather than "bargaining" to explain how congregants respond to death. For example, the following joke was told by Mr. Abraham in response to Fanny's announcement that she would be visiting her husband's grave shortly.

"Mr. Sacks," Fanny said, "there's something I want to tell you. I'm not going to be able to be here next week for the trip [to Long Island]. I'm making an unveiling. The rabbi is costing me a hundred and fifty dollars. It's for my husband, Dave, and also for my brother. But what am I going to do? You're busy, otherwise I'd have you do it. I like the way you do it better."

"Thank you, Mrs. Greenstein. But I'm sure the rabbi will do just as good a job."

"I'm sure he will too," Mr. Abraham pipes in. "Especially if he does it with his eyes closed."

"What do you mean, with his eyes closed?" Sacks asks.

"MAYBE IT'S BRODSKY"

"Don't you know the joke about the guy who goes to the cemetery for yortsayt and wants to have the *El Mole Rakhamim* recited. So he finds a zoger [usually an elderly man who recites the prayer in return for a few dollars] at the cemetery who does it, and he asks him, 'How much do you charge?' So the zoger says, 'Well, there's two prices. I got one price for the regular and one for a special.' 'What's the difference?' the guy asks. 'Well,' the zoger says. 'Not much really. The regular is five dollars. And the special is ten dollars. The only difference between them is for ten dollars I say the prayer with my eyes closed.' So the guy thinks for a moment and then he tells the zoger to go ahead and do the special. So the zoger closes his eyes and recites the prayer. When he finishes and opens his eyes, the guy who is supposed to pay him the ten dollars is gone. He took off." Sacks and Mr. Abraham have a good laugh at Fanny's expense. Sacks tries to reassure her.

"Well, Mrs. Greenstein. I don't know if the rabbi will do it with his eyes open or shut, but I'm sure he'll do a good job. He'll do what he has to do."

The joke, as Mr. Abraham explained to me, is about cheating a cheat. What he did not explain but which I later understood is that the joke's characters are symbolic figures: the visitor to the cemetery stands for any survivor; the reciter of the memorial prayers is death personified. The hero of the joke removes himself from the scene well before the primary culprit has a chance to demand payment. But implicit, too, is the fact that the hero must return to the cemetery at least once a year. Sooner or later the debt must be paid.

The survivor's sense of outliving another person and the accompanying sense of guilt that someone else has died in his place[6] carries with it a sense, too, of triumph. Hy Bohrer, the owner of a local dry-goods store, frequently visits the Intervale Jewish Center. When his father became ill, he kept congregants posted on the man's condition. One Saturday Hy arrived in synagogue and announced that his father had died. Mrs. Miroff, seeming distraught by the news, offered her condolences. "How old was your father?" she asked.

"Oh, he was pretty old. He was eighty-four," Hy replied.

Suddenly Mrs. Miroff's mood changed from sadness to triumph. A smile lit up her face as she announced proudly, "I'm eighty-five!" She has succeeded where someone else had failed.

That sense of having outlived someone else is a common theme of death jokes. For example, Sacks told a joke in which two men discuss a recently deceased friend: "Two old guys are walking and one says to the other, 'You going to Moishe's funeral tomorrow?' So the other one answers, 'Why should I go to Moishe's funeral? Would he go to mine?' " Or when I

THE MIRACLE OF INTERVALE AVENUE

ask Sacks whether he got along with his wife's relations: "Definitely! I've gone to every one of their funerals."

Whether the theme of cheating death lies behind all death humor I do not know. But for the Intervale congregation, cheating death has a very special meaning and has a good deal to do with why they stay in the area. As one man put it: "One advantage of living in such a dangerous neighborhood is that the malekh hamoves [the Angel of Death] is afraid to come here."

One Sunday, Mr. Abraham arrives in shul and approaches Mordechai: "Do you remember the guy who owned the hardware store around the corner from you? Well, I just heard that he died the other day. This guy never took a vacation in his life. Anyway, he and his wife decided finally to go to Miami Beach. So he's at the pool, and all of a sudden he says to his wife he doesn't feel good. She tells him to come upstairs to their room and she'll give him some milk of magnesia. The guy never made it across the lobby. He was dead before he reached the elevator."

"Imagine that," Mordechai replies. "You can live all your life among thieves and murderers and nothing ever happens to you. Then you go someplace else where it's supposed to be safe and you get killed or die."

Intervale's congregants are very proud of the South Bronx's notoriety. By taming a dangerous, life-threatening area, they have, if not conquered death outright, at least robbed it of some of its awesomeness. Ernest Becker in his study *The Denial of Death* writes about the fear of death as a driving force in human action. The hero, according to Becker, offers a counterpoint to our fear of death by facing death and returning. Or if he dies, then he gains a measure of immortality by facing death without sign of fear.[7]

The heroic aspect of living in Hunts Point is reinforced by family members or relief organizations with whom the congregation is in contact. A few minutes before the Kol Nidre service one year, Betty Flisser called the Intervale Jewish Center and asked me to walk up the hill to escort her husband to shul. She was afraid that, walking alone at dusk in the South Bronx, he might be in danger of attack. As we walked, Flisser complained that he had just received a call from his son: "You got little kids, you got little problems. You got big kids, you got big problems."

"What's the problem?" I ask.

"My son called to wish me a happy new year and to tell me that he's worried. I shouldn't go to shul because someone might try to hold me up or something. Of course, where he lives they don't got such problems. He lives in the suburbs."

Dave, for his part, takes a good deal of pride in the nightstick a policeman gave him: "The cop asked me what I'm doing in the area. I told him that I live here. So he says, 'Look, you better take this. It's filled with lead. If anyone bothers you, just show them this." Dave also carries a small arsenal of knives in his jacket pocket. One, a foot long, he refers to as "my penknife" and claims that he'll "use it on anyone who bothers me. My sister tells me I shouldn't go down to the stoop at night. I'm not afraid. Once somebody tried something. Or they would say 'Jew this' or 'Jew that.' So I just call them 'dirty Spic.' I'm not afraid. You got to be able to live with them."

Mrs. Miroff plays the role of "gun moll" surrounded by "bums and moiderers." She hesitates to leave friends alone with them in the shop, fearing that they might mistreat an unwary visitor. In one instance, Lawrence propped his body against the door and refused to let me leave the shop until I paid him a five-dollar fee he decided I owed him for allowing me to photograph him. I refused, remembering Mrs. Miroff's warning never to give the bums more than a dollar. But Lawrence was adamant, and Mrs. Miroff quickly realized that he meant business. "Give him the money," she advised me. I did. When Lawrence left, I asked her why she had given in to his demands. "They live by their own rules, not by ours. To be with them, you got to go by their rules. He thinks you owed him the money. He had made a deal with you. So he was going to get his money. He would have murdered you right here."

"I thought you told me no one would harm you or your friends?"

"That's true. But you have to leave the store to go home, and then he can do what he wants to you."

If the shop is a place of refuge, of order, it is by way of contrast with the chaos of the surrounding world. I once asked Mrs. Miroff why she prepared meals to bring to her children for the holy days rather than invite them to her place: "Are you kidding?" she replies. "What's the matter with you? Come to me? This neighborhood is so dangerous, if you come with a car, you're lucky if you leave with a bicycle."

Sacks, too, relishes the neighborhood's dangerous reputation. Though he feels relatively unthreatened by youths in the area, most of whom know him as Moish from the bakery, he nonetheless uses the neighborhood's reputation as a source of humor. He once described a conversation with a taxi driver who drove him home from a reception in Manhattan:

"I get into the cab and I tell the driver to take me to Hunts Point. The driver looks at me and asks, 'Is it safe to go there?' 'Sure, it's safe,' I tell him. 'I've been living there for more than thirty years.' When we arrive outside the apartment, I give him nine dollars for the ride that's on the meter, and I reach into my pocket and take out a handful of singles for the tip—how many I don't know—whatever's in my pocket. I give him the money and I ask him to wait outside for a few moments to see that I'm safe inside. The driver looks at the money I gave him and says, 'For a tip like that I'll walk you up to your apartment.' 'You don't have to walk me up to my apartment,' I tell him. 'Just stay inside the cab and if after five minutes you don't hear any screams, you'll know I'm safe and you can drive away.'"

On another occasion he was complaining about a pain in his leg caused, he felt, by poor circulation and "too much rest since I've been on vacation and the bakery has been closed." I suggested jokingly that he consider dispensing with leisure time altogether. "Why don't you try jogging?" I said. "Instead of lying down after work you could get rid of all that excess energy."

"You can't jog in this neighborhood. Here you can only dart."

"Dart?" I ask.

"Yeah, dart. This neighborhood is so dangerous you have to actually dart from one doorway to the next."

Most congregants treat the neighborhood's reputation as an indication of their special valor, comparable to what Becker refers to as a personal narcissism or heroism in the face of death. It adds special meaning to their lives because it makes their existence a testament to their courage and defiance. At the same time, just as old people feel they have outsmarted death by surviving, they are constantly reminded of the unpredictable nature of the enemy they face. Death can be kept at bay; it cannot be vanquished. Sacks tells a particularly poignant joke about this very dilemma:

"Sam is a retired man and he decides to live it up. So he buys himself a new suit. Then he gets himself a face lift. And he looks like a complete new man. Then he goes outside, and the first corner he crosses, a car comes and—*pow!*—kills him on the spot. So he goes up to heaven and he stands before God and he says, 'God, did you have to wait until I got a new suit and a face lift, and then go and do this thing to me? Why couldn't you do it before?' So God looks at him and says, 'Sam, I have to apologize to you. To tell you the truth, I didn't even recognize you.'"

Although jokes make death tangible, an adversary from without rather than an insidious threat from within, thoughts about death are nonetheless an ever-present source of anxiety for members of the congregation. But the concern generally has less the quality of a generalized fear of death than a desire either to defy or tame death by chipping away at its totality. The defiance of death separates congregants into individuals and their respective families; taming death brings them together into a religious community.[8] Both responses exist side by side.

When congregants discuss upcoming dates of yortsayt, they sometimes reflect on the number of years that have passed since that painful event.

"MAYBE IT'S BRODSKY"

At one kiddush, for example, Sacks reflects that his wife has been dead for twenty years. "Soon it'll be time for her to come back," Lena comments.

"She won't come back," Sacks responds. "It'll soon be time to see her upstairs. I have a plot here and in Israel. I got one in Israel because I figure when *moshiakh* [Messiah] comes I'm prepared since I won't be among the living ones who are still alive at that time. I bought the plot in Israel because I figured I would exhume my wife's body. But it turned out to be too costly. Instead I'll leave the money for the grandchildren."

Several members of Intervale's congregation are reasonably well off and could afford to live almost anywhere else in New York City. One woman, referred to as "the doctor's wife" because of her husband's profession, is undoubtedly not poor. Yet she lives in Hunts Point and dresses in old, worn-out clothes. Sacks, too, is rather prosperous. Some of his wealth comes from his weekly salary as a baker, some from Social Security, and some from his investments and various property holdings throughout the metropolitan area. He wears the same raggedy clothes as other congregants. His down vest is patched, and its blue color is rapidly losing ground to large black splotches. His winter coat is torn. Mrs. Miroff takes pity on his shabby appearance and periodically mends his pants or alters a suit for him.

At the same time, if a son plans to make a major purchase, Sacks may present him with part of the money for it. After one such gift, Sacks recalls: "I told my son that if I live another two years, it's a gift and it doesn't count. Otherwise it counts."

"What do you mean, 'counts'?" I ask.

"I mean it counts as part of the inheritance. I got another son and he gets part of the inheritance, too. If I die within the next two years, the amount I gave counts as part of the inheritance this son gets."

Sacks's savings are a legacy. They are a concrete way of keeping his memory alive long after he himself is gone. And it is, of course, the very anxiety about death that prompts parents to save and deny themselves luxuries despite the relative comfort of well-established children. Sacks's sons need no support from their father. Indeed, other congregants feel jealous, even betrayed, that he would shower his children with expensive gifts rather than use the money to help them or the synagogue. And they particularly resent his boasting about his generosity as if he were flaunting his betrayal. Sacks's accustomed role at the Intervale Jewish Center is that of provider to a congregation of dependents. But the symbolic rewards are destined for only short duration: Sacks is likely to outlive most of the other congregants. Consequently, his children are his key to immortality, and it is to them that he bequeaths his legacy.

Periodically Sacks's son, "the judge " or "hizzoner," as Sacks refers to

THE MIRACLE OF INTERVALE AVENUE

him, takes his father to spend the day with him and his family in Queens. It's usually on a Sunday. The son waits in the car outside the shul, and Sacks makes frequent glances at the clock as he rushes through the review of the parshe. One Sunday as we're talking, Sacks's eyes suddenly dart to the clock and, noticing that it's a few minutes past the time he's supposed to meet his son, he grabs his plastic shopping bag and heads outside. "I better get going. I don't want to keep hizzoner waiting."

In a similar way, Sacks's concern about recovering Lena's bank books when she died was only partly motivated by the thought that the money might be needed to bury her. He was also aware that whatever money was in the account was slated for the surviving family members. Since they, in turn, are the ones who will remember her, the recovery of the bank books was a way of rescuing Lena's immortality.

Elderly people have less of a need for physical comfort than they do for health and continued independence. Indulging in luxuries has meaning for the young—for those without a strong sense of their own mortality. But for the elderly, acquisitions or savings are considered as accumulated capital that can be passed down from one generation to the next. Material deprivations, particularly those which are self-inflicted, can have very great meaning.

There are many types of legacies. Sacks, for example, once talked about the special meaning invested in some of his cakes:

"Every year I give my son a fruit cake. It's just for him. He keeps it in the fridge and no one else is allowed to touch it—it's from father to son. When he finishes it, he tells me, 'Dad, I've finished the fruit cake.' And I give him another one. The other thing I do is every year I put one fruit cake in the fridge in the bakery. Even my boss and even the sales staff know they're not allowed to sell the cake. I figure this way if I die and they open up the fridge, they'll find the cake and something of me will still be there."

For Sacks, work and defiance of death are neatly intertwined. The long hours he puts in and the grueling pace he maintains to keep up with demand are a personal testimony to his vitality and indispensability. Baking is his key to immortality: "When I die, people will walk in here and they'll see the danish that I used to make and they'll remember me because they'll remember how good everything used to taste."

Legacies are ways of limiting the fear of oblivion. By defying death, however, they accentuate an adversarial relationship. Congregants know perfectly well that one day they will die (although they hope it will not be too soon); they need to make their peace with death, to turn an adversary into a friend. Intervale is a religious community. Its members may not be devoutly Orthodox, but they are nonetheless believers, and they expect, therefore, some sort of otherworldly life at the end of this one. So both

"MAYBE IT'S BRODSKY"

the ceremonies connected to the death of loved ones and, indeed, the concrete actions taken to ensure their own easy passage through death and burial are a way of making peace with death.

At one kiddush Sacks and Malachi discuss the date on the Hebrew calendar. "My birthday is coming up. It's in the tenth of Tammuz," Malachi comments.

"The tenth of Tammuz?" Sacks responds. "My mother's yortsayt is the twenty-first of Tammuz. So I'll have yortsayt then if I live that long. You know, when we wish our children long life, we don't just do it out of generosity. It's also out of vanity. It they have a long life, then they're here to remember us."

For congregants concerned about their legacy and needing the reassurance that they will be remembered, the Intervale Jewish Center has come to serve as a communal kaddish, guaranteeing to each member the recitation of the memorial prayers.

At the Intervale Jewish Center, everyone has special dates when they need to have memorial prayers recited. Together they form a cycle of mourning through which individual congregants count the passing time. Malachi's wife died five years ago on the eve of Passover. Sacks's wife died twenty-one years ago on the fifth day of Hanukkah. Lena Michaels died two days after Yom Kippur. "She died a righteous woman," Sacks announced the Sunday that he learned of her death. "She had repented for her sins, and she died before she had the chance to accumulate new ones."

For some congregants, yortsayt is a major reason for attending. Rose Cutler, well into her nineties, who until recently lived by herself on the twenty-first floor of a nearby housing project, stood impatiently in the rear of the shul, waiting for the recitation of the memorial prayer. Her neighbor told her to sit down: "Sacks will call you when it's time. Anyway, it's not even your yortsayt today."

"If it's not today," I asked, "why are you having the prayer said?"

"I'm over ninety years old," she answered. "Today's a nice day. I feel good. Who knows how I'll feel next week."

Ultimately, only the knowledge that one is part of something greater than familial bonds and obligations, something that reasserts the existence of a higher order of things, gives man the sense that death and life are linked, that they are both part of a divine plan, and that one gives meaning and purpose to the other. The communal rites of the shul provide that sense of order if only because they tie congregants to the world of their fathers and even, as I argued in an earlier chapter, to the world of their biblical forefathers.

There are several heroes who stand out in Sacks's recounting of the Bible: Moses, who led the children of Israel through the desert; Abra-

THE MIRACLE OF INTERVALE AVENUE

ham, their forefather; and Noah, from whom all living people are descended. The story of each has value to the everyday lives of Intervale's congregants. But the story of Noah is special in part because it is a story about righteousness in its most liberal definition and, therefore, the most applicable to Intervale. In part, too, it is special because, of all biblical stories, it approaches in a graphic sense the turmoil and devastation that Intervale's congregants have witnessed. In the story of Noah, there is a symbol of communal commemoration. The ark, after all, preserved the remnants of a doomed world. The Intervale Jewish Center is a vessel, too. And like the ark it contains a diverse crew—odds and ends of a ruined civilization. Surrounding it is a devastation so vast that it seems almost to be the will of God—as if He, angry with the world, chose to wipe it out as He had done millennia ago. ("God promised never again to destroy the world by flood, but He didn't say anything about fire," Sacks explained, referring perhaps to the devastation around him.) The story of the ark tells of God's covenant not to destroy the world entirely—individuals would die but humanity would live.

Rites of commemoration reflect that covenant. The kaddish, after all, is a doxology—a praising of God. The proper utterance in response to news of a death is the blessing *Borukh dayan emes* (Blessed is the true Judge). In commemorating the dead, we give praise to God. In that praise lies a deep need to overcome the sense of chaos that death imparts to the living. Merely uttering the praise of God is confirmation of a belief in order and divine will in the face of rampant disorder and unjust suffering.

Noah's ark, too, is a symbol of order, of structure in the face of chaos, of ultimate survival of the species in the face of general devastation. Like the ark, the Intervale Jewish Center guarantees the survival of its congregants. Sacks sees it in the physical properties of the place, what he refers to as the building's stones. "I don't want you to take this as sacrilegious, but every Saturday when I walk to shul, particularly as I get to the area around the shul where all the buildings are gone, even with all the garbage and the rubble, it reminds me of the area around the *kotel maravi*, the Western Wall, in Jerusalem. To me this place is my holy place. It's my kotel maravi."

Little wonder then that Sacks believes the very stones of the Intervale Jewish Center create the "miracle" by guaranteeing enough male congregants for a minyan. And the minyan is a symbolic indication of the viability of a community and, by extention, of a world.

And what world does the Intervale Jewish Center preserve? Perhaps the memory of a time and place gone by or perhaps simply the memory of one or another individual, which the Talmud tells us is equivalent to saving the entire world.

"MAYBE IT'S BRODSKY"

One Saturday, Sacks lifts the Torah, rests it on his shoulder, and announces, "Today is *khamishe oser be-shvat*. It's Old Man Brodsky's yortsayt. I'm going to say the *El Mole Rakhamim* for him."

"Go ahead," Mr. Abraham calls out. "Say the *El Mole. Gezunterheyt* [In good health]."

Sacks appreciates the remark. He cracks a smile and recites the prayer. I turn to Flisser, seated next to me, and ask what he remembers about Brodsky. "I'll tell you, Jack. The thing I remember about him is that he loved herring. Whenever we would go on a trip to another synagogue, as soon as he comes into the place he looks around to see whether they have any herring."

I prod for more details. "When was this?"

Flisser seems bewildered by the question. "When was this? When he was alive!"

Mr. Abraham, sitting to my right, has found an appropriate moment to jump in. "It's a funny thing," he says. "After Brodsky died, he lost his taste completely for herring."

Flisser laughs, then continues. "It's no good for you, all that salty stuff. Brodsky loved things that are bad for you. Herring. Pickles. He loved salty things. That's probably what killed him."

Mr. Abraham, the attorney, offers his own summation. "Imagine that. The poor guy was killed by a herring." Mr. Abraham offers his quips with a tone of reverence. They are meant as tribute from one jokester to another.

One Sunday, while reviewing the parshe of the week, Sacks recounts Noah's various attempts to find land until finally a dove returns bearing an olive branch in its mouth. Before Sacks can continue the review of the parshe, Kaplan interrupts: "I'm sorry for interrupting you, Mr. Sacks. But every year when we come to this parshe I'm reminded of a joke that Mr. Brodsky would make."

"Yeah," Sacks agrees, motioning to Kaplan. "I know the joke."

"Go on. Tell the joke!" Mr. Abraham urges. Unaccustomed to center stage, Kaplan hesitates for a moment. He defers to Sacks, who declines the offer and encourages Kaplan to continue. Kaplan clears his throat.

"The joke is, how is it that we know that the dove is a boy dove and not a girl dove?"

Mr. Abraham plays the straight man: "It's in Rashi?"

Sacks is sitting patiently. He lets the joke unfold, listening carefully to make sure Kaplan is telling it properly. He intercedes only when Kaplan is in danger of foundering. "Rashi doesn't say anything about the dove being male or female," Sacks advises.

"All right," Mr. Abraham concedes, "I give up. How do we know it's a male dove and not a female dove?"

THE MIRACLE OF INTERVALE AVENUE

"Because," Kaplan announces, beaming, "if it was a female dove, it wouldn't have been able to keep its mouth shut long enough to bring back the olive branch!" We all laugh. The three women who are present are, fortunately, sitting at a different table, out of earshot.

"Mr. Brodsky," Sacks shouts out, looking toward the ceiling, "with that joke you are immortal."

"That Brodsky was a funny man," Malachi commented. "He was always telling jokes."

The joke has become Brodsky's legacy and, too, the communal property of the congregation.

After services, Sacks and I make our weekly trek to the bakery. It is the Saturday of Brodsky's yortsayt. As we turn the corner onto 165th Street, Sacks begins to reminisce about his old friend:

"You know, this route is a short cut. But a short cut only in relation to a long cut along 163rd Street, which Mr. Brodsky always insisted was the shorter route. Mr. Brodsky's route made a perfect right triangle; somehow I could never convince him that the diagonal is the shortest line between two angles of a triangle. No matter how much I tried, he would insist I was wrong, 'It's shorter to go from one point to the next,' he would say."

I was curious to know more about the man whose place I might be filling in the minyan. (Brodsky had died shortly before I arrived at the Intervale Jewish Center, and I felt a certain connection between us.) When we reached the bakery, I encouraged Sacks to continue. What was he like?

"Brodsky was an old man who used to live in the area. He had a pickle stand on 165th Street, a block or two from the shul. It belonged to a brother or a brother-in-law, I'm not sure which. By the time I knew him, he was already a retired man. He lived alone on Bryant Avenue, not too far from where I live. I think he was the only one left in the building. He used to come into the bakery with his cane, sit down, and have a cup of coffee with a danish. But it wasn't at the bakery we met, it was in shul. When they closed Temple Beth Elohim, I started going to the Intervale Jewish Center. This was in 1962, just after my wife died. Brodsky was a congregant there. He would go to shul on the High Holy Days. Mind you, he wasn't a religious man, even though he died a religious man.

"You might think I'm bragging, but I had a part in that. I used to walk from my apartment on Faile Street along Hunts Point Avenue on the way to shul. Along the way I would escort three women—Blanche, who used to work in the bakery as a salesgirl, and two sisters, both spinsters who lived in the area. So I would encourage Brodsky to join us—less to go to shul than for the company. Once he got to shul already, he stayed.

"Brodsky was never married. He carried around a picture of himself as

"MAYBE IT'S BRODSKY"

a young man standing on some beach somewhere with a young woman. She must have been his girlfriend, but I don't know what happened. Somehow she wasn't lucky enough to get him to marry her. And for some reason he never married anyone else. So he had no children of his own. He was close, though, with his brother's children. One was a niece who lived in Coney Island or somewhere in Brooklyn. Eventually, he went to live with her. Before that, he lived in a deteriorating building. One day they broke in and vandalized his apartment. After that he couldn't stay there.

"I have a large four-room apartment—my wife was dead already many years, my children were grown up—so I invited him to live with me. Meanwhile, the niece in Brooklyn wanted him to live with her. So we compromised. Weekdays he lived in Brooklyn, weekends he spent with me. I gave him a key to the apartment, he was free to come and go as he pleased.

"By then he was a regular shul-goer. Saturday mornings sometimes Brodsky would look outside the window and say, 'Moish, it's raining. What are we going to do? We can't carry an umbrella?' So I would tell him, 'Don't worry. By the time we get outside it won't be raining anymore.' And the time it took us to get from my floor to downstairs, you'd never know it had just been raining.

"Brodsky would tell all the colored people in Mrs. Miroff's shop we're on our way to shul. He never realized they wouldn't know what a shul is. He was friends with all of them because during the day he was usually home. He was either downstairs in Mrs. Miroff's shop talking to her or to the 'bums,' or he was upstairs supervising the girl that cleaned the apartment. No matter how much she cleaned, it wasn't enough. He would stand there scrubbing the pot we used to boil water in after she had cleaned it, and would complain. If he would see what that pan looks like now, he'd probably turn in his grave.

"Anyway, Brodsky could never walk all the way to shul without resting. He could walk until we got to the dry-goods store. It was only two stores from the bakery, but he had to go inside and sit down in the armchair they kept by the door. He would sit there, and while he sat he would tell the owners the story of how the rain had stopped as we were out the front door. That made a real impression on him because he was never a religious man and now he was, and it was like the rain's stopping sort of confirmed him becoming religious. And as he was telling the story, he'd look out and see that it was raining again.

"After another five or ten minutes, the rain would let up, Brodsky was rested, and we continued to the bakery. I would put a chicken in the oven so we could have a bite after shul. He took with a bag of bread crumbs.

THE MIRACLE OF INTERVALE AVENUE

When we reached the park on Hunts Point Avenue and Southern Boulevard, all the pigeons would fly from the roof of the building facing the park as soon as they saw Brodsky. They knew he would feed them. They're still there today, so I guess they've found another Brodsky.

"When we got to shul, just as soon as we were inside the door, it would start to rain again. Brodsky never sat with me in shul. He used to say he didn't like the way I davened. He used to complain that I didn't read all the prayers. I tried to explain to him that I read without mouthing everything, I sort of scan. But I couldn't teach him to do it, so he sat by himself on a separate bench.

"But when it came to the dvar Torah, he was my best student. On Sundays I would go over the parshe, just like I do now. Brodsky would sit opposite me and fall asleep. I think being surrounded by holiness made him feel relaxed. Saturdays was the same thing; after shul we ate lunch in the bakery, and the three of us would fall asleep right at the table."

"You mean the two of you."

"Three. Brodsky, me, and Blackie, the cat I had at the time. Sundays, Brodsky would also come with me to the bakery on Sundays. He would sit there while I worked, usually fall asleep, and wake up just when it was time to go home. But we didn't go home together. I liked to walk, but he waited for a bus. Apparently he was too tired to walk. 'Moishe,' he would say, 'I get tired just from watching you work.' "

"Were you there when he died?"

"Not exactly when he died. But I saw him just before he died. One day I got a call from his niece, the one in Brooklyn, that Brodsky was in the hospital. He had a stroke. Maybe he recovered a little, because they were going to move him to the convalescent part of the hospital, but he died first from a heart attack. I went to see him before he died, and he said to me, 'Moish, you'll take care of me.' He meant when he dies.

"I don't know how much he really meant it, because when people are very sick, they talk like that. His funeral was downtown in Manhattan. I went with Dave. I said the *El Mole Rakhamim* and then I said a few words of condolences to his niece. Dave said the kaddish and the Ninth Psalm. And then we went home.

"Whatever Brodsky owned that was of value I imagine he left to his niece. He died a poor man. He did have some property in Atlantic City. It was never worth anything, but he held on to it. I think there was some plans to build a hotel on it. But nothing came of it while he was alive. Besides that, he had his personal effects. I still have them in the room I gave him. I can't bring myself to throw these things out. One of his canes still hangs from the door. Another one I have here in the bakery. He gave it to me."

"MAYBE IT'S BRODSKY"

"Why did he give it to you?"

"Why? I'll tell you. Brodsky only wanted I should walk with a cane. We used to fight over which of us was older, me or him. Actually we were about the same age, maybe two weeks' difference. But he liked to claim he was two weeks older than me and that's why he needed a cane. On the street, though, he was embarrassed he should need a cane and I shouldn't, so he kept buying me canes. The one I keep here, even my helpers know it's Brodsky's. Even my boss knows it's Brodsky's cane. Now and then they remind themselves of stories about him, how he used to do this or do that. They see the cane hanging from the pipe and they think about him. Now and then we use it, too. Sometimes there's a pan stuck too far in back or it's too hot, so one of the workers yells out, 'Get Brodsky's cane!' So he still comes in handy. We use it to pull the tray out of the oven."

Sacks pauses, and the pause grows into a lengthy silence. It is time for me to leave. I slip my tape recorder into my vest pocket and put my coat on. Sacks gets up from his chair. He walks me to the door and unlocks it. As I leave, he locks the door behind me and watches as I turn to walk away. I walk slowly down Hunts Point Avenue, retracing the route Sacks and Brodsky would take to shul. I reach the park and descend the stairs into the subway. Halfway down I stop, climb back up, and look around the park. The pigeons are still there.

The following week after shul, I take up the topic of Brodsky once again. "If someone comes along to replace a departed congregant, then whom did I replace?" I ask. "Brodsky died just before I arrived. Is there any connection?"

"No," Sacks replies, "there is no connection."

"But don't you insist that there is a connection between an old congregant dying and a new one arriving? Doesn't someone always come along just at the right time?"

"Not to take the place," Sacks corrected me. "Someone comes along. But no one can take the place of another person."

"So I didn't take Brodsky's place?"

"No."

Sacks and I parry with each other. I am vying for a place in the minyan, perhaps seeking my own immortality there. Sacks is bent on limiting my role, perhaps preparing for the likelihood that one day I will stop coming. The timetable for my leaving has a good deal to do with the progress of my book. Knowing that, Sacks asks one day how the writing is coming. I tell him that it's going well, and that I am writing about Brodsky.

"How can you write about him if you never met him?"

"I may have never met him, but I feel as if I did because of all that you've told me. It's as if Brodsky gained immortality through you and your memories of him."

Mention of the word "immortality" strikes a responsive chord. "You mention the word 'immortality.' It's true that I'm older than the others. But age is measured too by how long you work after sixty-five. I'm still working, so the others are likely to die before me. So I will remember them, and you might say I am their immortality. I wonder sometimes who is going to give me my immortality."

Sacks's comment takes me by surprise. "In Brodsky's case," I observe, "he had no children to remember him. So you have to remember him. But your immortality comes from your children."

Sacks is not satisfied by the reassurance. "That's not immortality," he insists. "Children and grandchildren remember out of duty and obligation, or because of materialistic reasons. Immortality you get from peers."

"Well," I try to comfort him, "you play a central role in my study. You're central to my book. Isn't that immortality?" Sacks thinks for a minute. He seems ready to concede, but he insists on having the last word. "Yeah," he says, "if I live that long."

One shabes, Dave busies himself shooing away a fly that keeps landing on the plate of cake while Malachi recites the kiddush. "Get out of here," Dave tells the fly, "you're not Jewish. You're not supposed to be here."

"Don't say that, Dave. You never know," Sacks admonishes. "You see, there's only one fly in here. It reminds me of the story of the Baal Shem Tov. He was traveling somewhere and he went in to daven, but there were only nine men. All of a sudden a butterfly comes into the room, flies to the aren kodesh [Ark], and flutters there throughout the service. Then, after the last amen of the last kaddish, it flies out the window. 'You see,' the Baal Shem Tov tells the others, 'we needed a tenth man for the minyan. Reb So-and-So who just passed away must have heard that we were missing a man, and his neshome [soul] came to daven.' So this fly is just like that butterfly. It's here because we needed a tenth man."

"We got more than that for the minyan," Dave advises. "There's rats here, too. Maybe they're kosher. We can include them, too. I'll ask Mrs. Miroff to make them yarmulkes and maybe even a talis."

"Now, that's more like heresy," Sacks admonishes. "A fly is like a butterfly because they both go between heaven and earth. So it's kind of like a neshome."

"So whose neshome is this fly?" I ask.

"I don't know," Sacks responds. "But let's leave the fly alone. We only had nine men today. Maybe it's Brodsky."

· 7 ·

THE MAKING OF
A MIRACLE

The film *The Miracle of Intervale Avenue* came about as most things do, by chance. Irving Rappaport, a film producer, and I had both been invited to a luncheon at a friend's apartment on Manhattan's Upper West Side. It was the first day of Rosh Hashanah, the Jewish New Year.

I arrive late, having gone with Sacks to *tashlikh* (the ceremony of casting off sins). Though it is normally held later in the afternoon, I lament not being able to witness the ceremony because of the luncheon engagement. Sacks is willing to accommodate religious custom to personal schedule. After services he rounds up a couple of congregants and we walk to an ugly bridge on a busy expressway that overlooks an industrial wasteland on either side of the Bronx River. Desolate, almost forbidding, the site looks custom-made for casting off sins. Sacks recites the prayer. Tossing the bread crumbs (our symbolic sins) into the water, Lena shouts down, "Here, fishies, eat. We'll be back next year." But I doubt there are any fish alive in those waters. I feel somewhat relieved as we head back to a mercifully sinful little park. Sacks will find a seat among the neighborhood types, the young black craps shooters long familiar with this old Jewish baker, and wait for other congregants to lead to tashlikh.

Back in Manhattan I apologize to the other guests for being late and take a chair next to Irving, who is explaining the differences he observed between services in New York synagogues and those in London, where he lives. More as a joke than as a serious offer, I suggest that if he were interested in seeing something truly different, he might want to visit the shul I have been studying for the past two years in the South Bronx. The following day he accompanies me to Intervale for the second day of Rosh Hashanah.

We arrive while services are under way. A Jewish policeman from the 41st Precinct is present in uniform. He stands several rows behind the other men, looking as if he does not belong, yet holding a prayer book and wearing a talis. I introduce myself, and he rather sheepishly apologizes for being on duty on the holy day, promising not to work on Yom Kippur. I assure him it's of no concern to me and invite him to join us at the table where I usually sit. I then go over to Sacks to introduce Irving.

"Gut yontov," I say. "I see we have a cop here. Is everything O.K.?"

Sacks seems a little surprised by my question. "Oh, yeah," he answers, "everything is fine. I always ask for police protection for the holidays."

"You mean," Irving asks more out of curiosity than alarm, "you think there might be some kind of trouble?"

"No. No trouble. Sometimes Dave works at the center, or Mr. Abraham can't make it and I'm missing a man for the minyan. So I call the 41st Precinct and I ask them to send me a man. If I'm lucky, they send a Jewish cop, so we have him for the minyan."

Irving and I wander over to the bench where I usually sit, and I decide to make use of the officer's presence to learn more about the area. The policeman confirms what I already know. The name Fort Apache is a vestige from the past:

"I started working in the precinct in 1968 when the gangs were at their height. Today, of course, the gangs are gone. It's the kind of thing that comes back every twenty years, kind of like a cycle. In those days the Savage Skulls were located just around the corner from the shul. They had maybe fifteen hundred members, broken down into divisions, battalions, and a gestapo squad to enforce discipline. A guy named Blood was their leader. There was another gang here that was pretty big too, the Dirty Dozens. They weren't right here, they were over in Longwood about twenty blocks from here. I arrested their leader, Big Eddie, for drugs and homicide. This guy was so well connected that when I busted him, he didn't even call a lawyer. He called the D.A. The D.A. must have owed him favors for helping with evidence on other cases. This time, though, his connections didn't do him any good. He was sent upstate to Ossining for five years."

Our conversation is interrupted when the policeman is called to remove the Torah from the Ark. He stands next to Malachi and Mordechai on the platform. I am amused by the palpable sense of astonishment on Irving's face as he takes in what to him must seem utterly outlandish: two black cantors, the light-skinned cantor a paragon of grace and dignity in an otherwise bizarre shul, the yeshiva-educated son, conversant in Yiddish, with the mannerisms and worldview of a hasidic Jew; a policeman in full uniform, with a loaded gun hanging from his hip and a talis draped over his shoulders, embracing a worn Torah *mantl* (cover); and the shul itself, everywhere displaying evidence of assault—windows covered by wooden planks, huge pieces of plaster fallen from the ceiling forming a vast diaspora of tiny fragments on the rotting wooden floors. Equally outlandish are the signs painted on the doors and hallway walls that read "Thank You, Come Again," "Glatt Kosher," and "Kosher Ladies Room," the last drawn inside an enormous red heart with Cupid's arrow pointing toward the lavatory. All are the handiwork of Dave Lentin, who approaches Irving now and then to run through his repertoire of bawdy comments and lewd gestures. And finally there is Mrs. Miroff, hard at work apportioning food onto paper plates for the meal that will follow the service, interrupting her work when we first approach her in order to switch from eighty-four-year-old grandmother to gun moll describing the latest murder on her block and her affectionate relationship with the street people. Irving doesn't have that much time to gawk. With a shortage of men, and extra *kibbudim* [honors] to give out because of the holiday, Sacks has him scurrying about to perform various parts of the service. "In London," Irving remarks, "I could wait in line for fifty years to be called to the Torah on Rosh Hashanah. I've only been here for a couple of hours and I've already been called up three times."

Irving returned to London soon after his visit to Intervale. A month later he called to let me know that he wanted to produce a film on the community. If I agreed, the filming would take place in the late summer or early fall. In the course of time, the project moved off the drawing boards. Irving approached Ken Howard, a British director, who was immediately interested in the project and offered to assemble a film crew. The two men next approached the BBC, which agreed to coproduce the film. The shooting would take place in the fall around the time of the Jewish High Holy Days. The following June, Irving and Ken arrived in New York. The three of us began to outline the film's structure, and I introduced Ken to the people who I thought would be most suited to appear on camera.

When Ken and Irving returned home, I asked Sacks whether he was looking forward to the film's production. I found him rather noncommittal: "It's a long way off; who knows whether or not I'll live that long." In either case, neither he nor the other congregants anticipated even the

THE MAKING OF A MIRACLE

slightest change occurring in their lives. Unlike younger people, the elderly do not tack fantasies of Hollywood careers onto the word "film." Their main concern is to keep on living the life they know. Asked about the future, Sacks usually responds, "If I live that long," or, "Young people think about the future. Old people think about the past."

At the time, I had known Sacks for just over two years. I had always considered him an optimist, undaunted by life's various pitfalls. But when the film production began, I was suddenly introduced to another side of Sacks, a dark side that I had not noticed before. At a loss how to deal with it, I responded by minimizing its import and ignoring every warning sign that things might not work as smoothly as I expected. Little did I know at the time that I was completely misreading a situation so volatile that it threatened not only the film but even the very close working relationship I had established with Sacks over the previous two years. Yet, had I known better, I may not have acted much differently, for it was Sacks rather than I who controlled the situation.

Despite his comments, Sacks's lack of interest in the film went beyond the usual refusal to look ahead. At the time he had suddenly developed a particularly dim view of life, largely because of an intense pain in his left leg. He reacted with an almost fatalistic resolve:

"Either the pain will get better or it will get worse. Either the pain will go away or the leg will go away. Life is an equation. It's all part of God's plan. It reminds me of what happened to my cat, Pinkie. The boss's wife put down some mouse poison, and Pinkie probably ate it and is dead because I haven't seen him all week. So that's a new equation.

"You know, I had five sons. Two are now alive. I had a three-year-old boy who died of appendicitis. He used to visit me in the bakery and say, 'Hello, Daddy.' Now people don't die of appendicitis. So they die of a double heart attack. No. Not even from that, but from a cancer eating various parts of the body. Whatever it is, you're still going to die."

Sacks's moodiness comes and goes. I ignore it. Amid ever-present morbid thoughts, a glimmer of optimism unexpectedly emerges. Each time, I assume the side of Sacks I am more familiar with will prevail. Even his none-too-well-masked ego surfaces now and then. Responding to a question I pose about any specific requirements on his part regarding the film's production, Sacks refers back to his hero and namesake, Moses. "Just remember to put the period in for the things that I do."

"What period?" I ask.

Sacks has in mind a bit of biblical exegesis: "The period in the Hebrew word for modesty. Although the Bible is perfect, it left out the dot from the word "modesty" when it described Moses. The rabbis interpreted that to mean that Moses was so modest that he even hesitated to have himself described as modest. But that doesn't mean you should go so overboard either. Otherwise they'll say that I'm a liar and no one will believe you. You know, when I was a young man, besides the different things I would do, I also worked in the bakery. Sometimes, when I would see my father, I would tell him how much I had made, how many of this or of that I had baked in a day. And he would say, 'Sha, Moishe! I believe you. But everyone else will think that you're lying.' "

For a while Sacks's mood switches back and forth between feelings of despair and moments of optimism and good humor. But two weeks before the crew is scheduled to arrive from London, his mood plunges into dark pessimism. Besides the continuing pain in his leg, two new developments contribute to increased feelings of desolation. Mr. Abraham, his closest friend, learns that he will need surgery to treat a malignant tumor. Mr. Abraham's condition seems to spark off morbid sentiments in Sacks that lurked just beneath the surface. Outwardly, Sacks voices his usual optimism, particularly when speaking to his friend. When Mr. Abraham informs him that the surgery will consist of a radioactive implant rather than a removal of the tumor, Sacks is quick to confirm the wisdom of the procedure:

"I had an aunt who was over eighty and was diagnosed as having cancer. The family asked the doctor what her chances were, and he told us, 'If we operate, she may live another five years. If we don't, who knows? The decision is up to you.' The family decided not to risk the operation, and the woman lived another fifteen years. The doctors couldn't explain it. They figured it must have something to do with metabolism. So you see, it's good that they're not operating. They'll put the thing in you and you'll be O.K."

The optimism is only show. Sacks continues to talk about death a good deal. He seems to fantasize that the circulatory problem in his leg is caused by a blood clot that sooner or later will dislodge and cause either a fatal heart attack or a stroke. The mood is reinforced by a threatened disruption of his normal routine. Vito, his assistant for the past twenty-seven years, is facing the likelihood of forced retirement because of increasing blindness. The condition isn't new. Vito's failings have long been a part of Sacks's personal folklore. He is a reliable assistant but only up to a point:

"Vito came in here unknowledgeable of any baking. He learned to a certain extent and refused to learn any more for the twenty-seven years that I've been working with him. He learned how to make a roll. He learned how to make challie dough, but he doesn't know how to braid a challie. He learned how to grease for me the pans and even make the mixes for the large cakes and make the butter cream and make everything necessary for the colors. But he will not go to take the cake and decorate it. He put a limit on what he wants to do, and that he doesn't want to do anymore. For me he was sufficient. The twenty-seven years he was working here I made him a union man. I made him get all the benefits of the union and everything. And he worked with me straight down. He drives a car and picks me up every night that we worked . . . picks me up at my home. And as he picks me up, the cops in their radio car follow us.

"Now, Vito is every bit a good man. But there is one thing wrong with him. He has only one eye. And that one eye (the other eye is glass, which is nothing), the one eye has been deteriorating till he's now officially blind. He was still taking me back and forth even with the official blindness. Even the vehicle bureau has taken away his license and everything else. But he is officially blind. He can't see anything. And when we made the turn from Hunts Point down the block, he never hit the cars because the cars had to miss him. Till finally it came to an impasse that he doesn't even see the shadow now. He absolutely cannot drive. And if his wife lets him drive from Jersey, she's actually telling him to commit suicide. So we had a discussion in here, in the bakery. We told him about it and everything else. By the way. He still owes me twenty-five dollars. And we told him that he can't come back to work. He's retired."

When Sacks first tells me the story, he is quite upset. In his view, Vito's retirement might well mean the closing of the bakery. I try to reassure him that it seems easy enough just to train a new man. I apparently hit a raw nerve:

"That's just what's bothering me. If Jerry, my boss, had mentioned anything about a new assistant, I wouldn't be so worried. But Jerry is in semiretirement. He would like to get rid of the place altogether. What does he need it for? His wife, Evelyn, she wants to keep it for the kids, she says. But Evelyn is a very sick woman. Besides, the lease will be up in two years. They had a fifty-year lease, so you can imagine what their rent must be like. When they try to get a new lease, who knows what will happen?"

"So they'll sell the place," I say. "What makes you think that the new owner won't want you?"

"I don't care even if he does want me," Sacks barks back. "I'm not interested in working for a new owner. If they sell the bakery, I leave!"

"How are you going to leave? Where will you go?"

Sacks, apparently, had already given a good deal of thought to that very question, suggesting, as I only realize later, the extent of his despair: "Actually I'm getting used to the idea of retirement. The bakery has been closed for vacation for the last two weeks, and it hasn't been so bad. I feel pretty good. My feet aren't bothering me anymore. So I spend the day in the little park over here reading Isaac Bashevis Singer. Besides, I'm well taken care of financially. I get Social Security and a pension. Plus I have income yet from some property I own in Brooklyn. I also got stocks and bonds. If I can't make do on that, then something is wrong. Besides, I got where to go. My son Arthur is thinking of leaving the city. He would like to move near his brother upstate. He's looking for a house. And he's looking for something where I could move next to. I tell him all I need is that I should be in walking distance to a shul where I could daven and a bakery store where I could work."

"But if you leave Intervale, won't you miss playing the kind of role that you play here?"

"I don't have to miss it. Look, there's a certain percentage of people who stand out as leaders in any crowd. These people are leaders no matter where they are. Do you think if I were in another shul that I wouldn't be active the way I am here?"

"Maybe you will. But what about the ones who remain here? Who is going to lead them?"

"Don't look to me like that. That's not fair to put so much responsibility on me." Sacks is agitated by my argument. It exposes something still unsettled in his thinking. But he has thought this through. "Besides," he continues, "Malachi can lead them."

"No, he can't," I counter. "People look to you as a leader. Like Moses."

"No, they don't. Bloch doesn't consider me Moses."

"Bloch does." I am desperately trying to win the point even if I have to stretch the truth. But I'm not far off the mark. Although he works on Saturday, Bloch is in all other respects Orthodox, and Sacks frequently defers to him before making decisions on ritual procedure.

"Bloch, for instance, won't go along with me in considering the minyan complete with only nine men." Sacks pauses for a moment, then adds in a self-congratulatory way, "But he respects me enough to accept my dispensation, or maybe I should say my not criticizing him for working on shabes."

"It seems to me that you've just contradicted yourself. Before you were telling me that Bloch doesn't consider you a leader. Now you tell me that he does."

"Maybe. But I'm not as important to Intervale as you make out. Anyway, I don't like people placing so much burden on me. It's not fair. It interferes with my ability to function." Sacks's desire to leave the area surprises me. It seems so much out of character with the man as I know him. He is resolute almost to the point of arrogance in his determination to keep the shul alive. Several years earlier, when the shul was repeatedly vandalized, a local minister offered the use of his church for Intervale's

Saturday services, even promising "to cover the cross so you can have the service in the way you want to have it." Sacks adamantly refused: "We're not moving from this place. If we're not safe here, then no one will be safe anywhere! Besides, you walk down the street, you see a building and you say, 'This used to be a shul.' Then you come to another one and you say the same thing. You come to the Intervale Jewish Center and you don't say, 'This used to be a shul.' Do you know why? Because this still is a shul!"

Since the possibility of his leaving never occurred to me, I feel inclined to dismiss what he is telling me and attribute it to a passing mood. I reassure myself with the thought that the optimistic side I'm familiar with will soon reemerge. Why not give it a little prompting? I try to cheer him up by talking about the plans for the film. It is a mistake. I do not comprehend the depth of despair, so I have no way of anticipating Sacks's response. It is like that of a bull to a red flag.

"I don't know if there's going to be any film," Sacks thunders.

"What do you mean?" I respond, my voice betraying an element of terror.

"Now isn't the right time to make it."

"Why not?"

"Because first let's see what happens in the bakery." Why should the future of the bakery affect the making of a film? I let the matter drop. The statement is ridiculous. The best approach is to continue with the plans. Time will bring Sacks around.

The following week I arrive for Saturday-morning services and go over to shake hands with Sacks. He looks even more agitated than when I last saw him.

"Look, Jack. You have to call the whole thing off. Vito is now completely blind, he can't work. Jerry says he's going to close the bakery."

Stunned by this sudden shift to a more aggressive offense, I feign incomprehension. "I don't understand. What should I call off?"

"The film! Call Irving and tell him he has to change his plans. He can't make the film now." Sacks's adamant opposition is something I hadn't anticipated. I begin desperately looking for some sign of flexibility.

"Well, I don't think it's possible. The crew has already been booked. Everything is ready. I don't think we can cancel now."

"It's up to you. But you'll just have to make the film without me. I can't promise you anything."

"We can't do that. You're central to the film."

"I'm not. You said you're calling it *The Miracle of Intervale Avenue*, not *The Miracle of Moishe Sacks*!"

"Well, let's see what happens." I try to get the last word in and leav

THE MIRACLE OF INTERVALE AVENUE

the issue open. A quasi-maybe is preferrable to an absolute no. But even that token victory fades as Sacks warns, "I'm telling you, Jack. You're wasting your time. You better cancel!"

The following day, Irving calls from London. I fill him in on the details of the shooting schedule. Toward the end of the conversation he asks whether I've allotted time for a lengthy interview with Sacks. I explain the problem I'm having but predict that Sacks will cooperate once production gets under way.

I sincerely meant what I said. But my reassurance stemmed in part from a somewhat arrogant assumption that what I thought would be good for my informants, they would consider good, too. That, though, was a minor misconception. Far more serious was my complete misreading of Sacks's stubbornness and the underlying cause of his behavior. I assumed Sacks's mood was irrational. True, the "blood clot" was a fantasy, and Mr. Abraham was not nearly so ill as Sacks feared he might be. However, Sacks's concern that the bakery might close was no mere fantasy. Jerry was anxious to retire. Neither of the two sons had much interest in running the place; both had business interests on the side. Evelyn's deteriorating health made her less and less able to keep a tight grip on things. Consequently, supplies dwindled and bills went unpaid. Sacks waged a constant battle with family members waiting impatiently to rid themselves of a business they had no interest in maintaining. So Vito's forced retirement set off omens of imminent doom in Sacks's mind. For a man accustomed to seeing the world around him bend to his imaginings, fearsome fantasies are far more worrisome than the most troublesome reality.

The following week I arrive in shul to find Deborah, a black Jewish woman who has recently moved from the area, visiting with her nephew Seth. I am about to witness firsthand the miracle of Intervale Avenue. At the kiddush, Bloch announces that he is being transferred to his company's main office in Manhattan and that next week will probably be his last visit to the Intervale Jewish Center. I expect the announcement will be a further blow to Sacks's spirits. I examine Sacks's face carefully for any signs of distress. There are none. I probe. "How do you feel about losing another member of the minyan?" Sacks responds without missing a beat.

"Bloch is leaving, so now we have Seth here. That's Bloch's replacement. It was the same when Horowitz went into a home. We got someone else to take his place," he says, referring to Rashim. "Now we'll just need someone to make the kiddush over wine. That was Bloch's job, so someone else will have to do it now."

"How about Malachi?" I ask.

"Malachi? No. He only does Rosh Khodesh [the new lunar month]." I

offer several other names, but Sacks dismisses every one I come up with.
It dawns on me that he would like me to volunteer for the assignment.
Less the participant than the observer, I do no such thing. Sacks lets the
matter go. He is obviously in a better mood than he had been in last
week. When we finish the wine and cake, he asks me whether I plan to
accompany him to the bakery. The question is hardly necessary since
Saturday afternoons in the bakery have long been a part of my routine. I
look forward to the food and banter, deriving particular pleasure from a
sense they give me of belonging to a private men's club. I want to reestablish that intimacy, and I am also hoping for a truce in a battle of opposing
wills. Sacks picks up his white plastic shopping bag with its "I Love New
York" logo, the repository of his valuables—baker's tools, synagogue receipt book, bank books. I pick up mine containing a *New York Times* and
tape cassettes. I am vaguely aware that the shopping bag is an affectation
on my part, an attempt to be like him. We walk side by side, gradually
making our way past the rubble-strewn lots now lush with vegetation and
dotted here and there with a plywood *casita*, the shelters Puerto Ricans
use as clubhouses. I keep an eye out for an occasional rat scurrying across
our path. Sacks is mindful of the broken sidewalk, concerned that a fall
might permanently rob him of his cherished independence.

"Are you still worried about the bakery's future?" I ask.

"Not at all. Jerry has already ordered cake from Zaro [a major New York
bakery], and Zaro is only too glad to give him what he needs. I just tell
Jerry, 'Look. You're the boss. Whatever you decide, you decide.' The
three weeks I've spent on vacation haven't exactly done me any harm. I'm
feeling good. My leg doesn't hurt. How do I look?"

"You look fine." I am not lying either. He does look good. His face has
shed its previous pallor, the cheeks have regained some fleshiness, and
the shadows under his eyes are gone. Even his pace is brisk. His leg no
longer hurts. I, however, am the one in pain. Thinking about Sacks's
refusal to appear in the film is literally causing my head to throb. "I'll
need some aspirins when we reach the bakery."

"You don't have to wait until we reach the bakery. I have some with
me."

"You're a walking pharmacy."

"I don't know if I'm a pharmacy. Aspirin I carry because I read
somewhere that they prevent blood clots." Like many old people,
Sacks has a vast repertoire of tricks to cheat death. After an elderly
man was struck and killed by a car whose driver claimed not to have
seen him crossing the street, Sacks was quick to put into practice the
lesson learned from the incident: he began to wear a bright red
sweater and scarf. I take the aspirin, feeling protected for the moment

THE MIRACLE OF INTERVALE AVENUE

from a fifth-column assault from my circulatory system. Sacks resumes the conversation, referring to Bloch's departure and the unexpected appearance of a likely replacement.

"So your miracle is intact," I comment.

"Of course it's intact!" Sacks shoots back. The conversation stops while we concentrate on dodging traffic as we cross Westchester Avenue at Simpson Street. Behind us, just down the street, is the 41st Precinct, "Fort Apache." It leers at us like a green-eyed monster. The building has become somewhat of a shrine, drawing media pilgrims the world over: German, French, and Japanese film crews, and now the BBC. Above us, casting a serrated pattern of light and shadow on Westchester Boulevard, stands the archaic steel framework of the el. We wind our way through a maze of steel pillars and automobiles piloted aggressively by Latin males, greeted as we reach the opposite side of the street by a tinny *salsa*-blaring loudspeaker mounted over the door of a butcher shop. The shop window has a prominent display of skinned pigs. Like the music, they are unkind reminders of change. I sense that Sacks, too, has the urge to seek refuge from the blaring noise and the dead animals, so we move rapidly like ships at sea, our progress hampered now only by the need to chart a zigzag course through street vendors with mounds of plantains or avocados stacked in grocery baskets. We turn the corner and we are on Southern Boulevard. Home turf. Its many Jewish storeowners are a great reservoir of potential congregants for the shul. The street is dense with shoppers, but the sidewalk is very broad. We can walk side by side. I resume the conversation.

"You know something? Today even with my headache I was sitting in shul and thinking that the place in its own peculiar way is kind of beautiful."

"That too is a miracle!" Sacks responds.

"What do you mean?"

"I mean it's a miracle that you, even with your headache, can open your eyes and look at the building inside and see that it's beautiful. Isn't that a miracle?"

"I don't know. Maybe it is." I begin hoping that if Sacks is so freely dispensing miracles, perhaps he'll throw one my way and agree to participate in the film.

"Anyway," Sacks continues, "I was telling you about Jerry and the bakery. So I stopped worrying about it. Whatever happens, happens. In the meantime, I'm getting the dough ready for when we start baking. Tuesday we open for business. And let me tell you, Intervale isn't the only miracle. Vito showed up at the store yesterday. His eyesight improved."

THE MAKING OF A MIRACLE

"So he'll be back at work?"

"Maybe. And there's another miracle too. Remember José?"

"You mean the guy you lent a thousand dollars to so he could go to Mexico to see his wife and children?"

"Yeah. Well, he came back and gave me the thousand dollars. Imagine that. Would anybody believe that someone would go away for a year and return to give me back the money? Vito did the same thing. On the last day he worked, he gave me back the last installment on the money I loaned him for the mortgage on the home he bought in New Jersey."

Sacks's stories about money always have a hidden meaning to them. They are boastful reminders of his net worth, a sign of worldly success. But they are also reminders of another sort. Here he is needed. Vito's reappearance has apparently sparked some optimism in Sacks; the blindness may not be permanent after all. We jaywalk our way through the heavy traffic of Southern Boulevard, sneaking across to wind the corner onto Hunts Point Boulevard. Another block and I can spot the bakery looking like a way station before a wide vista of abandoned buildings. Once inside, we set to work preparing lunch. Mr. Abraham joins us. I do not mention the film.

The following day I again visit Sacks at the bakery. I pound away at the gray metal door with its thick glass window. An impenetrable barrier to the world outside, the door cannot distinguish friends from enemies. The noise of my pounding goes unheard. I continue to bang on the door, many times, harder now. Sacks is in the rear in a separate room. Now and then I can see him scurrying about, moving huge, encrusted wooden trays. Perhaps out of the corner of an eye he sees me, or perhaps the pounding has had its intended effect. Sacks heads to the door to let me in. I follow him past the cafeteria section with its torn red Naugahyde chairs and equally worn linoleum floor tiles. The floor changes from linoleum to ceramic as we approach his workbench in the rear, as if it were stripping down for serious work. I remove my camera and tape recorder from my bag while he resumes his activity. The room is dark. The lone fluorescent bulb works hard, its light absorbed rather than reflected by the gray-painted walls and tin ceiling. A huge skylight occupying a sizable chunk of the ceiling and a small window attached to the back wall are now covered over to prevent unwanted entry. Light does not penetrate, as if it, too, were suspect. The only relief from the dungeonlike atmosphere is a lighted clock that hangs crooked high on a wall. On its face in red and blue lettering is the name of a prominent kosher meat firm. Sacks looks perfectly at peace with himself, as if relaxing in his living room. A scratchy-sounding radio near the workbench is tuned to classical music. The rhythm and tempo of sonatas create an illusion of art rather than craft as

THE MIRACLE OF INTERVALE AVENUE

Sacks takes a gooey mound of dough from the refrigerator and rolls it out with an enormous rolling pin. He seems to dance as he cuts the flat slab into small squares less than a quarter-inch thick. When the slab is completely rolled out and cut up, he lifts a large plastic container of cheese, holds it close to his nose, then takes a deep breath: "I think it's still good."

"Well," I comment, "you'll find out for sure when your customers taste it."

"I haven't had any complaints yet."

"Maybe they never live to talk about it." Sacks laughs and as usual manages to get in the last word:

"You know, I've never heard of anyone dying from baking, only from not baking."

"You're talking about your father who, you once told me, lost his interest in working when his wife died?"

"That's right. She was his downfall. He loved her so much that after she died he didn't want to live anymore."

"Is that why you've never remarried?"

"I've never remarried because I'm married to the bakery, to my job. This is all I need. And besides, the right person hasn't come along. When I quit here and I'm ready to retire and if the right person comes along, I'll get married again." At his age, it seems to me he's pushing his luck. I keep the comment to myself.

As we talk, Sacks is busy cupping his hands to squeeze small gobs of cheese filling from between his palms, then tosses them like projectiles onto the squares of dough. When all the squares are filled, he takes the opposite ends of each and pulls them to stretch the dough, then folds each corner past the middle before proceeding to the next diagonal to form a neat miniature box. Baking is Sacks's link to the universe, his way, too, of praising through imitation his Creator. I watch, both fascinated and envious. Years earlier I had worked as a potter. Reminded, now, of the tactile pleasure, I ask Sacks if I can try to make a few. Sacks humors me but corrects my first try. I make another one. He casts a disapproving glance: "They'll see that, they'll think, 'The old man is slipping in his old age!' " To distract Sacks's attention from my "handiwork," I try to resume our conversation about his father:

"Did you learn to bake these from your father?"

"Yes. But I also learned several other varieties." Again Sacks casts menacing glances at my work. I remain undaunted. Sensing that Sacks is in a better frame of mind, and determined to divert his attention elsewhere, I decide to head the conversation gradually in the direction of the film and the benefits he might derive from it. I mention the question of legacy.

"Do you see your children as an extension of yourself?"

"What do you mean, an extension of myself?"

"I mean a legacy."

"Nothing I do will last permanently. The only thing that will last are my children and the contribution they make to the world. That's my legacy."

"What about the shul?" I ask, curious about the omission.

"The shul doesn't need me. The miracle of Intervale Avenue, as you call it, is a miracle without me. I'm not even sad or worried that Bloch is leaving. In a way I'm glad because he'll be able to be shomer shabes [observe the Sabbath] as he believes, and that's good. So we're not losing Bloch. God is gaining him. Anyway we have Seth, the young colored boy, to take his place. So God makes the miracle, not me!"

"You keep denying the fact that you have an impact on other people."

"I have an impact on other people? Well, maybe on those women who come there to shul. They come in and know nothing about the Torah, and on Sundays I go over the parshe and that way they learn something. I don't know if you want to call that a legacy. Da Vinci's *Mona Lisa* or Rodin's *The Thinker* or Michaelangelo's *Moses*, those are legacies. They are great works of art that people remember, that the world is better for."

Sacks's humility seems a little out of character, so I try to press the point.

"Don't you think that the film also might be a legacy?"

"No. The film is a financial venture and not a work of art."

"Well, then, how about my writing about you?"

"That may be a legacy of sorts, but not necessarily my legacy. You're writing about the story of the Intervale Jewish Center, not Moishe Sacks."

"So you don't see yourself as central to the story?"

"No!" Sacks barks back. I still do not believe that Sacks is determined to write himself out of his own story, to disavow the central role he plays in the miracle. Exasperated by a logic I cannot understand, I decide to stop beating around the bush. I want a commitment of cooperation from him. "Now that the issue is settled with the bakery, will you appear in the film?"

"We'll see," Sacks replies. "Remember, I'm not promising you anything." The answer is less reassuring than I had hoped for. But I accept it gratefully as a grudging nod to move ahead.

The following week Irving arrives. After attending services, he asks to make a short speech to the congregation. Sacks is in excellent spirits; he even advises Irving how to tailor his speech. "As you all know by now," Irving begins, "tomorrow we start filming. I just want you all to realize that we are doing this from our hearts . . ."

Sacks performs *tashlikh*
at the Bronx River.

Sacks and Bill Abraham have lunch in Sacks's bakery.

THE MAKING OF A MIRACLE

"Stop right there," Sacks interrupts. "That's a perfect closing line for a speech."

Irving ignores the advice, and continues: "I just want people to know that they should act as if we weren't there and to understand that if anything goes wrong, it's our fault and not theirs."

"Well," Sacks comments, "that was an O.K. ending, too. But the other one would have been better."

Although in most synagogues the penitential Slikhot service is held at midnight on the Saturday before Rosh Hashanah, few of Intervale's congregants will venture out at night, so their Slikhot service is held on Sunday morning. A series of prayers rather than a holy day, the service offers none of the proscriptions on filming or similar activities that accompany most Jewish holy days. We decide to make good use of the occasion. To give us ample time to film, Sacks announced that members of the congregation should show up promptly at 9:30 A.M., much earlier than their usual arrival time for services. I was very pleased by Sacks's announcement. I was particularly pleased by the levity of his mood. It seemed to bode well for the two weeks of shooting that lay ahead. Then, as if from out of nowhere, Sacks turns to me and Irving and, in an uncompromisingly firm way, adds:

"You can film me in the shul tomorrow but that's it. No way will I let you film me at home. I'll only let you in as far as the entrance to the front door downstairs. You can film Vito or the cops giving me a ride, but you can't come upstairs to the apartment. And no filming in the bakery."

Sacks's sudden shift away from the good-spirited mood catches me by surprise. The proviso he adds about filming him at home and in the bakery seems artificial. I suspect that it will be rather easy to ignore. I was already familiar with similar provisos regarding my photographing him at work in the bakery. In fact, the proviso was repeated years later, even after I had photographed him numerous times inside the bakery. Once, after I had entered the work area with my camera, Sacks told me straightaway, "You can stand here and talk as much as you want, but the moment you start taking pictures, I'm walking out of here." I explained why I needed the photographs. Sacks was adamant: "You take pictures in here and you're liable to get a rat in one of them!"

"I should be so lucky. I've been trying for years to get a picture of a rat at the Intervale Jewish Center. They refuse to pose."

"Well, the rats in here pose!" I had a good laugh at the absurdity of the image, and Sacks joined in. The humor reinforced a common bond. Sacks began to change into cleaner work clothes. Donning a fresh apron and hat, he asked, "Why aren't you taking any pictures?"

"You told me not to."

THE MIRACLE OF INTERVALE AVENUE

"So who's telling you not to now?"

In the course of time I learned to ignore the provisos, and Sacks learned to ignore the camera. I assumed that his refusal to be filmed in the bakery was simply for the record. He could deny his culpability in case of a reprimand from his boss. So for the moment, I choose to let the matter drop.

When the kiddush is over, Sacks and I begin our walk to the bakery while Irving as "producer" must double as driver of the van. On the way, Sacks reviews the merits of Irving's speech, repeating once again his suggestion that "from the heart" would be a better closing line.

"You seem to be getting excited about the film," I comment.

"Excited? No. What will be, will be. I have a very fatalistic attitude in general. When a young child dies in your arms after the nurse tells you the child is going to die unless you can get him to defecate and he can't, and your wife also dies in your arms after a heart attack, at first you say, 'Why me?' Then after a few minutes you accept it." A typical Sacksism: fierce resilience in the face of adversity. Little wonder I respect him. But that continuing morbidity, what should I make of it? Will his fatalism work in our favor or against us? I don't know. At the bakery, Sacks delights us with stories of his past. The new year is approaching and his reminiscences are closely honed to memories of new years past. The food and banter put us all in a relaxed mood. Sacks seems pliable enough, although he does not give a firm commitment to participate beyond tomorrow's shooting. Soon it is time for us to leave. The film crew is about to arrive, and Irving and I are off to meet them. Heading toward the airport, we recount some of Sacks's anecdotes, wondering as we do which of them will find their way into the film.

The following day, Sunday, we begin to film. Sacks repeats his previous condition: he is making himself available to us for that day only; a fair compromise by his reckoning. For the rest we are on our own. We shoot a sequence of Dave opening the shul. As we film, other congregants begin to arrive, and Irving, the producer, has the unenviable task of trying to keep a cantankerous group of elderly Jews outside so they will enter one by one; the sequence could serve as a way to introduce the various members of the congregation. Suddenly, the calm entry scene is transformed into bedlam as people burst through the door and fall on top of one another in a mad panic to get downstairs. Lena is yelling, "They're shooting! They're shooting!" I assume she is referring to the camera crew, but the rush of frightened, screaming people and the panic in their voices tells me something else. A moment later a pudgy man in his late twenties wearing cut-off blue jeans and a white T-shirt, his leg oozing blood, lunges through the entrance, stops for a moment to peek through the crack of the door that he is clutching like a shield to see if he is still being pursued, then hobbles madly through the sanctuary and flees out the rear into the yard, where he falls to the ground, unable to move. The man had been shot several times through his left thigh, apparently, as we learn later, a warning about passing information to the police on drug dealing. I am completely bewildered by the incident. Well trained in the do's and don't's of documentary filming, the crew keeps the film rolling throughout. I join them outside the rear exit of the shul to interview the wounded man.

"Who shot you?" I ask.

"Four guys in a gang."

"Why'd they shoot you?"

"It's a long story." I am sure it is, but I let the matter drop. In considerable pain, the man is in no mood to talk. When the ambulance arrives, I head to the front of the shul, where a crowd of neighborhood people has gathered. Awed spectators to a drama of life and death, they linger to consider events so engrossing that they need to be reviewed again and again. A pool of blood dominates the entrance to the shul. Its message is as transparent as a flashing neon light on a cheap motel. The smell of blood is overwhelming. I have all I can do to stop from vomiting. I accompany the ambulance driver to help him carry the stretcher. His assistant is busy elsewhere. Sacks has steered him inside the shul to examine Rose Cutler, who has a rag pressed to her neck. She had been nicked by a ricocheted bullet, but she prefers to be left alone:

"I'm not going to no hospital. I don't need no hospital. Look, even the blood it doesn't come. I'll be all right."

Sacks convinces her to let the medic examine her, then apply a bandage to the wound. It was typical of the tenacity of these people. Hospitals are stages en route to nursing homes. They avoid them until severe illness or infirmity leaves no choice.

Later, when the police, paramedics, and various sleazy neighborhood types who had wandered inside the shul leave, Sacks goes to the bima. He is Moses now, the leader who guides his people through the Sinai wilderness. Sacks explains to the congregation that the synagogue is not only a holy place but it's also like the towns that Moses designated as places of refuge:

"Even a non-Jew knows it's a place of refuge. The man was shot and he came into the synagogue for safety. I can assure you that if a non-Jew knows this is a place of refuge, that is exactly what we have known all these years. Anyway, the excitement is good for you. It's good for your blood pressure. Nobody jumped up. We're used to it."

Sacks is in good humor. He seems to enjoy performing before the camera. He continues, still exuberant, while we film a sequence during which his son and daughter-in-law arrive to give him his birthday present, a hat. Sacks tries the hat on. It's too big and it sinks until it drowns his ears. "That's all right," Sacks announces. "By the end of the day my head will have swelled enough so the hat will fit." Later the bus arrives to take the congregation for an outing to the Plainview Jewish Center. On the bus he continues playing to the camera: he is funny and charming. At the outing he is even more flamboyant. Asked by the hosts to give his usual review of the weekly Torah reading, Sacks begins to orate much like a fire-and-brimstone preacher. His mood, though, is already changing. The humor is gone. As we prepare to leave, the film crew asks the bus driver to delay until they finish filming some cutaways for the leaving scene. Concerned with his own work schedule, Sacks becomes increasingly agitated by the delay. When we arrive in the Bronx and he steps off the bus, he advises us that he has done for the film all he intends doing: "That's it. I've given you everything I'm going to give you. You can forget about filming in the bakery or in my home. I got work to do now. I've got a lot to do to get ready for Rosh Hashanah. The rest you'll have to get from someone else, not from me. O.K.?"

"There is no one else to get it from," I reply. "Anyway, right now we're all tired. We'll fight this out tomorrow."

"There's nothing to talk about tomorrow. This is it." I try to argue, but it's no use. "The bakery is off limits. Jerry and Evelyn are against any filming in the bakery," he insists. "They're looking to sell the place and they don't want any publicity, particularly not something that might be seen by the health department."

He refuses to budge from his position. I try joking with him, hoping I can charm him out of his obstinacy. That doesn't work. I try reason: "Well, if the bakery is a problem, then we'll film after work on a Sunday or someplace else."

"There's no place else. You're not filming inside my apartment because I've had more leaks than Noah and I don't want anyone to see how I live." When his son offers the use of his own apartment in Queens, Sacks still refuses. Uncertain how to get around the obstacles Sacks is throwing at us, we decide that familiarity might breed some form of acquiescence, however grudging. It's a technique I've used before, so I have reason to believe it will work now. The front of the bakery is a self-service Jewish-style delicatessen. The only restaurant of its kind in the area, when it opens for business at 3:30 A.M., the place is like neutral territory in a war zone. Cops, muggers, sanitation workers, truckers, pimps, and prostitutes all line up for fresh danish and hot coffee. We figure we will have little problem blending in. The following day we arrive at the bakery for lunch. Bad luck. Sacks is in the front area talking to a customer. As soon as he sees us, he begins to scream loud enough for Jerry and Evelyn, who are sitting close by, to hear: "You're not filming inside the bakery!" I explain that we have come only to eat lunch, but Sacks keeps shouting and leaves the eating area to shut himself off in his private domain—the back room.

The episode leaves a pall upon the film crew. I am utterly bewildered, unable to explain Sacks's behavior, and even worse, I feel completely unable to change it. Mercifully, my sense of frustration is spared by a shooting schedule that channels our efforts for the next few days into other scenes in the film. But in the back of my mind remains the nagging thought that Sacks's obstinacy might hold through the film crew's entire two-week stay. I begin a furious campaign to line people up on our side, to bring pressure on Sacks. Everyone is reassuring: the cops from the 41st Precinct promise, "We'll talk to him." Other members of the congregation, including Mr. Abraham, say, "Give him time. He'll come around. He's just got his hands full now with what's going on in the bakery." Mrs. Miroff: "He left me the keys to his apartment, so the painter can get in to fix it up. Then he'll let you take pictures." Jerry, his boss: "It's my wife who doesn't want you to film. She leaves at three P.M. After that, do what you want." Sacks's son and daughter-in-law: "We'll talk to him." Then, later in the week: "We'll keep trying, but there's a limit to what we can do." The strategy is a dismal failure: it only challenges him to match his obstinacy against our pressure. Mountains are easier to move. For Sacks to concede would be an acknowledgment of weakness.

Strangely enough, Sacks's ambivalence is evident throughout. About a week into the filming we become desperate for a solution. We walk into the bakery and set the camera on the table, pointing at the counter area where Sacks often meanders. We order lunch. The cameraman can film while we eat, his head far enough from the viewfinder not to generate suspicion. Sacks comes out from the work area and sits down in the center of the room, right in the camera's line of vision. He acts as if he normally sits there to rest (although he does not), and as friends enter the bakery he motions them to join him at the table. Never once does he look directly at the camera or acknowledge our presence. The following day, still discussing his refusal to be filmed, he comments that he knew perfectly well that we were filming. A few days later, on Saturday, he unexpectedly allows us to film him inside the bakery (the bakery is closed on weekends). We are having lunch with him, ostensibly to discuss the problem his refusal to be filmed poses for us. Suddenly he comments:

"So who's stopping you from filming now?"

"You don't mind if we film now?" I ask, stunned.

"No." We whip out the camera, tape recorder, and lights. I ask questions. Sacks responds. The crew films. But it's all mechanical. It doesn't feel right. Sacks's affable mood slips away, a hopeful spark that lights no fire. The interview is over as unexpectedly as it began.

Toward the end of the two weeks, just after another futile round of bargaining in the bakery, Sacks calls me aside and asks me to deliver a message to a social worker assigned by the Jewish Allied Services for the Aged. Sacks had received a phone call that Lena Michaels, a black member of the congregation, was dying and friends of hers were concerned that she receive proper Jewish burial. Extremely busy, Sacks asks whether I would pass the message on. I promise to do so. The conversation feels like a truce to care for the wounded and bury the dead. But it serves, I think, as a reminder to both of us that our battle is quite trivial in the face of life's larger drama. A day or so later, Sacks mysteriously relents and agrees that we can film him just before closing time in the bakery. "But for one hour only. After that I'm throwing you out whether you got what you need or not!" At any rate, the one hour inside the bakery stretches into two. This time there is real magic. Sacks busies himself at the workbench, rolling out dough and simultaneously fielding questions. This is his show now. The storyteller has reemerged, and he is playing to an audience, wooing, teaching, scolding.

Although the crisis passed once Sacks allowed us to film him at work, the incident had created a serious enough breach in our relationship to cause him to ask me ten days later, when the film crew had already returned to England, whether I was still mad at him and whether I would keep coming on Saturday. I assured him that I had every intention to continue coming. The truth of the matter is that I was never angry at Sacks. I felt bewildered and somewhat humiliated by the futility of my efforts. Unlike the film crew, though, I saw Sacks less as a culprit than as a mysterious and enigmatic figure who in the end would, as in fact he did, give in.

Sacks's concern that I remain in the minyan may have had a good deal to do with his eventual participation in the film. It also had a lot to do with my willingness to push him into participating. After three years of my attending services on a regular basis, neither Sacks nor I believed that I kept coming back for purely professional reasons. In fact it was Sacks who suggested without my prompting that I come for my own personal reasons: "As an intelligent person you recognize your own mortality just like the old people," he said. "So you feel compelled to participate in the shul sort of as a way of making your peace with God."

There is more than a grain of truth in Sacks's statement. I had long ago gathered enough information about the service. Most of the information I still needed could be learned during occasional visits to Sacks's bakery or through telephone interviews. I continued attending services because I still enjoyed the company of various congregants long after I stopped needing them for information. So while, as an anthropologist, I might have had reservations about interfering in the life of an informant, pressuring him to do what he so adamantly refused to do, it wasn't the anthropologist who pressured: it was the part of me that felt like "family." I felt justified in crossing certain bounds of professional propriety since I felt like I was apprenticing in the "family business" (Sacks's speciality) of finagling God, Jewish relief organizations, and city agencies. There are, of course, good reasons for me to have felt like family here, beyond the bounds of the normal informant/anthropologist relationship. Elderly people, particularly when they share the same ethnic background, readily project a family relationship onto a young person and vice versa. They expect certain favors and make certain demands that they would be less inclined to make with someone from another ethnic background.

But I think my relationship went beyond that, and its particular quality stems from the fact that in the course of this project I began to see the anthropological enterprise as an apprenticeship with another culture. More than just accumulating knowledge, it involves the internalization of that information so that the anthropologist learns to think like his informants and thereby becomes an interpreter—a conduit for knowledge to pass between cultures. Particularly when groups are disappearing, though, the anthropologist must assume the role not only of conduit but also of repository. His knowledge may be the only surviving trace of a culture. And this, I felt, was precisely the case here in my relationship with the Intervale community. Consequently, there developed a certain blurring of identities, particularly on my part—so much so that I sometimes saw myself as Sacks. What I did not understand at the time, though, was that the relationship was only partly reciprocated: when Sacks assumed my role, he generally had a hidden agenda. During filming, for example, Sacks refused to explain the "miracle" of Intervale Avenue in his usual fashion: that God guaranteed the minyan despite the deaths or departure from the neighborhood of individual congregants. He insisted now that "there is no such thing as miracles. The synagogue serves the needs of each person who comes there." Sacks was playing anthropologist. Indeed, he had begun to attribute the idea of the "miracle" to me, since I had used the word in the title of an article about the shul. This seemed like a peculiar disavowal on his part, but upon reflection, I believe there was considerable motive here, although hidden perhaps, like a puppeteer pulling strings. By attributing his thoughts to me and by assuming the role of the outside observer, Sacks had in effect switched roles with me. Right at the outset, when he made it clear that he would not participate in the film, Sacks suggested that it should be me whom the director interview, since "Jack has all the information anyway." But this was not the only case of Sacks's asserting the ambiguity of our roles. Eight months later, a few days before a sneak preview of the film in New York, I asked Sacks what he planned to say to the audience when he got up to speak.

"That's easy," he answered. "I'll just tell them the story of the Khofets Khayim who was traveling from town to town with a *balegule* [coachman]. After hearing the Khofets Khayim give the same speech in town after town, the balegule says to him: 'You know, what you do isn't so hard. At the next town let me do what you do and you be the balegule.' So they switch places. When they come to the town, someone comes to the 'Khofets Khayim' and asks him a very difficult question on the Talmud. The 'Khofets Khayim' has no idea how to answer the question. So he thinks for a moment, then he answers the man, 'You know, that question is so easy that I won't even bother with it. I'll just let this simple coachman over here answer it.' So you see, if anyone asks me something I can't answer, I'll just tell them it's too simple for me to bother with and I'll tell them they should ask you."

That night, when I was asked to say a few words following the screening, I stole Sacks's lines from him. I told the audience the same story Sacks had told me, and then I introduced him as the simple coachman. Never one to be upstaged, Sacks later told me that he knew I would steal his lines and that's why he told me the story. So here was the puppeteer again. And I was just another of his marionettes.

The story of the coachman continues to have a certain appeal to me, perhaps because I feel myself acting out the coachman character through my relationship with Sacks. After all, I am the one who drives Sacks out of his own environment onto film or the printed page. And I suppose I envy him, too: his knowledge of rabbinic lore, his sense of completeness, and his satisfaction in the self-contained world of Moshman's bakery. So I have a "secret" longing to become Sacks, that is, to be a wise old Jew and a master craftsman.

For his part, Sacks probably has a longing to be young. He certainly has a desire to be a teacher (he was unable to pass the entrance exam on account of his "Lithuanian" accent). And I suppose, just like the Khofets Khayim, who agreed to make the switch, he probably has a secret yearning to determine his own fate entirely unaided by the coachman/anthropologist. But more than vanity is at work in Sacks's assuming the role of director/writer/anthropologist. As my chief informant, it is through his eyes that all of my research on the Intervale Jewish Center is filtered.

THE MAKING OF A MIRACLE

Moreover, the bulk of my information comes directly from him during our Saturday-afternoon feasts.

The closer my relationship with Sacks became, the more my observations took on the quality of what Clifford Geertz calls "looking over the shoulder" to jot down what he had to say.[1] This was not something I had to do on the sly. Sacks was not only aware of what I was doing; he began to save tidbits of information for me. But in the course of time, a more subtle and unspoken agreement arose between us, particularly after Sacks first saw me lecture and read my articles about the shul. He began to take a more direct role in gathering information and making sense out of it. So the line between us became in time increasingly thin.

But the blurring of identities is only a phase of ethnographic research. Empathy can get you only so far; distance and the reemergence of the self are vital, too.[2] The struggle with Sacks speaks to a more general point in the relationship between chief informant and anthropologist: through the conscious articulation of two distinct and often mutually contradictory worldviews, ethnography has the quality of a dialogue between two discrete cultural universes. Indeed, the breakdown within our relationship was a necessary reminder that the common identity I imagined existing between us is an ethnographer's fantasy: the agendas of informant and anthropologist can never be entirely the same.

Still, there is more here than just the personal dynamic of an ethnographer/informant relationship. There were after all numerous instances when our respective agendas were very much in sync. Sacks needed me for the minyan and I needed him to answer questions. Moreover, my presence within the community contributed something to Sacks's (and the others') self-esteem. It gave them a sense, to use Richard Schechner's words, that "someone else is interested, is listening."[3] Since old people need the life review as a way of establishing and reaffirming the meaning of their lives,[4] the questions that encouraged Sacks and the others to be reflexive served the community well. Why were our respective agendas out of sync now? Did Sacks have an agenda during the making of the film, or was his behavior mere fist-flailing?

What becomes increasingly clear in reviewing these events is that the stories people fabricate to impute meaning and order to their lives sometimes falter. If Sacks's grueling work pace despite his advanced age represents a heroic conquest of death, being deprived of the opportunity to work through the possible closing of the bakery is a rather clear symbol of the futility of that struggle. So Sacks's difficult behavior at the time represents a momentary disavowal of a narcissistic belief that he had control over his own life, that he could conquer death. And it hinted perhaps that even his miracle minyan might be on the verge of tottering. Sacks re-

sponded by seeking some way of restoring his sense of control. Consequently, the more we pressured, the more stubborn he became. At the
same time, the problems he caused for us were a way of lashing out, of
generalizing what to him was a specific problem that he alone faced.
Sacks's principal problem was the limitation old age imposed upon him. If
the bakery closed, he would have a hard time finding comparable employ-
ment. Even if he could find work, he would lose the status he enjoyed as
the man who almost single-handedly produced Moshman's baked goods.
Opening up his own shop was out of the question. Although he had the
funds to do it, he could feel his strength ebbing. "Besides," as Sacks once
explained, "it's one thing to work in a place and take on some of the
responsibility of running it. It's another thing to own the place and have
all the responsibility. I'm too old for that."

The situation with the bakery brought Sacks face to face with the
chilling realization that his options were limited. His ability to affect the
world around him was decreasing. The film crew, by comparison, was full
of vigor and in good health. Its members, for the most part, were coming
into their own as successful directors, cameramen, soundmen, and pro-
ducers. The world to them was limitless. So they would take what they
needed from Sacks and then move on in life. By behaving the way he did
and setting irrational limits, Sacks forced the film crew to experience life
the way he was experiencing it—as limited. For a brief two weeks, we
were all old people. We were all groping for a way to deal with the
unfairness of life's circumstances. And since the crew would return to
London at the end of their two-week stay, time became like a grim
reaper, threatening to cheat us of what we had set out to make. The whole
situation had the quality of a metaphor for the eternal struggle within
each of us between the will to live and the need to accommodate to the
inevitability of death.

But there is another level here, one in which the narcissistic belief in
omnipotence is not at all denied, but rather is confirmed. By denying that
the "miracle of Intervale Avenue" is the "miracle of Moishe Sacks," Sacks
was actually affirming and proving that very fact. He not only identified
himself as the central character, without whom there could be no "miracle," but also by extension staked his claim to being the creator of the
film. By refusing to participate, he was implicitly directing the film. And
when he finally agreed to take part, it was entirely on his terms, leaving
us to wonder whether he might suddenly change his mind or throw us
out. Sacks had effectively wrested control of a very complex situation, and
it probably helped restore his overall sense of power.

Nor is Sacks's assertion of control limited to the making of the film.
Sometimes in our relationship I have felt a certain disloyalty on his part,

using the advent of a journalist or photographer assigned to do a story on the shul to drive home the fact that whereas he is crucial to the story, I am expendable. The truth is, when Sacks comments that a poorly written article about the shul has some good lines in it—the ones in quotes (meaning his own)—he is both vain and correct. His is the only indispensable role. As storyteller or mythmaker for the community, he literally fashions through his imaginings a world of refuge for those around him. As storyteller, Sacks gives these people a place to come to and be needed; their individual eccentricities are integral parts of the miracle. Without them there would be no miracle, just as without Sacks there could be no myth of a miracle. In Sacks's mind I, too, am part of the miracle. Sacks repeatedly denies that he invented the phrase "the miracle of Intervale Avenue." By attributing the term "miracle" to me, Sacks is legitimizing its existence: "It's not a miracle. It's scientifically verifiable. In all the time you've been here, hasn't there always been someone new to take the place of a man who leaves the minyan?" But by denying authorship of his own creation, Sacks is actually "mystifying" it—giving it greater credence as a miracle. Therefore, I play a critical role in the legitimization and mystification of Sacks's myth. In that sense, my relationship with him is totally reciprocal.

I have remained at Intervale these many years to verify Sacks's miracle. I also wanted to see what would happen to the "miracle" as congregants die or leave the community. How would Sacks respond to a situation that mocks his peculiar view of reality? I discovered that the mockery is reversed: Sacks's fertile imagination generally got the better of reality. So I have come to actually believe in his miracle—not so much as a miracle but as part and parcel of Sacks's overall worldview, or what Erikson calls wisdom—the balance in old age between despair and hope.[5] The real miracle is of old people believing they can take control of their own lives and make things happen, that amuno (faith), as Sacks maintains, can indeed "make the miracle." Sacks's genius does not simply lie in his ability to overcome despair. It emanates rather from his ability to convince others to think like him, to believe in the same miracles, and in that way to extend one man's view of the world outward, to encompass an ever-widening circle of people. In the final analysis, this may well have been at the root of Sacks's capitulation. Despite his protests, he was and still remains captive to his own miracle. Myths, once created, do not easily shatter. Instead, they take on lives of their own, their credibility confirmed and enhanced by the number of their adherents. Perhaps it was his continuing faith in the miracle that whittled away despair and forced him to return to the fold. Or perhaps it was simply his desire to reassert a sense of control. For storytelling is the only enduring source of his or of any person's power. And for a man who is neither politically powerful, wealthy, nor in his prime physically, to be able to exert so much control over his surroundings, particularly over such bleak surroundings, could indeed be "the miracle of Intervale Avenue."

Nine months after the film was finished, I decided I would go to London for the premiere. My flight was on a Saturday night, so I was able to spend the early part of the day at Intervale.

During the kiddush, Sacks and I discuss my itinerary. While we talk, I manage to eat most of the pieces of chocolate babka, and I suspect that Sacks sees that as a sign that when I return from London I will continue to attend the minyan. When the plate is empty, I get up to leave. As I do, Sacks asks me about the plans for the premiere.

"I'm not sure what Irving's planning, although he did ask me to say a few words to the audience."

"Have you decided yet what you're going to say, or will you do like I do, be extemporaneous?"

"Actually I meant to talk to you about it. What do you think I should say?"

"Say what you think at the time. I told you I do things extemporaneously."

"Yes, but even when you speak extemporaneously, you have some idea of what you plan to say."

"That's true."

"Well, if *you* went to London, what do you think you would say?"

"I'll tell you what you can say. Tell them that we should all thank God that we have lived to see this day."

"You mean I should say the prayer *shekhiyanu*?"

"Yes. Say shekhiyanu."

"I will." I shake hands with everyone and wish them a *gut shabes*. When I shake Sacks's hand, he says:

"Jack, I want you to have a good time in London. But don't have such a good time that you forget about us. So drop us a line from time to time. Not too often, though. Otherwise we'll think that you're having a terrible time and you spend all day in your room writing letters."

"I'll write. And I promise not to write too often." I head to the stairs. Before I reach them Sacks calls out:

"And one more thing. When you talk to the audience, remember to tell them that in case any of them is ever in New York, we're saving a place for them here at the Intervale Jewish Center."

·8·

THE MIRACLE OF
INTERVALE AVENUE

In his essay "Conditions and Limits of Autobiography," Georges Gusdorf argues that the prerogative of autobiography consists in showing us "not the objective stages of a career . . . but that it reveals instead the effort of a creator to give the meaning of his own mythic tale."[1] Ethnography is very much like the study of autobiography; it seeks to decipher the story or mythic tale a people tells about its collective life. Indeed, mythic tales are of enormous significance for the interpretation of cultures. They reflect "group fantasies" (to borrow a term from psychohistorians) governing much of human behavior and beliefs.[2]

But where do mythic tales come from? Are they a passed-down heritage or are they created anew in each generation? The answer is: both. Every age experiences tradition as an immutable thing that is ever in danger of dissipating (inheritors of a tradition never think they have quite the thing their ancestors did). At the same time, each generation brings to culture a unique historical context and its own range of extraordinary individuals. There is a dialectic here between culture as given and culture as created. Although culture is always changing, the changes may occur without conscious effort, or they make take place through the intervention of master storytellers who assemble the group's mythic tales and reinvigorate them by identifying and asserting the timeless values they contain.

THE MIRACLE OF INTERVALE AVENUE

Despite his frequent denials, the miracle of Intervale Avenue is indeed the miracle of Moishe Sacks. It is his mythic tale, a story that reveals his passionate need to create out of the disparate events of the surrounding world an overall structure within which his life and the lives of those connected to him are infused with meaning. But it also reveals the power of a man's imagination and, by actively asserting itself, its ability to substantially sculpt reality.

The tale begins in the story of his own life, where the events and personages who emerge are foils rather than essential elements in the formation of personality. Sacks's life story reads like an unfolding of inherent talent and ingenuity rather than a gradual process of learning and mastering the various domains of adult knowledge, as if he were both father and mother to himself and those around him. His bosses at the bakery appear in his narratives as little more than children who cower in the face of his greater prowess; he provides extra income for some of the actors within the Intervale drama; and he sees to the needs of all for the stimulation of special foods and entertainment. Convinced as he is that his craft is both a calling and a chance to make his mark on the world, his identity is inseparable from his work. Indeed, Sacks seems to perceive the entire world as a bakery: people and circumstances are raw ingredients waiting to be shaped and molded by his hands. At the same time, that power to create generates a certain belief in his own sleights of hand to magically transform raw material into finished products. For him there is something cosmic in that act, analogous to God's creation of order out of chaos at the dawn of creation.

If there is any one place in which Sacks has been given a free hand to sculpt reality outside of the bakery, it is inside the Intervale Jewish Center. Consequently his strategy is to use his own intellectual resources, his astute sense of psychology, and his expertise in rabbinic tradition to assemble a Jewish congregation out of an assemblage of diverse people. Sacks's efforts demonstrate his resilience and fierce determination to combat death. But they also show his skills at leadership. In order to maintain the minyan, Sacks must go to extraordinary lengths, even inventing ways to twist religious law. If, for example, there are nine men for services, Sacks does what is common practice in other synagogues with a dwindling minyan: the Ark is opened and God is invited to stand in as the tenth man. If there are fewer than nine, Sacks sometimes suggests ways of counting a minyan that have no precedent in rabbinic rulings. Recognizing the extreme differences in religious observance of members of the congregation, though, Sacks must balance his ability to find such rationales with the realization that his finagling might prove too extreme for some. Although Sacks and Malachi are able to strike a balance between their respective views, other divisions over belief within the congregation are more complicated. Only careful diplomacy prevents congregants from viciously turning on one another for not living up to their own individual ideals of what constitutes a Jewish congregation. Fortunately for Intervale, Sacks styles himself a diplomat—a cross between his namesake Moses and a more contemporary role model, Henry Kissinger. Diplomacy, though, is not the only key to Sacks's success. Much of it stems from his role within the congregation as godfather and rebbe, addressing both their physical and spiritual needs in struggling with old age. As godfather, Sacks is the community's broker to the outside world. He sees that relief organizations provide basic services, while at the same time he supplies a rationale for accepting charity that enhances rather than diminishes congregants' pride by confirming the reciprocal relationship between donor and recipient.

As rebbe, Sacks is the community's intercessor before God: standing on the bima, he pleads their cases and assures individuals that their prayers have been heard; he recites the memorial prayers and enables congregants to faithfully fulfill their obligations to the dead; and, in a way that is reminiscent of hasidic tales, it is Sacks who finds higher spiritual meaning in the eccentric behavior of various congregants. Sam, busy sweeping the shul or banging a nail into the Ark, is, according to Sacks, praying to God in his own unique and perfectly acceptable way. Moreover, Sacks casts individuals who are perhaps too eccentric to play anything more than a marginal role in any other shul, as central figures in Intervale's ritual. Dave, the irreverent trickster at the very margin of acceptability as a congregant, has become through Sacks's prompting Intervale's kaddish-sayer, the reciter of a prayer that joins congregants to their deceased loved ones and brings them to the shul. "Even a whistle from Dave, God listens to. He means it. It's from the heart." Even the decrepit condition of the Intervale Jewish Center takes on, through Sacks's storytelling, a degree of sacredness. Reflecting on the *kines* (prayers of lamentation) recited on Tisha be-Av in commemoration of the destruction of the Temple in Jerusalem, Sacks comments:

"When the Temple was destroyed, all the people were standing around and crying. As they watched they saw a red fox come out of the ruins. Jeremiah was standing there, and when he saw the red fox, instead of crying he began to laugh with joy. All the people asked how he could laugh at seeing an animal in the ruins of the Temple. And Jeremiah answered that seeing the red fox proved the prophesy that one day the Temple would be destroyed and only wild animals would inhabit its ruins. If that prophesy came true, he was now certain that the other prophesies would also come true and that one day the Temple would be rebuilt.

"So we don't have to go to the ruins of the Temple in Jerusalem. We can look right here at the Intervale Jewish Center to see the prophesy come true. We go to daven, and sure enough we see a furry animal or two come out from where it's hiding in the ruins here."

The mechanism Sacks uses to impute such meanings into behavior is his tendency to see existence as an ongoing dialogue between man and God. The Bible for Sacks is not a historical text of one-time events; it is a narrative of paradigmatic events repeated constantly in the lives of people. Dave and other peculiar participants in the shul, including various non-Jews or quasi-Jews, are analogous in Sacks's eyes to the rabble, the so-called mixed multitude that Moses led out of Egypt. Seen in that light, the Intervale minyan is like a reenactment of the birth of a people on its journey through the Sinai. Indeed, it is here where Sacks's playful musings as storyteller take root and blossom. By dispensing altogether with the divisions separating biblical time from the present, Sacks continually blends the two into a single fabric in which the threads of yesterday are so tightly interwoven with those of today that the past is informed by the day-to-day events of the present (Jacob, according to Sacks, was mugged by an angel) and the present assumes some of the biblical aura. There is even some of that in Sacks's insistence that the shul be painted and the roof be repaired:

"When the Messiah comes, all of the synagogues will pick themselves up and be transported to Jerusalem. I want this place to look nice, and besides, we shouldn't have leaks during the rainy season there."

Consequently, congregants are left with a sense that at the very moment when they are utterly vulnerable to physical attack and even more insidiously to illness from within, they can take comfort in a belief that they have entered into a unique partnership with God. "You see where the piece of plaster fell from the ceiling?" Zelda asks, pointing to a gaping hole in the ceiling. "Well, it didn't fall while anyone was inside the shul. It waited until no one was around to get hurt. You see, God protects us."

As a cultural system, Intervale is faced with the task of responding to the biological limits of human existence. But as a community of elderly people, the needs individuals have are twofold: one is to live out their final years with a sense of dignity; the other is to gain reassurance that death is not oblivion. The belief in the miracle, that despite the departure of individual congregants the minyan will continue, casts congregants' lives in a similar mold as those of their biblical forebears; at the same time it removes the threat of oblivion and affirms the triumph of life over death. In a peculiarly paradoxical way, the Intervale minyan is death's nemesis. Congregants assemble each Saturday, for the most part, because of their desire to recite the memorial prayers: death gives life to this community.

If the miracle is a group project, a collective protest against the tyranny of death, there are at the same time individual protests carried out by each and every congregant. Indeed, for all, merely choosing to remain in the South Bronx, rejecting their children's offer to house them or shunning homes for the aged, is a personal protest against passivity. Sam, for example, made the following comments after listening to Horowitz's description of the old-age home he had entered: "There everything is regimented. They put name tags on their clothes. They tell them when they can go out and when they have to have their meals. That's not for me. It's like being in the army."

Perhaps the loudest of these protests is the one made by Mrs. Miroff, a woman who abhors any association to death. Mrs. Miroff literally flaunts her skills at managing forces that most people would find wild and destructive—the street people who hang around her shop. Controlling them confirms her sense of being in charge at the very time when old age threatens to deprive her of the strength and stamina to affect the world around her. For all congregants, remaining in the South Bronx and surviving where most New Yorkers fear to tread offer a sense of personal conquest over that dark, relentless force within them called aging that threatens to rob them of independence and ultimately of life itself. At the same time, surviving in the Bronx enhances their pride: it allows them to feel special, to attain a level of heroism by demonstrating defiance in the face of death.

But the conquest of death is only one factor keeping these people here. Because advanced age in American culture is generally associated with a gradual disengagement from the social and economic spheres of life, old people are considered somewhat superfluous. Ceding power, they also lose status. As one woman explained to me: "My daughter would like me to move in with her. But I don't want to, even though she has a nice house in the suburbs with plenty of extra room. You see, I'll never forget the time I went there to visit and one of my grandchildren saw me through the living room window. He went running to tell everyone, 'Guess who's coming? Grandma's coming!' He was so excited. Now, if I lived there, that wouldn't happen. So you see, I like to be like a guest."

Indeed, the elderly frequently become burdens to family members, particularly so when they join their children in single-family surburban homes. Without public transportation and separated from their friends, they are often unable to establish a network of peers for support and friendship. As Mrs. Miroff explains, "My son tells me he's holding a room for me in his house anytime I want to move in. I tell him I don't want it.

THE MIRACLE OF INTERVALE AVENUE

When I go there, all day long I'm alone. The children are in school. My son and his wife go to work. So I sit in the yard and hear the dog bark. We got dogs in the Bronx, too."

Many congregants, Mrs. Miroff included, consider their work a way to bring leverage in life. Work for them is an organizing principle that creates a sense of order out of chaos: it is a nexus point between them and the universe. Mrs. Miroff's *axis mundi* is sewing; Sacks's is baking; Dave's is sign painting; Sam's is carpentering. These are more like callings than trades. They are symbols, too, of independence and self-assertion as mature human beings. Little wonder that they are almost always reluctant to give them up, that they see their continued survival intricately bound to their continuing to perform some form of work. As Mrs. Miroff put it, "When my machine goes, I go." (She keeps a spare machine hidden in her bedroom, "just in case.") Indeed, for Mrs. Miroff and Sacks, their places of work have a good deal to do with why they remain in the area. In Mrs. Miroff's words, "Here on my Social Security check I have a four-room apartment and a separate tailor shop. If I moved somewhere else, I couldn't afford to keep a shop. All day long to be locked up in a one-room apartment is like to be in a grave."

Despite congregants' fierce resistance to change and their determination to endure, they are forced to recognize the nearness of death: they observe the constant diminution of the congregation, and they must cope daily with the gradual attrition of their physical selves. They respond to that awareness by attempting various ways to prepare for death or at least to include it within the realm of social life. Indeed, the rites of commemoration are central to the ritual life of the Intervale Jewish Center. They establish a framework within which death, the ultimate example of nature intruding upon culture, is itself transformed by culture.

Jokes do the same thing. Death humor is a major part of the joke repertoire of these people, largely because it makes the awesome seem, if not entirely friendly, then at least familiar. At the same time, by acting familiar with a subject that is frightening to others, the elderly acquire for themselves some of death's power. The humor suggests another element in how congregants respond to their own continued survival: they apparently believe that in continuing the life they have always known and remaining in the South Bronx, they have in a sense cheated death. No wonder they are reluctant, particularly now, to move. And there is another good reason not to squander their remaining resources by changing where and how they live. Congregants look to legacies as a hedge against mortality. Consequently they are less interested in material comforts than in accumulating financial legacies that, passed down to succeeding generations, will rescue them from oblivion.

THE MIRACLE OF INTERVALE AVENUE

Realizing that their contest with death is an unequal one which they will eventually lose, congregants also try to make their peace with death. Ultimately, this is why they come to the Intervale Jewish Center. Indeed, for those without children, and for others uncertain of their children's devotion, the congregation must sustain their wish for immortality. It is here that the kaddish is recited and here, too, where the memories of those who have died are preserved and passed down to newer members. That sense in which the memories of individuals become the communal property of the congregation stems in part from the organizing theme of the community: individuals die, but the group survives, and in so doing, individuals, too, survive.

The miracle of Intervale Avenue is a myth created by a master story-teller. It is his way of bringing meaning to life's vicissitudes, to create order out of chaos. But stories are only stories. They may affect the people who hear them, thereby indirectly changing reality, but they do not themselves constitute reality. All storytellers must at times feel remorse that the world they create through narrative is real only in their telling it. Much as he relishes the role of Moses, Sacks knows that he cannot perform real miracles the way his biblical namesake could. Perhaps for that reason he sometimes loses patience with an enterprise that may not survive him, with the possibility that his life may not be of similar magnitude as that of his biblical namesake. Aware—occasionally acutely aware—of the proximity of death, Sacks is brought face to face with the knowledge that the story of the miracle is no more than that: ultimately, his efforts may produce nothing lasting. Not surprisingly, such despair generates a profound urge to flee, to distance himself from the very things he, like all people, creates as symbolic buffers against oblivion. So there are moments of resignation when even fighters such as Sacks contemplate the futility of the struggle and consider abandoning the arena for a less challenging environment. But the symbols and myths through which culture is constructed are rather durable. Besides, all people need to feel heroic in the face of death,[3] and a man who looks to life as a source for the "good fight" finds only hollow solace in the possibility of flight. The urge to flee is a whim that soon vanishes, while he, even in the depths of despair, wrestles with those around him, determined to reestablish and expand his overall sense of control. He succeeds, in part because of his continuing faith in the miracle and in part because so many people who surround him have come to believe in the same miracle. Myths are invented by men, but once they are created, they take on a life of their own, entangling their creator, too, in their web.

There is an underlying theme to this book, which stems from my initial interest in this community. What we of all ages have to learn from Sacks,

Sidney and Betty Flisser walk home from *shul*.

Dave recites the *kaddish* for members of the congregation.

Sam Davis holds the *ets khayim,* the wooden frame for the Torah scroll.

Celebrating the miracle of Hanukkah.

Mrs. Miroff, Dave, Sam, and all the other members of the Intervale Jewish Center is not only about successful aging under seemingly adverse conditions, but also about the eternal human struggle to defy the limits imposed upon us by nature.

The Intervale community is to some extent exceptional: it is located in North America's most desolate urban landscape, a forbidding place in which only the heartiest or the most desperate dwell. And then, the community has come under the spell of a truly charismatic leader, who, though savvy in the ways of man, a great finagler of God, is ultimately most talented as a storyteller who can impart meaning to events that, if left to speak for themselves, might not confirm a divine order in existence but would hint rather at the chaotic nature of things. Although storytellers exist among all peoples, not always do they have the chance to leave so deep an imprint upon others, to invent, so to speak, their own culture. Sometimes, like Moses, they do. They can radically transform society, creating whole new ways of seeing humanity's place in the universe. More often, like the hasidic rebbes who followed the Baal Shem Tov, they reinterpret and in so doing reinvigorate old stories formulated by much earlier storytellers. Sacks is like the latter, although circumstances rather than personality are probably more the issue in limiting his impact. The Intervale community is tiny and is far from isolated from the rest of the Jewish world. Nevertheless, all storytellers have their impact, transforming, if conditions allow it, not only the group to which they belong but all those who come in contact with them. They are valuable resources through which cultures are created, regenerated, and sustained. They encourage people to experience their own lives on a grander scale than ordinary reality, comparable to the lives lived by the heroes of myth.

What the miracle of Intervale Avenue teaches us is the importance of stories as a regenerative force in the lives of people. Without them, we are left to our own wits to derive purpose and a higher order of meaning from experience. Stories are a group resource, and they reinforce through the numbers and devotion of their adherents the veracity of the universal truths they propound. Although all people struggle with the need to formulate structure and meaning, the task becomes all the more pressing toward the latter stages of the life cycle.[4] Consequently, the need for stories grows with age. The search for meaning, though, begins much earlier in life, generated the moment one begins to recognize the fact of one's mortality.

Not surprisingly, then, the elderly themselves constitute a significant resource for younger people, concerned with their own formulation. And I would argue that in any consideration of how to treat the elderly, our task must be only partly based on what we can do for them. The elderly are necessary for us, and it is to our benefit when we encounter them, whether as family members, health care professionals, or anthropologists, to pay very careful attention to how they reflect upon their lives, for in relating to us their formulations, there is much that they can do for us.

One Sabbath Sam Davis and Moishe Sacks stood outside the shul and examined the metal-covered door of an unused entrance that had been partially damaged the day before. I stood there, too, contemplating the motives for the damage and listening to their conversation.

"Mr. Davis, did you bring your hammer?"

"Sure, I did. When a soldier goes to war, he brings his gun. My hammer is my gun. This is a war!"

Mr. Sacks liked the metaphor. He thought for a moment, smiled, and then commented: "You're right. This is a war. Your hammer is your gun, and my prayer books are my gun. And his"—he pointed to me and hesitated because I did not have my tape recorder with me that day— "whatever he has, that's his gun." I, too, was pleased with the metaphor, realizing even then that I would remember it for a very long time.

NOTES

1. FORT APACHE: THE BRONX

1. *Encyclopaedia Judaica*, vol. 12 (Jerusalem: Keter, 1972), p. 1106.

2. Deborah Dash Moore, *At Home in America: Second Generation New York Jews* (New York: Columbia University Press, 1981), p. 73.

3. Ibid.

4. Ibid., p. 74.

5. Marshall Berman, *All That Is Solid Melts into Air: The Experience of Modernity* (New York: Simon and Schuster, 1982), p. 326.

6. *New York Times*, June 21, 1980.

7. I rely here on the excellent catalogue *Devastation/Resurrection: The South Bronx* (Bronx Museum of the Arts, 1980). See in particular the essays by Lloyd Ultan, "1776–1940: The Story of the South Bronx," and Donald G. Sullivan, "1940–1965: Population Mobility in the South Bronx."

8. Lloyd Ultan, "1776–1940: The Story of the South Bronx," in *Devastation/ Resurrection*.

9. Moore, *At Home in America*, p. 33.

10. Donald Sullivan, "1940–1965: Population Mobility in the South Bronx," in *Devastation/Resurrection*.

11. Robert Caro describes the process of destruction in East Tremont, a few subway stops from Intervale:

> More people moved out of the buildings bordering the expressway. Some of the vacancies were filled by the type of family that would have filled them in the days before there was an expressway. . . .
>
> But, with the noise, most moved out again—as fast as they could. And the families that replaced them were the families from the other side of the park. Muggings increased, and there began to be reports of robberies, thieves breaking right into your home. Before long, the old residents of the 3,000 apartments bordering the expressway were gone, moved away. Then the residents of the apartments next to those began to move, and then the residents of the apart-

ments next to those. [*The Power Broker: Robert Moses and the Fall of New York* (New York: Knopf, 1974), p. 889]

12. Moore, *At Home in America*, p. 36
13. Herbert Meyer, *Fortune*, November 1975, p. 145.
14. Robert Jensen, "Introduction," *Devastation/Resurrection*, p. 54.
15. See, for example, Robert Jensen's discussion of federal antipoverty and slum clearance programs, ibid., p. 53.
16. Ibid., p. 54.
17. *CBS Reports*, March 22, 1977.
18. "The City Disease," *Newsweek*, February 28, 1972, p. 96.
19. "Free Fire Zone," *New York Times*, July 11, 1975, pp. 40; 46–51.
20. Op. cit., p. 141.
21. *New York Times*, October 25, 1977.

3. "THAT'S THE SHUL I DON'T GO TO"

1. Victor Turner, *Dramas, Fields, and Metaphors: Symbolic Action in Human Society* (Ithaca: Cornell University Press, 1974).
2. Erving Goffman, *The Presentation of Self in Everyday Life* (New York: Doubleday Anchor, 1959), pp. 111–12.
3. Barbara Myerhoff, *Number Our Days* (New York: Dutton, 1979), p. 185.
4. Moreover, the conflict did not break down into a black/white confrontation since there are no other like-minded blacks laying claim to Judaism and willing to wage outright war for possession of the shul. Nor did it escalate into an observant/nonobservant confrontation—a potential subdivision at the Intervale Jewish Center. There simply was no danger of the shul's dividing into two discrete and mutually hostile units. See, for example, Lewis Coser's model on types of limited conflict that are not dangerous to the survival of a social group, *The Functions of Social Conflict* (New York: Free Press, 1956), pp. 76–77.
5. Quoting from the poet W. H. Auden, Turner admonishes us to learn to "think of societies as continuously 'flowing,' as a 'dangerous tide . . . that never stops or dies and held one moment burns the hand.' " *Dramas, Fields and Metaphors*, p. 37.

4. REBBE AND GODFATHER

1. See, for example, Karen Jonas and Edward Wellin, "Dependency and Reciprocity: Home Health Aid in an Elderly Population," in *Aging in Culture and Society*, Christine L. Fry, ed. (New York: Bergin, 1980).
2. See Samuel Heilman's discussion of itinerant beggars at synagogue services in *Synagogue Life: A Study in Symbolic Interaction* (Chicago: University of Chicago Press, 1976), pp. 112–26.
3. Within the framework of a game, behavior may occur that is of a very different order than would normally occur outside of it. Citing the anthropologist Gregory Bateson's theory of play, Erving Goffman argues that "games place a 'frame' around a spate of immediate events, determining the type of 'sense' that

would be accorded everything within the frame." *Encounters: Two Studies in the Sociology of Interaction* (Indianapolis: Bobbs-Merrill, 1961), p. 20.

4. By condemning individual shnorrers, the congregants are also able to disassociate themselves from what they have all, in a sense, become. As Barbara Myerhoff notes:

> In fighting with each other, the old people established a negative identification, proclaiming who they were by asserting who they were not. By treating their fellows as antagonists they emphasized the distance and differences among them and so were saved from seeing themselves as reflected in their peers, most of whom they regarded as pathetic, weak, and lonely. As long as they fought, they knew certainly that they were "not like those others." [*Number Our Days*, p. 184]

5. Lewis Hyde, *The Gift: Imagination and the Erotic Life of Property* (New York: Vintage, 1983), p. 4.

6. As Myerhoff notes, the anger may serve another purpose:

> . . . among people who are not inevitably bound together, anger may become a refutation of the possibility of separation. Anger is a form of social cohesion, and a strong and reliable one. To fight with each other, people must share norms, rules, vocabulary, and knowledge. Fighting is a partnership, requiring cooperation. A boundary-maintaining mechanism—for strangers cannot participate fully—it is above all a profoundly sociable activity. [*Number Our Days*, p. 184]

7. The impetus to prestation follows Marcel Mauss's notion about alms as "the result on the one hand of a moral idea about gifts and wealth and on the other of an idea about sacrifice. Generosity is necessary because otherwise Nemesis will take vengeance upon the excessive wealth and happiness of the rich by giving to the poor and the gods" (*The Gift* [New York: Norton, 1967], p. 15). Similar logic may be used to explain the need for rituals regarding the dead. By surviving and by being in good health, the living need to repay the dead for having endured the bad fate that they (the living) have been spared. To the individual, the tying of death and life together strips death of its randomness and subconsciously reassures the living of their continued existence. The idea of life as a limited resource implies, according to anthropologists Maurice Bloch and Jonathan Parry, that "one creature's loss is another's gain" (*Death and the Regeneration of Life* [New York: Cambridge University Press, 1982], p. 8).

8. Although the appreciation of the trickster does say something about the ironic sensibility of a given social and cultural tradition (Robert Pelton, *The Trickster in West Africa: A Study of Mythic Irony and Sacred Delight* [Los Angeles: University of California Press, 1980], p. 242), it is evident that the trickster as a personality type is not restricted to any one area or even type of social organization. All cultures have tricksters. Some cultures, however, are closer to the trickster's sensibility than others. Vulnerable and constantly aware of the cat-and-mouse game they play with death, old people have a greater sense than most other people of the ironic twists of fate, making them perhaps as a group

tricksterlike in their exploitation, to use Barbara Myerhoff's words, "of cultural freedom and confusion" ("Rites and Signs of Ripening: The Intertwining of Ritual, Time, and Growing Old," in *Age and Anthropological Theory*, David Kertzer and Jennie Keith, eds. [Ithaca: Cornell University Press, 1984], p. 308).

9. See Freud's observations on the character of the dirty joke in *Jokes and Their Relation to the Unconscious* (New York: Norton, 1963), pp. 97–98.

10. This, too, is a hasidic notion about *kavone,* devotion in prayer. See, for example, the hasidic tale "The Yom Kippur Flutist" in which the slow-witted son of a village Jew blows a powerful "note" during the *Neilah* service: "And the Baal Shem, contrary to his custom, finished his prayer quickly and said: 'This boy with the voice of his flute lifted up all the prayers and eased my burden.' " In *Gates to the Old City: A Book of Jewish Legends*, Raphael Patai, ed. (New York: Avon, 1980), p. 672.

5. "EVEN SOLOMON WOULD HAVE TROUBLE"

1. Barbara Myerhoff, "Rites and Signs of Ripening," p. 325.

2. Mircea Eliade, *Patterns in Comparative Religion* (New York: Meridian, 1974), p. 430.

3. The scenarios even of fairy tales, according to Mircea Eliade, "are the expression of a psychodrama that answers a deep need in the human being. Every man wants to experience certain situations, to confront exceptional ordeals, to make his way into the Other World—and he experiences all this, on the level of his imaginative life. . . ." Cited in Bruno Bettelheim, *The Uses of Enchantment* (New York: Vintage, 1977), p. 35.

4. Sacks generally mixes Ashkenazic and modern Hebrew pronunciations. The quality of the sound recording, particularly with background noise, makes accurate transcription difficult.

5. Sacks is conflating two verses: *Yayoymru mi ya'akhileynu bosor* [Num 11:4] and *Zokharnu es-hadago asher-noykhal* [Num. 11:5].

6. Samuel Heilman, *The People of the Book* (Chicago: University of Chicago Press, 1983), p. 62.

7. Sacks is making reference to the local and express stops on New York City's subway system.

8. Max Weinreich, *The History of the Yiddish Language*, trans. S. Noble and J. Fishman (Chicago: University of Chicago Press, 1980), p. 208.

9. According to Victor Turner, such performances are examples of "public reflexivity . . . in which a group or community seeks to portray, understand and then act on itself." "Frame, Flow and Reflection: Ritual and Drama as Public Liminality," in *Performance in Postmodern Culture* (Madison: University of Wisconsin Press, 1977), p. 33. See also Clifford Geertz's examination of the role of the cockfight in allowing the Balinese "to see a dimension of his own subjectivity," in "Deep Play: Notes on the Balinese Cockfight," in *The Interpretation of Cultures* (New York: Basic Books, 1973), p. 450.

10. Myerhoff, "Rites and Signs of Ripening," p. 324.

11. The case demonstrates what Samuel Heilman refers to as "traditioning." *The People of the Book*, p. 62.

12. Bettelheim, *The Uses of Enchantment*, p. 37.

13. Ibid., p. 41

14. Erik Erikson, *Adulthood* (New York: Norton, 1978), p. 26.

15. Walter Benjamin, "The Storyteller," in *Illuminations* (New York: Schocken, 1969), p. 94.

16. In Erikson's words: "Wisdom . . . is the detached and yet active concern with life itself in the face of death itself, and that it maintains and conveys the integrity of experience in spite of the Disdain over human failings and the Dread of ultimately non-being" (*Adulthood*, p. 26).

17. *Illuminations*, p. 96.

18. Conflated verse: cf. Exod. 14:9.

6. "MAYBE IT'S BRODSKY"

1. Becker argues against one component of classical Freudian theory:

Man's body was "a curse of fate," and culture was built upon repression—not because man was a seeker only of sexuality, of pleasure, of life and expansiveness, as Freud thought, but because man was also primarily an avoider of death. Consciousness of death is the primary repression, not sexuality. As Rank unfolded in book after book, and as Brown has recently argued, the new perspective on psychoanalysis is that its crucial concept is the repression of death. This is what is creaturely about man, this is the repression on which culture is built, a repression unique to the self-conscious animal. [*The Denial of Death* (New York: Free Press, 1973), p. 96]

2. Quoted in Becker, p. 2.

3. See Barbara Myerhoff's discussion of the central role that the quest for continuity plays in the ritual life of the Aliya Center in Venice, California. *Number Our Days*, pp. 108–10.

4. See Elisabeth Kübler-Ross, *On Death and Dying* (New York: Macmillan, 1969), chap. 5, pp. 82–84.

5. Kübler-Ross describes one patient who made various promises if only she could live long enough to attend the wedding of her oldest son: "I will never forget the moment when she returned to the hospital. She looked tired and somewhat exhausted and—before I could say hello—said, 'Now don't forget I have another son!' " (ibid., p. 83).

6. Robert Jay Lifton argues that there exists a universal experience of survival guilt:

Since survival, by definition, involves a sequence in which one person dies sooner than another, this struggle in turn concerns issues of comparative death-timing. Relevant here is what we have spoken of as guilt over survival priority, along with the survivor's unconscious sense of an organic social balance which makes him feel that his survival was purchased at the cost of another's.

He adds:

To be sure, there are differences in degree: we noted in Hiroshima the special intensity of the guilt of parents surviving their children. But even when the young (seemingly appropriately) outlive the old, there are always reasons for them, as survivors, to find fault with the comparative timing, to emphasize the "untimeliness" of death. No survival experience, in other words, can occur without severe guilt. [*Death in Life* (New York: Simon and Schuster, 1967), p. 489]

7. Becker, *The Denial of Death*, pp. 11–12.
8. Since, as Becker notes, "Every society . . . is a 'religion' whether it thinks so or not: Soviet 'religion' and Maoist 'religion' are as truly religious as are scientific and consumer 'religion' " [ibid., p. 7.], the turn to the sacred community to find meaning in death may take many different forms.

7. THE MAKING OF A MIRACLE

1. Clifford Geertz, "Thinking as a Moral Act: Ethical Dimensions of Anthropological Field Work in the New States," *Antioch Review* 28, no. 2 (1968): 151.
2. See, for example, the stages of fieldwork as outlined by William Shaffir et al. in *Fieldwork Experience: Qualitative Approaches to Social Research* (New York: St. Martin's Press, 1980).
3. Richard Schechner, "Collective Reflexivity: Restoration of Behavior," in *A Crack in the Mirror*, Jay Ruby, ed. (Philadelphia: University of Pennsylvania Press, 1982), p. 80.
4. See Barbara Myerhoff's "Surviving Stories," in *Between Two Worlds: Essays on the Ethnography of America Jewry*, Jack Kugelmass, ed. (n.d.).
5. Erik Erikson, *Adulthood*, p. 26.

8. THE MIRACLE OF INTERVALE AVENUE

1. Georges Gusdorf, *Autobiography: Essays Theoretical and Critical*, ed. by James Olney (Princeton: Princeton University Press, 1980), p. 48.
2. See Howard Stein's use of the term in "Judaism and the Group Fantasy of Martyrdom: The Psychodynamic Paradox of Survival Through Persecution," *Journal of Psychohistory* 6, no. 2 (Fall 1978).
3. As Ernest Becker argues in *The Denial of Death*:

It doesn't matter whether the cultural hero-system is frankly magical, religious, and primitive or secular, scientific, and civilized. It is still a mythical hero-system in which people serve in order to earn a feeling of primary value, of cosmic specialness, of ultimate usefulness to creation, of unshakable meaning. They earn this feeling by carving out a place in nature, by building an edifice that reflects human value: a temple, a cathedral, a totem pole, a skyscraper, a family that spans three generations. [p. 5]

4. See Robert Butler's observation on the role of reminiscing among the elderly in "The Life Review: An Interpretation of Reminiscence in the Aged," in *Middle Age and Aging*, Bernice L. Neugarten, ed. (Chicago: University of Chicago Press, 1968).

GLOSSARY

The Yiddish or Hebrew origin of each word is given in parentheses, but the reader should note that a number of words listed as Hebrew are in fact integral parts of spoken or written Yiddish. They derive from the prominent role that *lernen* or the study of sacred texts played in Ashkenazic culture. [See Max Weinreich's *History of the Yiddish Language* (Chicago: University of Chicago Press, 1980).]

Adoshem (Hebrew) A name for God.

Alevashulem (Hebrew) Rest in peace.

Aliya (Hebrew) An honor in which one is called to the Torah to recite the blessings before and after the Torah reading.

Amuno (Hebrew) Faith.

Aren kodesh (Hebrew) Ark; the cabinet where the Torah scrolls are stored.

Avrom Ovinu Lit: Abraham our father. The biblical Abraham.

Baal koyre (Hebrew) A designated individual who reads aloud directly from the Torah scroll.

Baal Shem Tov Rabbi Israel ben Eliezer, the eighteenth-century founder of Hasidism.

Baal tefile (Hebrew) Prayer leader.

Babka (Yiddish) A yeast cake with a chocolate filling.

Bar mitzvah (Hebrew) The ceremony in which a thirteen-year-old boy becomes counted among adult Jewish males.

Bas, bat (Hebrew) Daughter.

Besmedresh (Hebrew) Synagogue or study house.

Bima (Hebrew) The elevated platform in the center or near the front of the synagogue where the Torah is read.

Borsht (Yiddish) A soup made from beets.

Borukh dayan emes (Hebrew) Lit: Blessed is the true Judge: a prayer recited upon hearing bad news.

Boytchik (Yiddish) A yiddishization of the word "boy" with a Slavic diminutive suffix.

Breshis (Hebrew) Genesis, the first book of the Bible.

GLOSSARY

Brokhe (Hebrew) Blessing.

Canaan Pre-Israelite Palestine.

Cantor A designated person who sings the prayers during the synagogue service.

Challah, challie (Hebrew) A braided bread eaten at Sabbath and holiday meals.

Daven (Hebrew) To pray.

Dayan (Hebrew) Judge.

Dayenu (Hebrew) Lit: That would suffice us; a phrase from the Passover Haggadah.

Diaspora The world Jewish community outside of the land of Israel.

Dor (Hebrew) Generation.

Dvar Torah (Hebrew) A sermon on the meaning of a Torah portion.

El Mole Rakhamim (Hebrew) A prayer recited in honor of the dead.

Elyohu The prophet Elijah.

Emes (Hebrew) Truth.

Erets Yisroel (Hebrew) Land of Israel.

Esav The biblical Esau.

Gabbai (Aramaic) Sexton; lay person who coordinates parts of the service, such as the distribution of *kibbudim* (honors).

Gan eyden (Hebrew) Garden of Eden.

Gezunterheyt (Yiddish) Lit: In good health; may you be healthy.

Goyim (Hebrew) Non-Jews.

Gubernye (Russian) Province.

Gut shabes (Yiddish) Lit: Good Sabbath; a Sabbath greeting.

Haftorah (Hebrew) A portion from the Prophets read after the reading from the Torah on Sabbaths, festivals, and fast days.

Halakha, halokhe (Hebrew) Jewish law.

Hamevorekh (Hebrew) Praised be the One who is blessed (God).

Hanukkah (Hebrew) A Jewish holiday celebrating the Hasmonean victory and the rededication of the Temple.

Hitl (Yiddish) Hat.

Kaddish (Hebrew) Memorial prayer recited daily for eleven months following the death of a loved one.

Kashres, kashruth (Hebrew) The Jewish dietary laws.

Kavone (Hebrew) Lit: Devotion; a term associated with hasidic prayer.

Khanukas habayit (Hebrew) Rededication of the Temple.

Khasene (Hebrew) Wedding.

Khay (Hebrew) Life.

Kheyder (Hebrew) A traditional Jewish elementary school.

Khofets Khayim Rabbi Israel Meir ha-kohen, the great twentieth-century East European rabbinical scholar.

GLOSSARY

Khumesh, khumoshim (pl.) (Hebrew) Lit: The Five Books of Moses; the Torah.

Khupe (Hebrew) Canopy under which Jewish weddings are celebrated.

Kibbudim (Hebrew) Synagogue honors such as reciting the prayers before and after the reading of a section of the Torah.

Kiddush (Hebrew) The blessings recited over wine on Sabbath and holidays. It includes the light food, particularly cake and challah, that accompanies the wine.

Kines (Hebrew) Prayers of lamentation recited on Tisha be-Av to commemorate the destruction of the First and Second Temples in Jerusalem.

Kohanes, kohanim (Hebrew) Priesthood that originally served the Temple in Jerusalem.

Kotel maravi (Hebrew) The Western Wall of the Temple in Jerusalem.

Koved (Hebrew) Honor, respect.

Kovner maggid A well-known religious teacher from Kovno.

Lamdn, lamdonim (Hebrew) Scholar(s).

Lernen (Yiddish) Lit: Study; referring to the study of sacred texts.

Levi'im (Hebrew) Those who assisted the kohanim or priests in the Temple.

Malekh hamoves (Hebrew) Angel of Death.

Mamele (Yiddish) Mother.

Mantl (Yiddish) Torah cover.

Mashgiakh (Hebrew) Supervisor of the ritual purity or kashres of food.

Maven (Hebrew) Expert.

Mekhitse (Hebrew) A curtain or wall that separates the men's and the women's sections in an Orthodox synagogue.

Menorah (Hebrew) Candelabrum.

Midrash (Hebrew) Commentary on the Bible.

Migdash, mishkan (Hebrew) The Temple in Jerusalem.

Minyan (Hebrew) A quorum of ten men required for Jewish prayer services.

Mishpokhe (Hebrew) Family.

Mitsrayim (Hebrew) Egypt.

Mitzvah (Hebrew) Lit: A positive commandment; a good deed.

Mizrekh (Hebrew) East; also, a sign designating the eastern wall which Jews face while praying.

Moishe The biblical Moses.

Moshiakh (Hebrew) Messiah.

Mun (Hebrew) Manna, the "bread from heaven" described in the Book of Exodus.

Neilah (Hebrew) Final prayer service of Yom Kippur, the Day of Atonement.

GLOSSARY

Noyakh The biblical Noah.

Parshe (Hebrew) Weekly portion of the Torah read at the Sabbath service.

Rashi Rabbi Solomon ben Isaac, the great Medieval French Jewish scholar and biblical commentator.

Rebbe (Yiddish) A hasidic leader.

Rokhel The biblical Rachel.

Rosh Khodesh (Hebrew) The beginning of a new lunar month for which special prayers are recited at the Sabbath service.

Rosheshone (Hebrew) Rosh Hashanah, the Jewish New Year.

Rugelakh (Yiddish) Pastry made with cinnamon and nuts.

Seder (Hebrew) Festival meals held on the first and second nights of Passover.

Sha! (Yiddish) Quiet!

Shabes goy (Yiddish) A non-Jew who performs essential tasks that Jews may not perform during the Sabbath such as lighting a fire or extinguishing lights.

Shavuot (Hebrew) Pentecost, or the Feast of Weeks.

Shekhine (Hebrew) The Divine Spirit.

Shekhiyanu (Hebrew) Part of a prayer recited upon one's first encounter with something new.

Sheliakh (Hebrew) Messenger.

Shiksa (Yiddish) Non-Jewish woman.

Shiva (Hebrew) Lit: Seven; the seven days of mourning observed by the family of a deceased person.

Shmeer (Yiddish) Spread.

Shnorrer (Yiddish) Lit: Beggar; a term of derision.

Shokl (Yiddish) To shake or sway.

Shomer shabes (Hebrew) One who observes the commandment to abstain from work-related activities on the Sabbath.

Shofar (Hebrew) The ram's horn which is sounded during Rosh Hashanah and at the end of the Yom Kippur service.

Shul (Yiddish) Synagogue.

Slikhot, slikhes (Hebrew) Penitential prayers.

Smikha (Hebrew) Rabbinical ordination.

Soreh The biblical Sarah.

Talis, Taleysim (Hebrew) Prayer shawls worn by adult Jewish males during prayer.

Talmudist An expert in the Talmud, the codified oral tradition.

Tammuz A month of the Hebrew calendar.

Tashlikh (Hebrew) Part of the celebration of Rosh Hashanah in which sins are symbolically cast into a river.

GLOSSARY

Tefillin Phylacteries: two small black leather boxes containing passages from the Bible which are bound by leather straps to the left arm and forehead and worn during weekday morning services.

Tefiles (Hebrew) Prayers.

Tisha be-Av The annual fast day to commemorate the destruction of the First and Second Temples.

Treyf (Hebrew) Nonkosher food.

Tsaddik (Hebrew) Righteous man.

Yakov The biblical Jacob.

Yarmulke (Yiddish) Skullcap.

Yasher koyekh (Hebrew) Lit: May your strength increase; a traditional Jewish congratulatory phrase.

Yitshak The biblical Isaac.

Yizkor (Hebrew) The memorial prayers recited on Jewish holidays.

Yortsayt (Yiddish) Lit: Anniversary; the annual commemoration of a death.

Yoysef The biblical Joseph.

Zoger (Yiddish) Lit: Reciter; generally referring to cemetery attendants who recite memorial prayers in Hebrew for a fee.